END
OF DISCUSSION

END
OF DISCUSSION

How the Left's Outrage Industry
Shuts Down Debate, Manipulates Voters,
and Makes America Less Free (and FUN)

MARY KATHARINE HAM
and
GUY BENSON

CROWN
FORUM
NEW YORK

CROWN FORUM with colophon is a registered
trademark of Penguin Random House LLC.

Library of Congress Cataloging-in-Publication Data
is available upon request.

ISBN 978-0-553-44775-0
eBook ISBN 978-0-553-44776-7

Printed in the United States of America

Jacket design by Michael Nagin

10 9 8 7 6 5 4 3 2 1

First Edition

To our parents, from whom we learned our values. And to all those whose commitment to free expression entails far more personal risk than merely writing a book. We admire your courage and pray for your safety.

"Liberals claim to want to give a hearing to other views, but then are shocked and offended to discover that there are other views."

—*William F. Buckley, Jr.*

"We must picture hell as a state where everyone is perpetually concerned about his own dignity and advancement, where everyone has a grievance, and where everyone lives the deadly serious passions of envy, self-importance, and resentment."

—*C. S. Lewis, Preface to* The Screwtape Letters, *1960*

CONTENTS

WELCOME TO OUR BOOK

reetings, friends, acquaintances, fellow conservatives, curious liberals, and people who feigned gratitude upon receiving this book as a gift from a right-wing relative! Welcome to our conversation about America's dysfunctional national conversation. Before we dive right in, we want to begin by thanking you for (theoretically, at least) caring about how we as Americans debate issues and exchange ideas. If you're on the conservative end of the political spectrum, we suspect that you'll agree with much of what you'll read over the next three hundred or so pages, but fair warning: you will almost certainly object to some of our analysis and may even find yourself shaking your head in disbelief at some of the people we cite in a positive context. Feel free to keep a running list of our RINO ("Republican in Name Only") apostasies and enumerate them in an angry e-mail—but please try to commit to at least finishing the book prior to clicking send.[1]

If you're not a self-identifying conservative, and *especially* if you place yourself on the left side of the political spectrum, we're exceptionally glad you're here. Seriously. Investing the time to ingest tens of thousands of words written by two "right-wing bloggers"—people employed as talking heads on "Faux News,"[2] no less!—is probably well beyond the scope of your comfort zone. We'll forgive you if you choose to shed the cover when carrying this book in public, so as to avoid some seriously judgmental side-eye from your friends and/or fellow public transit enthusiasts. In the likely event that you end up disagreeing with much contained in the pages that follow, please do hold your nose and soldier on. We're confident that there are enough morsels of intellectual honesty, self-criticism, and (hopefully) amusing content to sustain you along the way. We believe in you.

All right. *Let's do this.*

---

[1] We can be reached at Filthy.SpinelessRINOs7@gmail.com (we cannot actually be reached here).
[2] This play on words ceased being clever circa October 1999.

1

HEAD EXPLOSIONS

You're perched in front of your laptop, eyes boring holes into the screen. A familiar, uneasy feeling swells inside you. Moments ago, you logged in to Facebook, where a gray-lettered prompt in small font beckoned you with four innocuous words: *What's on your mind?* Something *is* on your mind, as it happens; it pertains to a viral national controversy, and a lot of people in your feed have been buzzing about it. You've entered a few sentences reflecting your opinion into the status field, and now you're anxiously eyeing the post icon. One click, and your take will officially be on the record, permanently. Sure, there's an edit button, and a delete function, but the Internet is forever. You've posted hundreds of statuses before, accumulating countless "likes" and sparking a handful of debates, but this time feels different.

The hot story *du jour* is fraught with . . . let's call them *sensitivities*. A significant number of people in your "friend" orbit aren't going to agree with your minicommentary. That's fine with you, in theory, but you're increasingly aware that disagreement of this type may not end well. You've seen it happen: angry comment "flame" wars erupt, friendships are strained or dissolved, heavy-duty names are called, and motives are impugned. HR departments have even gotten involved on occasion.

Here's the thing: you don't want to be lumped into the "bad person" camp—a fate that awaits those who fail to convey the proper feelings on a matter of public debate. You're confident you don't deserve it, and you know what is, and is not, in your heart. But other people might not, and some won't care. They might seize on a word or a sentence fragment in your post, and things could spiral from there. Posting a selfie, or a music video, or that adorable photo of your dog is far less likely to get ugly (one doesn't typically get called a bigot posting about one's puppy[1]), so you select the text you've entered and trash it. *It's just not worth it.* You click away from the page and move on.

A growing number of Americans are beginning to sense an insidious strain of self-censorship in themselves, either explicitly or subconsciously. You find yourself keeping your mouth shut about controversial issues like gay marriage or so-called women's issues because you'd rather not suffer the social costs of being cast as the enemy by the increasingly aggressive thought police. They have enforcers everywhere—at the office, at dinner parties, and all over the media. This silencing impulse isn't born out of normal or healthy self-reflection and restraint; it arises out of fear. Nor is it part of a free society's natural process of discarding truly pernicious ideas after open discussion, making marginalization the rightful cost of losing to better arguments. Instead, outrage mongers turn this process on its head, disqualifying ideas *without* debate instead of after debate.

The fear to speak is cultivated by people who actively work to raise the social cost of engaging publicly on any number of issues. We call them the Outrage Circus. They are highly ideological, often deeply partisan, and relentless in their vigilance, ever on alert to name and shame violators of their approved order. Once you've violated one of their capricious and fluid "rules"—even unwittingly—malice is attributed, and restitution is demanded. Nothing short of full, professed repentance shall suffice.

But sometimes even *that* is not enough, as the relentless, pedantic

---

[1] Though that "Yo quiero Taco Bell" Chihuahua could be of questionable cultural sensitivity, so watch out.

hall monitors of our discourse often see fit to exact economic costs for perceived social transgressions. Think or express the wrong ideas, and they'll come after your livelihood. Play the wrong Top 40 hit at a club? Pink slip for you, as one college DJ found out in North Carolina. Uncomfortable with hosting a same-sex marriage ceremony in your own home? That'll be a $13,000 fine, as a couple with a small business in New York discovered. Display the wrong piece of modern art on an American campus, and you'll bring scandalized activists and professors down on you, as Tony Matelli realized when his realistic tighty-whitey-clad statue *Sleepwalker* was shunned and vandalized on the Wellesley College campus after being deemed potentially traumatic for women on campus.[2] Hell, even *Vagina Monologues* playwright Eve Ensler has had her work banned because it's not *sufficiently inclusive of women*.

Thought policing is strictest on America's college campuses, so much so that the idea of a campus as a place of freewheeling free inquiry and speech is almost a laughable relic of a bygone era—a theme we'll expand on in chapter 5. The outrage industry's most loyal adherents and enforcers are leftist activists, often trained on campus to believe that protecting certain people from offense in the public sphere is a higher calling than defending free expression. Thus, seemingly without irony or familiarity with Orwell, free speech becomes an exercise not in pushing boundaries but in creating new ones, openness is about closing off, and radicals become more puritanical by the day.

In leftist circles, participants vie viciously for the title of most socially aggrieved in pursuit of the ultimate social windfall—the sanitization of the public square of the arguments of one's adversaries. We're not the only ones who've noticed. A bevy of liberals in good standing, Bill Maher and Dan Savage among them, have felt the sting of violating the grievance hierarchy. Jonathan Chait, in a 2015 essay for *New York* magazine, called the "new p.c." a "style of politics in which the more

---

[2] "Liberals" against art!

radical members of the left attempt to regulate political discourse by defining opposing views as bigoted and illegitimate." This system, he wrote, "makes debate irrelevant and frequently impossible."

It might be fun to watch this snake devour itself from the tail in a paroxysm of censorship if it weren't for the fact that the Outrage Circus is so intent on exporting these practices to the rest of society. And unhappily for us, their regulations are most unsparingly enforced against conservatives of all stripes.

Commenting outside of the ever-shifting lines of "correct" thinking and preapproved terminology has always been a problem sweated by politicians and their publicists. No more. While public figures still bear the brunt of the Circus's acrobatics, "normal" people are no longer exempt. If moments of heterodoxy among liberal lights are punished, imagine what, say, a libertarian homeschooling mom might be in for. Thus, some are turning to self-censorship as the hassle-free, easy way out of being attacked. But it also results in being left out of the conversation. This move toward acquiescence isn't just limiting. It's dangerous for society.

North Korean and Islamist terrorists brought new attention to the problem in 2015 in dramatic and tragic fashion, throwing into stark relief the choices and dangers free society faces. In the case of Sony's *The Interview* and French satire magazine *Charlie Hebdo*, those who found artistic speech offensive launched criminal and unspeakably violent attacks with the object of preventing such speech in the future. A disturbing number of free society's spokespeople and publications failed to defend that speech, some even arguing for self-censorship, in the face of these attacks. If we're not willing to fight bullies with keyboards and petitions, we're certainly not going to stand up to bullies with machine guns.

THE BUSINESS WE'VE CHOSEN

To our occasional shame, we work in politics. We chronicle, quote, and quantify our country's least edifying industry. We entered this sordid fray, ironically, based on a belief that said industry should be as unobtrusive to its citizens and their daily business as possible. (We're conservatives. That's kind of the whole idea.) To the detriment of our mental health, our job requires us to pay lots of attention to the goings-on of Washington, D.C., every single day. We routinely survey the state of our "national conversation" with great frustration and occasional alarm. As close friends with preternaturally similar worldviews, we often find ourselves on near-daily phone calls that feature some variation of this exchange:

> *"Wait, is this a thing now? I think this is a thing."*
> *"WHY is this a thing?!"*

We call these cathartic venting sessions "head explosions," which often commence with some variation of the "I can't even" meme. There's much pacing, occasional unparliamentary outbursts, and rending of tiny garments, as Mary Katharine does her baby's laundry with the phone on speaker. Regardless of how productive our head explosions may be, they're certainly cheaper than real therapy. Frankly, though, we shouldn't be surprised by almost anything anymore. We work in an industry whose number-one export is outrage, yet we are consistently amazed at how little it takes to create "an outrage." Efficient at nearly nothing else, Washington excels at the world's worst kind of alchemy— what was formerly mundane becomes "a thing" to talk about. Washington is where the oddities of campus oversensitivity and leftist outrage come to get weaponized—something to freak out about, something to obsess over, and most important, something over which to bash political enemies and fellow countrymen.

Pause. Did you see what we just did? Did you catch *the thing*? We wrote "countrymen" instead of using a gender-neutral term (which is, what? "Countrypeople"?)[3] A rational human being might assume we meant no harm by using "countrymen," out of a customary assumption of good faith, or an examination of our nonmisogynistic careers, personal lives, and public comments. Our political adversaries instead might choose to deem this an attack on women, and with a helpful assist from their allies in the media, brand us infantry officers in the right's mythical war on women (see chapter 6). Braying like carnival barkers, they'll pound the table about our "revealing" alleged gaffe until the use of one word eclipses the balance of our careers and lives. The object is not to declare our words or actions offensive, which would be preposterous enough given their innocuous nature, but to slowly but steadily declare our very *existence* offensive.

To understand how little material the Left's choreographed outrage brigades require to make a ruckus that completely obscures the record, one need look no further than the 2012 presidential election, and one of the silliest attacks in modern political history, as substance-free as it was ubiquitous.

Let's try this thought experiment: Please tell us what's offensive about the phrase "binders full of women," employed by Republican nominee Mitt Romney in an October 2012 presidential debate. As a refresher, Romney was touting his documented track record of hiring women to high-ranking positions when he uttered the offending phrase. He explained that he used binders filled with qualified women's résumés for his gubernatorial cabinet after his first round of recruitment was male dominated. He awkwardly consolidated that thought into "binders full of women."

Seriously, tell us what is offensive about that. No, really. Try. Was the allegation that the former presidential candidate kept *actual* women in binders, like some ghastly scene out of the *Saw* franchise? That the clumsy phrasing indicated some sort of odd objectification

---

[3] Our lawyers inform us that the correct term is *fellow citizens*. We regret the error.

of women, in which they become mere office supplies in the eyes of a ruthlessly sexist CEO? It couldn't possibly have been an indication of his unwillingness to actually hire women, because he used the phrase to describe his *uniquely successful* efforts to get more women into his gubernatorial cabinet. The Center for Women in Government & Civil Society noted his administration's peak 50 percent representation was the nation's closest "to parity in terms of the degree to which women are represented in top policy positions."[4]

So, what was it? It was Romney's clumsy omission of one word: résumés. It was beyond obvious what he meant, but the mistake played into a Democratic attack line (namely, that Republicans are anti-women). The Left found it convenient to be offended, and the circus went to work. As a result, the microscopic gaffe became a meme. If it had remained a goof, that'd be one thing, but it was deemed indicative of "larger truths," if not prima facie sexism by Mitt Romney.[5]

This sequence of events wasn't accidental. Media circuses and "things" may appear chaotic to the untrained eye, but they're often intricately choreographed events, led by designated ringmasters. In the political realm, a network of well-trained operatives, nonprofits, special interests, PR firms, universities, "thought leaders," and the media stand at the ready to manufacture and amplify fury over pretty much anything, or nothing at all. One of the most useful things about employing the entirely subjective "offense" of the listener to draw the limits of acceptable speech is that literally anything can be offensive to someone. The same exact words or thoughts are deemed offensive from someone of one political or ethnic identity, but not from another.

---

[4] In 2012, a look at nine governors in the Democratic Governors Association's leadership ranks showed the average percentage of women in cabinet positions was a mere 24 percent.

[5] In an incident of achingly poetic irony, "Binders Full of Women Writers," a private Facebook group for the type of female writers and activists who objected to Romney's phrasing, itself descended into "bitter identity-politics recriminations, endlessly litigating the fraught requirements of p.c. discourse," according to Jonathan Chait's 2015 reporting for *New York* magazine. Perfect.

Again, the idea is to disqualify a target's views as unacceptable contributions to the public discourse. To demonize and caricature the target, transforming him into a punch line or persona non grata. To establish a cost associated with crossing society's self-appointed high priests. By disqualifying someone as prima facie bad, wrong, and backward, you've shut down their ideas without much intellectual exertion, guaranteeing that they don't receive a fair hearing.

As we mentioned, the mob may focus most of its attention on public figures, but its effect on others is undeniable. It's one thing if your humble authors get excoriated for what-have-you. It's not pleasant, but we signed up for it in a way that the reticent Facebook user we described earlier did not. To quote *The Godfather II*, "This is the business we've chosen." We actively decided to jump into the political fray and live relatively public lives. Nonetheless, average people are more aware than ever that their association with the "wrong" fried chicken joint, Internet browser, breast cancer charity, packaged pasta, children's toy, Halloween costume, TV channel, TV show, word, diaper, school, and even comedian can be the source of potential scrutiny and judgment. Choose incorrectly on any of these fronts, and you're liable to be branded a hater, a racist, a troglodyte.

The weaponization of outrage for ideological and partisan ends is out of control. Widespread use of social media as a debate forum (and an efficient multiplier of outrage), an increasingly sophisticated political organizing class that knows how to build mere offense into campaign offensive, and a twenty-four-hour media environment that thrives on anything that resembles outrage has whipped up a perfect storm of perpetual, mechanized offense.

Its unavoidable by-products are a hypersensitive citizenry, a country where reasoned, open debate is stymied, and a culture in which good people are reluctant to contribute to the dialogue for fear of what they might be labeled. Where mild trivialities are cynically elevated and exploited for partisan ends, and scorched-earth politics infects every corner of our lives. The actions of the outrage machine are corrosive to our freedom, and make America a worse place to live and think and work. This is the end of discussion.

OUTRAGE CONFESSIONAL

W e know what some of you are thinking: you guys keep excoriating the Left, but the Right does this, too! Yep. And we generally suck at it. Sure, we have our share of outrage merchants, but they're far less effective and are afforded far less credibility than their counterparts on the other side. Conservatives are the hopelessly outmaneuvered President Garrett Walker[6] to the Left's Frank Underwood when it comes to this game, though we are not without our Underwood aspirants. There is a sometimes heated internal debate playing out among right-leaning strategists—it boils down to this quandary: learning to better exploit our "outrage" and punish the Left could be detrimental to speech, but doesn't declining to fight back using their tactics amount to unilateral disarmament in the face of those who are already damaging speech?[7] Is doing battle on their terms—by their standards—necessary, or does it just make everything worse?

While the Right is hardly blameless, we do believe that end-of-discussion-style silencing is a phenomenon primarily escalated and enforced by the political Left. In his 2013 book, *Bullies*, author Ben Shapiro hits on an important point that helps illuminate and explain the clout disparity: "Power derives from institutions. The right thinks individually; the left thinks institutionally. And so the left wields more power, and therefore has far more opportunity to bully," he writes. Because of their indisputable dominance in academia, media, and entertainment, liberal outrages have a natural advantage of amplification.

---

[6] The original president in Netflix's *House of Cards*. Admit it, you forgot his name, too, he's such a spineless nonentity.

[7] We'll grapple with this question at greater length at the end of the book.

But that doesn't mean we'll avoid calling out our own side when appropriate. For instance, genuine opposition to war has too often been cast as opposing "the troops." Conservative supporters of Israel are sometimes too eager to reflexively brand criticism of Israeli policy as anti-Semitism. That's unfair, even if many Israel critics have richly earned that abominable designation. These dismissals are meant to silence and short-circuit debate. The Right has also occasionally dialed up its complaints loud enough to get people fired. The unseemly pound-of-flesh extraction scorecard may be lopsided, but it reflects a bipartisan pastime.

It would be tacky and incomplete of us to simply cast stones at "some on our side" without taking a measure of personal ownership, too. Even though we generally try to remain levelheaded and fair-minded, we've each had our moments. For instance, Guy recalls hosting a live radio show in Chicago on the evening of March 21, 2010—the night Obamacare passed the House of Representatives, guaranteeing that it would become law. He uncorked a furious rant that he'd probably like to return to and dial back a bit, if given the chance. As we've grown more aware of the implications of the endless politics-as-bloodsport cycle, we've worked to alter our own behavior. Maybe we've mellowed out a touch as a result. (Our friends on the other side of the Right's internal debate about this might say we've "gone squishy.") Our aim has been to become more conscientious, more circumspect, and more self-aware in confronting whatever controversy the latest news cycle visits upon the commentariat.

That doesn't mean we won't screw up and expose ourselves to charges of hypocrisy from time to time, nor does it mean that we need to cut outrage out of our political diet altogether. Well-placed, deserved indignation is unavoidable and sometimes necessary when you're invested in a subject like politics. Sometimes people *do* say things that are beyond the pale. Sometimes people *do* need to lose their jobs. But in the vast majority of cases, the appropriate response to opinions that offend or annoy is to offer *more speech*—rebuttals, refutations, counter-arguments, and expressions of disagreement.

"I'LL DEFEND TO THE DEATH YOUR RIGHT TO SAY IT . . ."

According to the Internet, which is unfailingly accurate, the oft-invoked axiom "I disapprove of what you say, but I will defend to the death your right to say it" is credited to Voltaire. In fact, it was written by Evelyn Beatrice Hall in 1906 to sum up Voltaire's beliefs on freedom of thought. The sentiment it expresses encapsulates a central tenet of pluralism and small-"l" liberalism: We tolerate and strive to welcome dissenting speech. When we disagree, we'll say so, but we won't try to muzzle or punish your viewpoint. We're not pretending that the last few years have marked a sudden departure from some mythical golden era of mutual respect and free expression; American history is littered with examples of groups trying to suppress and stifle others. But the current climate does seem increasingly poisonous, as this axiom is all too frequently turned on its head. "I disapprove of what you say, so I will explore various ways of punishing you for saying it." The concilia-tory *but* is being supplanted by a vengeful *so*.

As we were researching the provenance of what turned out to be Voltaire's apocryphal declaration, we happened upon an obscure, long-forgotten Internet eruption that typifies the abandonment of Vol-taire's mind-set. The kerfuffle played out at *Daily Kos*, a Far Left on-line community, where several featured writers and commenters went to war with one another over one diarist's use of an offensive word (*fag*, which he employed in the context of illustrating a self-critical point). After exchanging blows in a series of livid recriminations, one concerned diarist appealed to his fellow liberals' alleged reverence for inclusiveness by invoking an iteration of the "defend to the death" quote. The very first response to this plea wound up representing the consensus:

> Pfft. *I don't defend your right to call other people hypersensitive, irony impaired ninnies just cuz you're in the mood for it, just as I don't defend similar wingerisms. Because that's what it is: flatout wingerism. You have no respect for other people. Fine with me. Stay away from other people then.*

"Wingerism," for the uninitiated, is a derogatory term for arguments and ideas advanced by right-wingers. For challenging the word police, this individual was informed that he has "no respect for other people" and should therefore "stay away from" them entirely. That's the solution. *Shut up*, they explained, *and kindly remove yourself from society*. That comment ended up getting up-voted by dozens of users, and down-voted by zero. Incidentally, the date of this nonexchange of ideas? July Fourth. God bless America!

We both earn a living writing on the Internet, so we'll be the very first to acknowledge that judging a website or a political movement based on Internet comments is basically the least fair thing ever. We often dispense, and too often ignore, the sage advice to *never read the comments*. (Especially, for whatever reason, on YouTube.[8]) But the pile-on described above is hardly out of the ordinary. Aggressive, unabashed speech stifling is becoming the rule, rather than the exception, in and out of comments sections.

The political Outrage Circus is at once a high-level coordinated effort and an ad hoc grassroots endeavor. Grievance mongering, apology demanding, and scalp collecting are modeled at the national level by ruthless professionals, then replicated straight on down the line.

We relish debate. We use words for a living and would prefer that

---

[8] If you're ever feeling too chipper about the state of humanity, remove all sharp objects from your immediate vicinity, then take ten minutes to peruse some YouTube comments at random.

fewer of them be banished from our collective lexicon for dubious, ideological reasons. We've each convinced others of the rightness of our positions through the years, and we've been convinced by others, too. That sort of authentic exchange isn't possible when everyone involved is fearfully walking on eggshells. (Decency note: Intentional, jarring rudeness for its own sake, or as a "protest" against political correctness, isn't typically very productive either.) We personally hope to talk, argue, and persuade our way through the coming decades in a free and prosperous country, and then pass those underpinnings of genuine freedom on to the next generation.[9] So rather than continue to simmer and stew in private, we've decided to share our head explosions with all of you. *You're welcome.* You may disapprove of some of what you'll read in the chapters that follow, but we hope you'll come away strenuously defending our right to say it—and nagging your friends and family ("to the death!"[10]) to buy this book.

---

[9] References to "the next generation" in political books and speeches are usually pretty trite and blowhardy. We use the (applicable) term in this case with a soupçon of self-loathing. Mary Katharine has actually grown and birthed a literal member of the next generation, so we've got that going for us, which is nice.

[10] Figuratively, of course! Contrary to popular belief, we Republicans don't actually love violence and war (the other side of the "you hate the troops" demagoguery coin).

2

EVERYTHING'S A THING

Combating the Politicized Life

Among other wonders, 2014 gave us the Rob Lowe Directv ad campaign, in which the handsomest man on the planet humorously advocates for satellite TV service over cable. In one commercial, Lowe portrays himself, a satellite subscriber, as well as Painfully Awkward Rob Lowe, an alter ego who subscribes to cable.

Painfully Awkward Rob Lowe, among other social afflictions, can't "go with other people in the room," he proclaims while standing awkwardly in front of a urinal. This was a problem for someone.

Steven Soifer, president of the International Paruresis Association, demanded the ad be pulled for disrespecting those who deal with the real affliction of shy bladder.

"We don't mind if people have a little fun with it," Soifer told the Associated Press. "It's a situation that a lot of people don't understand. In this particular case, the portrayal is making it look ridiculous, that this guy is a loser for having a problem."

THE CULTURAL FLOP

Soifer had executed a dramatic cultural flop. In the sports world, *flop* is the term given to a player's theatrical fall designed to draw a referee's attention to a rather minor or even nonexistent foul. Soccer is the sport most famous for its flops but the practice has enthusiastic practitioners in American football and basketball.

There is rarely any penalty for flopping, and there is great potential upside—yardage, free throws, possession—if a referee is convinced of an athlete's performance.

When it comes to speech, America is turning into a country of floppers, figuratively grabbing our shins in fabricated agony over every little possible offense in hopes of working the refs.

Was anyone truly offended by Painfully Awkward Rob Lowe, even within the tiny subset of Americans who suffer from shy bladder? Was any real damage done? Of course not, but there was no penalty for Soifer grabbing his emotional hamstring and writhing on the floor dramatically. Indeed, there was a tremendous upside—all of America talked about his shy bladder support group for one day.

In this case, Lowe and Directv responded appropriately. Directv declined to remove the ad and Lowe tweeted, "[T]here are those who really need to lighten up" along with a crack about his own bladder:

@RobLowe: For those wondering, my bladder is gregarious.

If an organization as obscure as the shy bladder association can make national headlines for a perceived slight so tiny, the power of the cultural flop to monopolize the nation's attention is immense, and many have learned how to use it.

Imagine a basketball game in which thirty-eight minutes are just LeBron James lying on the floor getting awarded call after call.[1] That's what living in a culture of constant outrage feels like. These people aren't making plays; they're trying to win via constant finger-pointing and insincere whining.

This phenomenon has gone by many names as cultural observers

---

[1] Or just rewatch Game 6, 2013 Eastern Conference Finals, Pacers vs. Heat.

have tried to put their finger on what is changing: the "politicized life," the "culture of shut up," the "extinction of context," the "outrage economy."[2] *Slate* assembled the "Year in Outrage," an exhaustive and exhausting compendium of everything Americans were angry about in 2014, which illustrated just how pervasive outrage has become in the news cycle and, consequently, our daily lives.

Instead of engaging in the rich American tradition of a loud, raucous, messy, free speech free-for-all, we have begun to spend a disturbing amount of our speech just flagging the speech of others. The object is no longer to argue one's own side of any issue passionately, but to argue that the other side should not argue. What used to feel like a national experiment (and source of national pride) in joyously pushing limits now feels like an exercise in imposing new limits. That's why we call it the End of Discussion, because ultimately, that's what it is designed to do. And far too often, it works.

This is not healthy for the country. It is demoralizing, and it's creeping far beyond discussions of public policy. While politics is the natural home of the cultural flop and the stultifying debate it produces, America seems to have decided exporting that way of doing business to every other conversation in our lives is wise. It is not.

With a nod to a form of communication to which so many in our generation are receptive, the listicle, we now present: Six Ways Outrage Culture Is Turning Your Entire Life into a Political Campaign.

1. Every Person a Public Figure

The U.S. Marines have a famous saying that governs their training—every man a rifleman, meaning every single marine regardless of his ultimate job is trained as a rifleman. In our outrageously outraged

---

[2] Those terms were coined by Sonny Bunch (*Washington Free Beacon*), Jon Lovett (the *Atlantic*), Alexandra Petri (*Washington Post*), and Alyssa Rosenberg (*Washington Post*), respectively.

culture, all individuals have the potential to be treated as public figures regardless of whether or not they've volunteered to run for office.

The mere existence of a personal website, Facebook page, or Twitter account, even protected or private in nature, has made the ruminations of regular citizens plausibly "public" in a way they've never been before. But just because regular citizens have the amazing power to publish independently any thought that's in their heads doesn't mean they should have to answer for those remarks in exactly the way a political candidate would. Yet increasingly, that's what our culture asks of every single one of us.

As duly noted earlier, your humble authors signed up for this game. Our thoughts are generally geared to public consumption, delivered with the expectation that they'll be subject to criticism, ridicule, and possible professional and financial consequences if ill-considered. We are compensated for wading into the discourse.

But what about someone like Justine Sacco, who was working a decent job in tech PR before she tweeted the wrong joke, jumped on a transatlantic flight without Internet, and landed to find she was an internationally hated pariah with no job? It was the doldrums of the Christmas news cycle in 2013 when Sacco tweeted this before boarding a flight to South Africa:

@JustineSacco: Going to Africa. Hope I don't get AIDS. Just kidding. I'm white!

Gawker blogger Sam Biddle published the tweet, treating it as if it were a racist statement meant to be taken at face value instead of a satirical skewering of what a racist would say about AIDS in Africa. Before Sacco landed, the hashtag #HasJustineLandedYet was trending worldwide. Companies were using her international humiliation for their own PR, and AIDS charities were fund-raising off the perceived gaffe. She landed and promptly deleted all her social media accounts, provoking even more Internet ire. Things got so bad, her company's press release announcing her firing included a request that the world avoid "wholesale condemnation of an individual who we have otherwise known to be a decent person at core."

Sacco released a sincere apology to international media and promptly faded into obscurity as the culture moved on to another outrage.

Granted, Sacco was a person whose job required some Internet savvy and attention to words, but there is no credible argument that her willfully misunderstood or bad taste Twitter joke should have made her the center of an international firestorm. Rarely do even a presidential candidate's tweets get such a high-profile dissection and demonizing.

A year after Biddle somewhat unwittingly set off this firestorm, he wrote about Sacco again, this time after meeting her. In a piece entitled "Justine Sacco Is Good at Her Job, and How I Came to Peace with Her," he explained the phenomenon that caused the row and ruined her life:

> *Twitter disasters are the quickest source of outrage, and outrage is traffic. I didn't think about whether or not I might be ruining Sacco's life. The tweet was a bad tweet, and seeing it would make people feel good and angry—a simple social and emotional transaction that had happened before and would happen again and again. The minimal post set off a 48-hour paroxysm of fury, an eruption of internet vindictiveness . . . Jokes are complicated, context is hard. Rage is easy.*

A year later, in a twist of outrage karma, Biddle himself got into a similar situation over a dashed-off tweet. Sacco—who it turns out is a kind person, not a racist monster—offered him advice and support as he made his way through the storm. Both of them remain employed.

Theirs is a rare story of redemption in outrage culture, but that story will never reach as many people as #HasJustineLandedYet. How many people watched Sacco lose her job and become a famous racist and decided just to shut up lest they risk a similar fate?

2. An Ever-Shrinking Sphere of Privacy

As soon as everyone can be plausibly treated as a public figure, they are also granted a constricting sphere of privacy. We do some of this to ourselves, of course, posting blithely to Instagram, Facebook, and Twitter our locations and pictures of our kids and beer-pong tournaments.[3]

But more and more, even the most private of exchanges are fair game for national consumption and condemnation as long as the perpetrator can be shown to have acted like a jerk in said private exchange.

Though a billionaire racist is surely an unsympathetic figure, many were nonetheless disturbed by the implications of the way former Clippers owner Donald Sterling's offending comments came to light. His girlfriend/assistant recorded them in his home without his knowledge and they were released to the media.

"Ultimately, I don't think he should have lost his team," comedian Dave Chappelle told *GQ* in the aftermath of the Sterling story. "I don't like the idea that someone could record a secret conversation and that a person could lose their assets from that, even though I think what he said was awful."

In the Sony hack of 2014, possibly perpetrated by agents of the North Korean regime, private e-mail exchanges became public fodder regardless of how they were obtained or their newsworthiness. Though the media had lectured all of us righteously about the dissemination of illegally obtained nude photos of female celebrities like Jennifer Lawrence just months prior, there seemed to be no such consideration given to e-mails that were just as private and wrongfully disseminated.

Why? Because a couple of Sony executives made insensitive racial

---

[3] Preferably not in the same picture.

jokes about President Obama, and the e-mails revealed juicy gossip and salary information about famous people. Leaks are nothing new. They're sometimes justified and genuinely newsworthy. But outrage by outrage, we shrink our space to be candid, real people, even behind closed doors.

As comedian Neal Brennan put it, arguing with Jon Stewart about the Sterling case, "George Orwell predicted a future in which the government polices our every word and thought. But we don't have Big Brother. We have millions of Little Brothers . . . using their phones to record our every misdeed."

3. Everything Is a Thing

Do you have a position on every single story in the news on any given day? Do you have a clear understanding of the political implications of every product you use or buy? You'd better. To steer clear of the outrage merchants, you must choose the correct opinion on every subject under the sun and profess it loudly. The thirst for outrage, and the surge of Internet traffic and self-satisfaction it provides, means new fronts for potential "wrongdoing" open every day. Did you know you can choose the wrong pasta or hand soap to pass muster? Not to worry. There's an app for that!

"Bet the last time you were sipping Campbell's soup or popping Pringles chips it never occurred to you that your eating habits could be political," writes Al Kamen in the *Washington Post*, introducing the BuyPartisan app.

Matthew Colbert, a former Capitol Hill staffer, built the BuyPartisan app to allow users to scan the barcodes of any product they buy to determine just how "Republican" or "Democrat" that product is. For instance, scanning the code on a lotion bottle, as Kamen did, will bring up the political contributions of the lotion's parent company, Johnson & Johnson (slightly more Republican than Democrat), its employees (about even), and its board. Weirdos can then make buying decisions about a beauty product based on whether they can countenance the personal politics of the people behind the product that moisturizes their countenances. After all, it's hard to put on lotion if you can't look yourself in the mirror, *amirite*?

The goal of the company, Colbert told the *Washington Post*, is to make "every day Election Day" through "spending choices." Well, that sounds terrible. One writer took the challenge, using the app to determine "How Republican Is Whole Foods?" in *Fast Company* magazine. In a piece that is mostly tongue-in-cheek, the writer seems nonetheless quite surprised and perturbed to find that, in a country that is split evenly between two parties, many products at a grocery store are made by a diverse group of people who give to both parties. "Spoiler: it's almost impossible to buy anything in Whole Foods without, in a roundabout way, supporting the Republican Party." *Quelle horreur!*

"Down this path lies madness," the writer John Brownlee rightly concluded after his attempt to shop in this assiduously politicized style. And, yet, this kind of life is encouraged as a reasonable, even a virtuous choice, according to many of our cultural and political leaders.

First Lady Michelle Obama famously gave a speech at UCLA asserting as much on the campaign trail before her husband was elected in 2008:

> *Barack Obama will require you to work. He is going to demand that you shed your cynicism. That you put down your divisions. That you come out of your isolation, that you move out of your comfort zones. That you push yourselves to be better. And that you engage. Barack will never allow you to go back to your lives as usual, uninvolved, uninformed.*

Again, that sounds terrible.

In a political campaign, there is a paradoxical demand for immediate commentary on every little thing, paired with a strenuous requirement that speech be perfectly calibrated in both position and tone. Political candidates have entire staffs of obscenely paid consultants and volunteering college students to help them navigate these minefields. It's a constraining, exhausting, and demoralizing system, even for a candidate. But at least there's some ostensible reason for it. The electoral system is built to evaluate people who may have an impact on policy and our lives, so assessing their views on issues becomes important. But to what end are we making regular citizens live by this standard?

The *Washington Post*'s Alyssa Rosenberg wrestled with this notion upon realizing that when she writes about art and culture, she increasingly finds she can't escape politics: "When we criticize politicians for similar slips of temper or public statements, we do so in part because we believe they have revealed something about how they will make policy and enforce the law. But artists do not behave like politicians." She also noted, "We treat people whose interpretations differ from our own as if they are acting in bad faith. We focus on gaffes and supposed gaffes. And we demand that significant figures in cultural commentary have something to say about every big event so we can check their reactions against our sense of what they *ought* to feel to remain in good standing."

Regular citizens shouldn't be required to live this way. When we demand as a culture that everyone's life be run like a campaign, we will get the conversation of politicians—stilted, rehearsed, black-and-white, and adversarial. Sonny Bunch, a conservative writer and cultural critic with the *Washington Free Beacon*, calls this phenomenon "the politicized life": "It treats politics as a zero sum game or a form of total warfare in which the other side must be obliterated. It alters every aspect of your being: where you shop; what you watch on TV; what sort of music you listen to; who you associate with." Once more, that sounds terrible.

4. Every Choice Is Between Good and Evil

Not only is everything a thing, but everything is binary. There are not merely two sides to an argument but a Good side and an Evil side, and making clear you're on the Good side is vital.

Writer Mollie Hemingway of *The Federalist* uses Václav Havel's essay "The Power of the Powerless" to address this tendency. Her subject is gay marriage, which having undergone a sea change in public perception over recent years has left many of its opponents unsure of how to voice their opinions in public.

> *To explain how dissent works, Havel introduced the manager of a hypothetical fruit-and-vegetable shop who places in his window, among the onions and carrots, the slogan: "Workers of the world, unite!" He's not actually enthusiastic about the sign's message. It's just one of the things that people in a post-totalitarian system do even if they "never think about" what it means. He does it because everyone does it. It's what you do to get along in life and live "in harmony with society." (For our purposes, you can imagine that slogan is a red equal sign that you put up on your Facebook page.) The subtext of the grocer's sign is "I do what I must do. I behave in the manner expected of me." It protects him from supervisors above and informants below.*

Those who assume all opposition to gay marriage must be rooted in dark bigotry are surely playing the world's smallest violin for their counterparts in this debate, but the concerns of gay marriage opponents aren't exactly unwarranted. As we will discuss later in more depth, Josh Barro, a writer for the *New York Times*, declared that those who disagree with his liberal position on gay marriage ought to have their attitudes "stamped out, ruthlessly." Brendan Eich was briefly CEO of the company he founded and had run with no indication of any discrimination against coworkers before being pushed out. His sin? He donated to Proposition 8 in California six years before his promotion, and he declined to recant his views on the matter once they were brought to light. Even passionate gay marriage advocates expressed concern over the precedent set and the message sent by Eich's raucous, public demotion.

The message to regular citizens was clear: If you hold a minority view on a policy, zip it, because there are plenty of people who think your point of view should make you lose your livelihood.

There's a term for this. Researchers call it the "spiral of silence," "the tendency of people not to speak up about policy issues in public—or among their family, friends, and work colleagues—when they believe their own point of view is not widely shared," according to the Pew Research Center's Internet and American Life Project. The phenomenon was established before the rise of social media, but a 2014 Pew experiment found that despite hopes to the contrary, social networks like Twitter and Facebook haven't conquered the problem and may have reinforced it. Pew surveyed 1,800 adults about Edward Snowden's leaked revelations about NSA surveillance programs—an issue on which the American public was about evenly split, according to the organization's other polls.

They found people far less willing to discuss the Snowden case online than in person, with 86 percent willing to discuss it in person, but only 42 percent online. Pew found, despite a hopeful hypothesis, Facebook and Twitter were not giving those unwilling to discuss the issue in person an alternative "discussion platform." And a person's perception of whether his or her view is in the majority or minority drastically changes that person's willingness to engage.

"For instance, at work, those who felt their coworkers agreed with their opinion were about three times more likely to say they would join a workplace conversation about the Snowden-NSA situation," Pew found. Further, social media use seemed to lessen the likelihood an individual would discuss this issue in person. This kind of self-censorship can be detrimental in a system that depends on an informed citizenry where an "informed citizenry depends on people's exposure to information on important political issues and on their willingness to discuss those issues with those around them."

Pew theorizes on several reasons people might not be open about what they believe to be minority views—they don't want to lose friends, disappoint family, or create a searchable record on the Internet of such thoughts. One of the theories is experience with the Outrage Circus itself:

> *[W]e speculate that social media users may have witnessed those with minority opinions experiencing ostracism, ridicule, or bullying online, and that this might increase the perceived risk of opinion sharing in other settings.*

It would be hard *not* to have witnessed it. And, as the Havel essay relates, when the stakes are high, it's often not enough to simply keep quiet. Lest one be mistaken for a dissenter, one must hang one's sign. One must change one's Twitter avatar to green or slap an asininely named twibbon upon it, lest the rest of the world might assume you hate the troops, or the transgender, or both.

In 2014, in the wake of the Sony hack, this tendency resulted in a particularly ludicrous spectacle in Hollywood. George Clooney, one of the most powerful men in a town allegedly dedicated to art and free speech, could not get anyone to sign onto a petition to support Sony if it decided to release *The Interview.* The Seth Rogen vehicle had upset North Korea enough to launch the hack against the company. Though it seemed a clear-cut issue of protecting artistic expression against assault by foreign despots, no one would join the petition. Clooney explained to *Deadline*:

> *Here's the brilliant thing they did. You embarrass them first, so that no one gets on your side. After the Obama joke, no one was going to get on the side of Amy, and so suddenly, everyone ran for the hills. Look, I can't make an excuse for that joke, it is*

what it is, a terrible mistake. Having said that, it was used as a weapon of fear, not only for everyone to disassociate themselves from Amy but also to feel the fear themselves. They know what they themselves have written in their emails, and they're afraid.

Again, this is exactly the way a political campaign functions. Candidates must constantly signal their social acceptability to a diverse group of consumers. Neither silence nor a lack of an opinion is an acceptable answer on any subject. And, in order to reduce the chances of losing their livelihood for transgressing, they default to shallow, safe, rehearsed, and socially approved messages. It's not a question of whether you sympathize with gay marriage opponents, who up until very recently made up the majority of this country. It's about what you lose if you cross the line. We have this wide-ranging Internet of infinite possibilities at our fingertips, but we're intent on shutting many of those possibilities down. *First, the spiral of silence came for the gay marriage opponents, and I did nothing, for I was not a gay marriage opponent,* etc.

5. Vetting Yourself

To be properly engaged in the outrage culture, one must pick one's side and then cull all associations that would taint that allegiance. In the way that a candidate must drop problematic board positions and investments before running for office, outrage culture demands regular citizens vet their own likes and dislikes to remain in good standing.

For writer Kevin Blackwell, a self-professed "black, male geek," vetting himself meant publicly disavowing his former hero Dr. Ben Carson. Carson, you see, cannot both be respected for being an incredibly accomplished pediatric brain surgeon who ascended to the top of his profession and also profess conservative views. No, according to Blackwell, Carson, who previously was a paragon of high-profile black intellectual achievement, is now a man who just says what the right-wing nuts tell him to so he can bring home some extra cash and hold court every now and then. On the blog *Ordinary Times*, Blackwell fumed, "Dr. Carson's willingness to sell out the truth for some media appearances and/or a political career is a sign of severe moral bank-ruptcy . . . To my mind, this outs him as a craven, opportunistic hack willing to compromise his integrity for a little money, attention, and power." Of course Blackwell would never assume that Carson assessed the facts and simply came to a different conclusion from his. Instead, the guy who is so successful that he was played by Cuba Gooding Jr. in a television movie about his life is probably just bowled over by the chance to rub shoulders with the likes of Representative Louis Goh-mert (with all due respect to Congressman Gohmert).

There are probably some things we would put on our list of dis-qualifiers for mentorship and admiration—the attempted bombing of American citizens and soldiers on the soil of the United States of America among them,[4] but we digress. Mere disagreement with the other half of the country on some policies does not discredit someone's stature. If either of us tried to purge our idea or media consumption of all traces of left-leaning bias or influence, we would consume nothing but think-tank podcasts and Toby Keith (the boot-in-your-ass era, obvi-ously, not the touchy-feely stuff of the later aughts).[5] Perhaps because so many of the people who provide the music, TV, movies, pop culture, and news in this country are liberal, conservatives are typically bet-ter at compartmentalizing their outrage. It's a survival mechanism of sorts.

---

[4] Bill Ayers didn't ghostwrite *our* book, we'll have you know. Yes, we're trolling here. But Barack Obama really did launch his political career with a fund-raiser in the living room of two unrepentant domestic terrorist bombers. That really *was* a thing. We're sure the detail that a Republican presidential candidate hosted his first political event at the home of an unapologetic abortion clinic bomber would elicit shrugs from much of the media, right?

[5] Tragically, even Toby Keith is tainted. His record company for most of his career was founded by Democratic megadonor Jeffrey Katzenberg.

Guy here: I once got into a Twitter dispute over poverty rates in the Reagan era with acclaimed chef Tom Colicchio, the chief judge on the Emmy Award–winning reality series *Top Chef*, of which I am a longtime fan. Colicchio and I had a productive, if slightly adversarial exchange, concluding with some quasi-obsequious fanboy tweets from yours truly. Some of my Twitter followers who'd witnessed the back-and-forth demanded to know why I kept watching a "liberal show" like *Top Chef* and encouraged me to boycott Colicchio's Craft restaurants. I'll pass, thanks. The show is enjoyable, and the man cooks one hell of a steak. As I wrote at the time, "living an intensely partisan life is exhausting and limiting." I also gained an entrée, so to speak, to honestly communicate conservative ideas to Colicchio, who'd likely never heard them framed in that way before.

Liberals profess tolerance but often have no occasion to practice it in everyday life, as conservatives do. Hence, Blackwell's rejection of Carson, or Steven Lloyd Wilson's rejection of Orson Scott Card. Card, the author of one of the most universally loved science fiction works of all time—*Ender's Game*—has written (sometimes harshly) against same-sex marriage, and homosexuality generally, in the decades since his masterpiece and its sequel were published. Upon the long-awaited announcement of a movie version of *Ender's Game*, the sci-fi nerds who would normally be weeing their pants at every behind-the-scenes glimpse and trailer leak decided to mount a boycott. "Card's political views have come to the forefront over the last year, as a film adaptation of *Ender's Game* has gotten under way, and especially in the last month when DC announced that Card would be writing for the *Superman* comic," Wilson wrote in his official denunciation of a formerly favorite writer.

Card's views on gay issues became problematic enough that "DC caved to pressure . . . and announced that Card's story had been scrapped." Almost like when a political candidate advances far enough to run for high enough office, and suddenly the vetting process makes every foible an issue.

Sure, you have the right to boycott all day long. If you desire to deprive yourself of an artist whose work you enjoy, and that artist of a living, because you disagree with her political views, it ain't a freedom of speech issue. You can use PR and market forces to punish people who disagree with you to your heart's delight. What we are saying is it may make you miserable.

Not all conservatives shrug off political differences in their day-to-day lives either. We often get blowback when we tweet or write about anything outside of conservative politics as if mere engagement in the culture at large—with which one must connect to win elections, mind you—is a betrayal of conservative values in and of itself. [6]

In the days following Obama's reelection, the *Washington Times* reported on a libertarian Romney voter who decided to excise all the Democrats from his life. Eric Dondero will not speak to his brother. He handed out Halloween candy under the banner REPUBLICAN FAMILIES ONLY. When it comes to music, Dondero had to give up Bon Jovi, but was still evaluating John Cougar Mellencamp, producing one of the saddest sentences we've ever read: "John Cougar Mellencamp is an interesting situation. He is a big-time Democrat, and I absolutely hate him. But a couple of years ago, he had some nice things to say about Sarah Palin. So, he is kind of dicey." He also told the *Washington Times* he's ashamed to drive a Chevy truck, but he grandfathered it in because he bought it pre-bailouts.

Seek help, we whisper gently.

6. The Professionalization of Outrage

The Internet has given us many great things, among them the ability to join together with those of similar interests in ways far more varied

---

[6] If this book had a comments section, roughly half of the comments would be some variation of, "STICK TO THE ISSUES!!!!1!!1!!"

and tailored than the Rotary Clubs and Ladies Who Lunch groups of days past.

The Web also allows these groups to quickly mobilize via e-mail, Twitter, and Facebook. We hope they would choose to lift up humanity, but they can also use the technology to register offense. Unfortunately, there are plenty of people interested in orchestrating such action, for attention, for social capital, for entertainment, for catharsis, and for political ends.

So, just as an Internet campaign can bring much-needed attention to kidnapped Nigerian schoolgirls, or create pro–free speech flash mobs in France, or move a school board to examine its zero-tolerance discipline practices, it can also be used to get a college DJ fired for playing a Top 40 hit.[7]

The point of politics and advocacy is to slice and dice the electorate, identify and get as many people as possible into a camp, moving from casual observer to engaged volunteer to insufferable proselytizer. That's why Michelle Obama declared her husband will not let you go back to your life as usual. Politicians need you living as an activist so that they can thrive. Our society is very skilled at the business of politics, for better or worse. Other countries come to our consultants to learn how to slice and dice their own electorates and hone their messages. Our media is also very happy to cover political campaigns, or anything it can squeeze into that template. It creates a vicious cycle: Have something that needs attention? Well, the media covers epic, emotional, good-versus-evil fights heavy on outrage and run like professional political campaigns. Therefore, make your issue into a political campaign so the media will cover it. The media then covers your issue in the style of a political campaign, thereby amplifying all the negative attributes of politics mentioned above.

This is bad for our brains. Literally.

---

[7] We've now alluded to this twice, and it really did happen. We'll discuss it in chapter 4.

OBSESSIVE POLITICS WILL BREAK YOUR BRAIN

There's a growing body of research that suggests partisan politics, that American tribal pastime, actually makes one unable to discern facts accurately. Here's the deal, as explained by *National Journal*'s Brian Resnick, who had his head examined in an MRI machine to determine the extent to which politics had ruined it:

> *Research at NYU and elsewhere is underscoring just how blind the "us-vs-them" mindset can make people when they try to process new political information. Once this partisanship mentality kicks in, the brain almost automatically pre-filters facts—even noncontroversial ones—that offend our political sensibilities.*

In experiment after experiment, once you cross the partisan threshold "it's almost like the whole brain becomes recoordinated in how it views people," NYU researcher Jay Van Bavel told *National Journal*. For instance, in one experiment, Democrats and Republicans were asked about the same, concrete, indisputable fact—the trajectory of the unemployment rate—in two different ways. "Would you say that compared to 2008, the level of unemployment in this country has gotten better, stayed the same, or gotten worse?" and "Would you say that the level of unemployment in this country has gotten better, stayed the same, or gotten worse since Barack Obama was elected president?"

To the first version of the question, partisans of both sides answered about the same. When the president was added to the question, the responses split on party lines. Even when Democrats in the room were given the raw numbers in the sentence directly before the partisan-primed question—unemployment had gone up, according to the raw numbers at the time—60 percent answered in the president's favor anyway. Gloat not, Republicans. This is not a phenomenon limited to Democrats, of course.

When Resnick asked the researchers what can fix the problem of the partisan brain, the answers that showed promise were all about jarring the brain out of its tribal political reflexes. For instance, a 2013 study at Princeton found "all it took was $1 or $2 to dramatically improve the chances of a right answer."[8] Another experiment required partisans to ruminate on their own humanity and individualism before watching a political debate, which led to a more accepting attitude toward the opposing candidate.

After his somewhat depressing quest to understand the partisan brain, Resnick asked, "Can we reshape our political environment to access the better angels of our neurological nature?" Instead, what we're doing increasingly is reshaping our cultural environment to access the nastier devils of our neurological nature.

This is the opposite of what we should be encouraging, as Jon Lovett explains in his "The Culture of Shut Up" piece mentioned earlier; it was adapted from a speech at Loyola Marymount University's First Amendment Week:

> *We need to learn to live with the noise and tolerate the noise even when the noise is stupid, even when the noise is offensive, even when the noise is at times dangerous. Because no matter how noble the intent, it's a demand for conformity that encourages people on all sides of a debate to police each other instead of argue and convince each other. And, ultimately, the cycle of attack and apology, of disagreement and boycott, will leave us with fewer and fewer people talking more and more about less and less.*

In short, in a culture suffused with politics and smartphones, every citizen must become a minipolitician, to one degree or another. Here's what happens when everyone starts to act like a politician. Jon Lovett again: "It replaces a competition of arguments with a competition to delegitimize arguments. And what's left is the pressure to sand down the corners of your speech while looking for the rough edges in

---

[8] Don't ever change, Americans, you beautiful, capitalist bastards.

the speech of your adversaries. Everyone is offended. Everyone is offensive," precipitating "cycles of pearl-clutching followed by either abject sorrow or banishment."

When we police the speech of people who care about what others think about them so intensely that they don't want to talk about anything of importance, we cede the debate to those who don't care whom they offend. And the fate of the country is too important to be left exclusively in the hands of trolls and floppers.

3

ANATOMY OF AN OUTRAGE

How the Racket Operates

The modern Left is largely bereft of new ideas, so its adherents are necessarily wedded to status quo policies that have failed the country for decades. Upgrades and revisions to this tired agenda often boil down to four words: larger government, more spending.[1]

To compensate for their intellectual torpor, liberals operate a ruthlessly effective demagoguery machine that shoots to kill, politically speaking. The machine's twin objectives are to isolate and polarize conservative figures, and just as important, to bypass meaningful debate via hype and outrage. So beware of those on the left calling for "national conversations" on difficult issues. Your working definition of a national conversation might involve the various sides presenting evidence, sharing concerns, and seeking areas of compromise to address intractable problems. *Their* idea of a national conversation entails them talking, and you listening. If they deign to allow you to speak, you must stick to permissible narratives, using only preapproved nomenclature. Only they know all the rules, and only they can grant waivers to said rules. (You are not eligible for a waiver.)

---

[1] "More money" is particularly problematic when the country is already grappling with a long-term spending and debt crisis—a reality that many on the left simply deny. The debt denialists can't hear your concerns about unpaid-for federal promises because they're straddling their high horses, loudly congratulating one another for being so "pro-science."

We've spent a fair amount of time in the previous two chapters de-crying the cynical manufacturing of "things." But how are those things created, especially in our politics? **Step One** is sort of the Paul Re-vere stage. Someone notices a conservative's comment or action that they recognize as exploitable, then races around the Internet (glee-fully) warning that an outrage is coming! An outrage is coming! **Step Two:** More town criers lend their voices to the growing throng, en-suring that the faux pas, no matter how trivial or unfair, filters into the lefty media bloodstream. In **Step Three,** "victims" are deployed to crank out perfunctory expressions of outrage. Relevant interest groups and "Absolute Moral Authority" figures (think Cindy Sheehan until she turned on Obama) issue statements and demand action. **Step Four:** Mainstream media, which all too often takes its cues from its ideologi-cal brethren on the left, jumps into the fray, often prompting official concern trolling from elected Democrats. By this point, the circus has achieved peak outrage. **Step Five** is the endgame: The sound and fury grow louder until the allegedly aggrieved parties claim their proverbial pound of flesh. This can take various forms, from firings, to boycotts, to social embarrassment. At the very least, the objective is to erode the target's reputation and to make him or her think twice before crossing the circus again.

Let's explore one example of how an attack is hatched, and the con-tagion spreads. As you've gathered, we're conservatives. We are ideo-logically inclined toward the Republican Party, despite a number of philosophical and tactical differences with the party as it exists today. Among the elected Republicans we admire most is Representative Paul Ryan of Wisconsin, one-half of the GOP's defeated 2012 presidential ticket. He is an influential member of Congress and a rumored future presidential candidate in his own right (though he's publicly passed on 2016). He's captain of the Right's wonk team on Capitol Hill, having spent the last decade or so offering conservative solutions to address some of the nation's toughest challenges—from Social Security's and Medicare's unsustainability to entrenched poverty.

For the purposes of this book, we're not going to rehearse the details of Ryan's various policy prescriptions, nor are we going to sketch out a modern governing agenda for the Republican Party. If you're interested in that sort of thing, we'd recommend checking out the YG Network's "Room to Grow" project, reading *Grand New Party* by power wonks Ross Douthat and Reihan Salam, and following the work of scholars from Jim Capretta to Avik Roy to Ramesh Ponnuru. Their work is invaluable and granular in detail—plus, they're smarter than we are. We're more keen on explaining how the Left tends to respond to Paul Ryan's ideas. We'll do so by performing a postmortem of one conversation-ending, contrived "outrage."

"INNER CITIES" AND BOGUS BIGOTRY

On the morning of Wednesday, March 12, 2014, Paul Ryan appeared on Bill Bennett's *Morning in America* radio program on the Salem Radio Network. Bennett cited a speech Ryan had delivered at the Conservative Political Action Conference (CPAC) several days earlier and asked him a series of questions about his latest project of tackling poverty in America. Ryan riffed on the value and dignity of work, prompting the host to jump in with a point about hard work being a learned trait. Here is the transcript of the resulting exchange:

> **Bennett:** We had a report yesterday, Paul, from the Pew
> [Research Center] on the Millennials. We're setting records
> in terms of people not working. Part of it is the economy, part
> of it is policy. But there's a cultural aspect to this, as well,
> right? Boys, particularly, learn how to work. Who teaches
> boys how to work? You lost your dad at an early age. Who
> taught you how to work?
>
> **Ryan:** Mentors and my mom. My dad's friends, his buddies
> taught me how to hunt and taught me a lot of things, and my
> mom. And so—

Bennett: Hunting is not working, is it?

Ryan: Well, no, but you can learn—by the way, you can teach your kids character in the woods. A lot of good life lessons are learned in a tree stand, Bill.

Bennett: You still haven't sent me that ad, but I know. But the fatherless problem is a big one. This has something to do with people's attitudes. I asked my boys the other day, you know my guys, "what do you remember me saying most often?" And of course, they gave me a bad time and said lately it is: "What's that? What'd you just say?" Pretty funny, but they say: "Do your job, do your job."

Ryan: I remember more my mom was: "Suck it up, deal with it, and tough." Those are the things I remember her saying to me a lot.

Bennett: Suck it up, deal with it, tough—Betty Ryan. But I mean, a boy has to see a man working, doesn't he?

Ryan: Absolutely. And so, that's this tailspin or spiral that we're looking at in our communities. You know your buddy Charles Murray or Bob Putnam over at Harvard, those guys have written books on this, which is we have got this tailspin of culture in our inner cities, in particular, of men not working and just generations of men not even thinking about working or learning the value and the culture of work; and so there's a real culture problem here that has to be dealt with. Everybody's got to get involved. So, this is what we talk about when we talk about civil society. If you're driving from the suburb to the sports arena downtown by these blighted neighborhoods, you can't just say: "I'm paying my taxes, government's going to fix that." You need to get involved. You need to get involved yourself—whether through a good mentor program or some religious charity, whatever it is, to make a difference, and that's how we help resuscitate our culture.

To summarize: intergenerational poverty and a culture of workless-ness can inflict lasting damage on communities, "in our inner cities, in particular," and it is the responsibility of civil society to both help people in need and work to "resuscitate our culture"—beyond the limited confines of government intervention. Despite the commonsense nature of Ryan's observations and the uncontroversial nature of his "let's get to work helping each other" call to action, the Outrage Circus sprang into high gear as soon as that sentence escaped Ryan's lips.

Steps one and two of the aforementioned outrage chain unfolded simultaneously and almost instantaneously. "Paul Ryan Blames Poverty on Lazy 'Inner City' Men," blared a headline at *ThinkProgress*, a branch of the Center for American Progress and a core member of the left-wing Democracy Alliance network (we'll address this more later on). The wildfire quickly set the entire lefty blogosphere ablaze, hitting *Daily Kos*, *FireDogLake*, and *Democratic Underground* within hours. Each of these sites accused Ryan of blowing racial "dog whistles" (more on that term to come), and inserting "inner city" as a substitute for "black people." According to the *Daily Kos* write-up, the phrase "dignity of work" has insidious racial implications, too. Several of these screeds accused Ryan of "doubling down" on the 1996 bipartisan welfare reform law passed by a Republican Congress and signed into law by President Clinton. These critiques presupposed that the 1996 law, which beefed up work requirements for welfare, has not seen empirical successes. The opposite is true. After the reforms were enacted, poverty rates plunged to five-decade lows and remained fairly stable until spiking as a result of the 2008 financial collapse. According to poverty scholar Robert Rector, "in the four years after welfare reform, the caseload dropped by nearly half. Employment surged and child poverty among affected groups plummeted."

Viral lefty blog hyperventilation, coupled with an exploitable racial angle, yielded the inevitable incessant and breathless coverage about the interview on MSNBC. According to an iQ Media Corp archive search conducted by the *Washington Free Beacon*'s David Rutz, the cable network devoted at least thirty segments to Ryan's remark over a four-week stretch. This included multiple cracks at the topic by hosts Melissa Harris-Perry (she who wore tampons as earrings on-air in support of late-term abortion, lectured parents that they ought to shed the provincial notion that their children belong to them, rather than to the community writ large) and Al Sharpton (he who owes millions in back taxes, perpetrates vicious racial hoaxes, foments race riots, and routinely loses nightly battles with his own show's teleprompter[2]). Without a shred of shame or irony, Sharpton slammed Ryan's off-the-cuff analysis as "vicious and divisive."

Quick, but relevant, side rant: MSNBC serves as a clearinghouse for liberal-left attacks and acts as something of a messaging petri dish for developing and/or amplifying Democratic Party talking points. It frequently bridges steps two and four in the outrage-creation racket we've described. Yes, some would argue that our network, Fox News, furnishes the Republican Party with the exact same sort of media mouthpiece, but independent research has found that MSNBC *far* outpaces Fox on opinion programming,[3] and the network's coverage during the 2012 election's home stretch was literally as unbalanced as humanly possible: 100 percent pro-Obama and anti-Romney. We'd also recommend checking out the *Columbia Journalism Review*'s worthwhile 2012 profile of Fox's sizable liberal on-air contingent, which noted that "though MSNBC has a handful of moderate conservatives— namely *Morning Joe*'s Joe Scarborough—Fox stands out for the prominence it awards its on-air naysayers, many of whom occupy regular roles on the network's most popular shows."

To that point, liberal Juan Williams guest hosts the top-rated

---

[2] Do yourself a favor. Search YouTube for, "Al Sharpton versus the Teleprompter." Allow several minutes for uncontrollable laughter—more, if you watch the follow-on installments. They never get old. *"Sigannoy Weaver!"*

[3] We'd direct you to the nonpartisan Pew Research Center's analyses of American cable news. Pay special attention to the opinion versus hard news ratios they track, as well as the breakdown of positive versus negative coverage for Barack Obama and Mitt Romney during the 2012 election cycle.

O'Reilly Factor regularly. Remember those times when Rachel Maddow handed the reins of her show over to a conservative? Neither do we.

Okay, back to the Ryan "outrage." Once established as "fact" on the blogs, the opprobrium over Ryan's racist remarks jumped seamlessly from the lefty media echo chamber to official Democratdom. Here's how steps three and four played out: congressional Democrats pronounced themselves scandalized by Ryan's comment, with the Congressional Black Caucus leading the charge. Representative Barbara Lee (D-CA) fumed that what Ryan said was a "thinly veiled racial attack" that "cannot be tolerated." Nancy Pelosi, the highest-ranking House Democrat, piled on, denouncing Ryan's remark as "shameful, disturbing and wrong." Sensing an opportunity to make a buck off a race-baiting slander, the Democrats' fund-raising arm jumped into the fray, blasting this "petition"-style e-mail to supporters:

> *You won't believe what Paul Ryan is saying to justify his radical agenda. This week, Ryan told ultra-conservative radio host Bill Bennett that poverty in America is caused by a "culture problem" of "inner city" men too lazy to work. Ryan's comments are plainly a dog-whistle to ugly racial politics . . . If Paul Ryan and his Republican buddies are going to use thinly veiled racial attacks to justify their radical agenda, let's tell them they're the ones with the real "culture problem": Let's get 100,000 strong denouncing Paul Ryan for this thinly veiled racial attack. Click here to automatically add your name.*

Depressingly, most political fund-raising e-mails are similarly frantic in tone.

Let's remember that at no point did Paul Ryan even come close to accusing anyone of being "too lazy to work." *ThinkProgress* invented that phrase in its headline. Hours later, the official Democratic Party apparatus was ripping off that mischaracterization verbatim. This was no coincidence.

The story was revived a few days later when a *ThinkProgress* "tracker" filmed one of Ryan's black constituents confronting him about his comments at a town-hall-style meeting. The man accused the congressman of employing "code words," and asserting, "You said what you meant." This clip quickly made the rounds, touching off another blitz of attention, including coverage from a number of mainstream outlets. In all the stories and blog posts we read about the exchange, none bothered to mention that the featured constituent, Alfonso Gardner, happened to be a "longtime community activist," as described by a 2009 *Racine Post* account.

Delving into the archives, we discovered that Mr. Gardner was at the center of another race-based controversy in 2004. At a city council meeting that year, Gardner accused an alderman of cutting him off before his full public comment period had elapsed. His accusation evidently had racial overtones. The alderman responded with an extremely awkward joke about his watch "having a black face—this is not a prejudiced watch," noting that Gardner had been given precisely the same amount of time as everyone else. (According to the official record, he was actually granted more time than others.) As a result of this unfortunate comment, the NAACP got involved, and local media quoted Gardner demanding that the alderman "apologize to the black community," calling for a summit to address the city's "race problem." Just your average citizen.

Don't misunderstand; Mr. Gardner was and is absolutely entitled to his opinion, and he had every right to question Paul Ryan the way he did. But the resulting coverage presented the scene as an embattled congressman taking organic heat from a random constituent. Mr. Gardner was not random. He was an activist with a history of making accusations of racism. His anger wasn't piqued *by* the Outrage Circus. As a low-level lefty activist, he was *part of* the Outrage Circus. If we could discover as much over an hour of googling and following links, the media that chose to highlight the episode could have ascertained the same context. They didn't care, or didn't try.

Sometimes political stories go viral because of genuine news value or inherent shareability. "Outrages," like the one over Ryan's comments, though, are often inorganic. While both major political coalitions have their respective chains of outrage, Democrats have mastered the process. In this case, the opposition research branch of an organization funded by anonymous, deep-pocketed liberals—and led for years by John Podesta (previously of the Clinton administration, currently of the Obama administration)—decided that a turn of phrase by Paul Ryan during an interview about fighting poverty could be presented as "racist" and could thereby be used to discredit him. They went to work and made it "a thing," to the point that Ryan felt compelled to meet with the Congressional Black Caucus to try to smooth things over, apologizing for "inarticulate" phraseology. One CBC member condemned Ryan as ignorant: "He probably doesn't know anything about people, African-American men or the Latino men, in the inner city. He doesn't know," asserted Representative Emanuel Cleaver (D-MO).

The irony is that Paul Ryan, more than most politicians, *does* know. Not because he grew up in the inner city (though his background is hardly the stuff of silver spoons), but because he's consciously and faithfully sought to understand poverty in this country. In April 2014, *BuzzFeed* reporter McKay Coppins published a seven-thousand-word story chronicling Ryan's quest to internalize how America's have-nots exist and subsist day to day. He's undertaken this journey quietly, attending numerous events at churches and shelters across the country, away from the cameras. His mentor throughout this process has been Bob Woodson, a septuagenarian community organizer who's dedicated his life to helping people—mostly from, er, inner cities—escape cyclical poverty and crime. Coppins describes the moment that catalyzed Ryan's passion and conviction on these issues:

> *Ryan's fixation on fighting poverty began with a laying on of hands. It was Oct. 24, 2012, and he was sitting in a high-ceilinged backstage room at Cleveland State University's Waetjen Auditorium. Woodson had arranged for about a dozen*

activists to meet with him, and Ryan spent the half hour he had managed to carve out of his campaign schedule listening to stories about homelessness and addiction and redemption and relapse. When the testimonials came to an end and Ryan rose to leave, a hulking tattooed minister who had come to the meeting via motorcycle asked if he could bless him before he went. Ryan was taken aback by the request, and not entirely familiar with the ritual, but he obliged.

The group encircled him, and the minister placed his hands on Ryan's shoulders, as the candidate made the sign of the cross. While they prayed over him, he thought about the stories he had just heard: of people miraculously escaping the pit of poverty and then reaching down to pull their brothers and sisters out as well. Several people in the room, including Ryan, grew emotional. "To me, that moment is how the things we believe in and what we're trying to do can really revitalize our country," he recalls now.

Weeks after he lost the election and returned home to Wisconsin, the prayer stuck with him as the single most powerful experience he had on the campaign trail. By the time a close confidant called him over the holidays, Ryan was speaking with the passion of a convert. "I want to figure out a way for conservatives to come up with solutions to poverty," he confided to his friend. "I have to do this."

Such a racist. Ryan told Coppins that prior to the "inner cities" supposed gaffe, he'd been called virtually every name in the book, but the "scarlet R" was a new one, and it stung. Which was the entire point. Most of these people didn't *really* believe that Paul Ryan's heart was filled with secret racial contempt, surreptitiously conveyed to fellow racists using special code words. Their umbrage was an act. Our proof on this point comes from a decidedly unlikely source . . .

BUSTED AND SPEECHLESS

Comedian Bill Maher, an ultraliberal and aggressive religion basher, raised the issue of Paul Ryan's comments on his HBO program *Real Time*. The left-leaning members of Maher's panel—including the president of the Center for American Progress (there they are again), Neera Tanden—predictably savaged Ryan for sowing racial divisiveness, blaming the victims, and so on. Maher egged them on. "Here's something else Paul Ryan said: 'When it comes to getting an education, too many of our young people just can't be bothered. They're sitting on couches for hours playing video games, watching TV. Instead of dreaming of being a teacher or a lawyer or a business leader, they're fantasizing about being a baller or a rapper,'" Maher concluded, allowing a beat of silence before his big reveal. "Oh wait, that wasn't him. That was Michelle Obama. Michelle Obama said that." Nobody spoke. "Hushed silence!" Maher exclaimed, staring defiantly at his notoriously rabid studio audience, which laughed uneasily. Recovering from momentary cognitive-dissonance-exploding-brain lock, one guest jumped in to try to salvage the situation:

> **W. Kamau Bell** (*comedian*): I don't think this is a Republican or Democrat issue. This is a people issue.
> **Rick Lazio** (*former GOP congressman*): Wait a minute, you just called Ryan a racist . . .
> **Maher:** Yeah, suddenly . . . [laughs]
> **Bell:** Did I actually say he was a racist?
> **Tanden:** No.
> **Lazio:** Basically.
> **Bell:** He was talking about black people . . . [crosstalk] . . . you're either a racist or not a racist.
> **Maher:** Come on. I just read this, and you thought it was Paul Ryan.
> **Bell:** Because you told me it was!

Maher: For a reason! I'm just asking. Is something less true if a
white person says it about black people?

Bell eventually settled on the excuse that the first lady made her
remarks "in front of black people . . . we talk to each other differently
than we talk in front of you." The crowd roared with approving laughter, relieved to no longer have to think too hard about what had just
happened. The *Wall Street Journal* found an even more fitting quote
comparison in a March 20, 2014, house editorial (we've added the bold
for emphasis):

> "*We know **young black men are twice as likely as young
> white men to be 'disconnected'—not in school, not work-
> ing**. We've got to reconnect them. We've got to give more of these
> young men access to mentors. We've got to continue to encour-
> age responsible fatherhood. We've got to provide more pathways
> to apply to college or find a job. We can keep them from falling
> through the cracks.*"
>
> *Those were the words of President Obama, speaking less
> than a month ago about his "My Brother's Keeper" project to
> help "groups who've seen fewer opportunities that have spanned
> generations," especially boys and young men of color. "It's going
> to take time. **We're dealing with complicated issues that
> run deep in our history, run deep in our society, and are
> entrenched in our minds**.*"

Curiously, *ThinkProgress* didn't assail Obama for blaming lazy
"young black men" for their lot in life—and his comments were *explicitly* racial. His wife's comment, cited by Bill Maher, was very clearly
an admonition against laziness, with a bonus deployment of both basketball and rap references. Where was the parade of hand-wringing
MSNBC segments about that? Don't bother. Rhetorical question.

FORWARD

The simple truth is that many members of the Left didn't, and still don't, want to engage Ryan's ideas, nor do they want to be held to account for their own failures. So they go the cheap, delegitimization route, correctly concluding that it'd be easier than defeating Ryan's proposal on the merits. *Decades* after Democrats declared their multitrillion-dollar "war on poverty," approximately 50 million Americans are struggling below the poverty line, according to 2013 data. Big government has spent a fortune, and politicians have spoken countless words, yet the results speak for themselves. Paul Ryan is trying to do better,[4] and what better way to try to silence him—or at least distract from his serious work—than to drum up a pretext to yell "racist"?

"I know who I am and I know who I'm not," Ryan said in the *BuzzFeed* interview, refusing to assist the Left in executing step five of the vilification process. "If we're going to get to fixing this problem, we need to allow a good conversation to happen without, you know, throwing baseless charges at people." As for the "dog whistle" charges, Ryan said that he hadn't even encountered that phrase until this episode. We caught up with Congressman Ryan and asked him whether, upon further reflection, he agrees that the objective of the firestorm was to preclude the "good conversation" he craves. His short answer: Yes, and the problem is getting worse.

"I see it as an accelerating trend," he told us, citing his two decades in political life as a basis for comparison. "We are in the age of Obama and the progressives who choose [these] tactics, who cling to modern liberalism—which is intellectually pretty much exhausted, so they

---

[4] His good-faith stab at this complex challenge took the form of a detailed, budget-neutral (no cuts) antipoverty agenda released in the summer of 2014, which drew on ideas and reforms from both ends of the ideological spectrum. Many of the usual suspects objected furiously, because that's their raison d'être. Also, like clockwork, a certain segment of conservatives stamped their feet over Ryan's ideas not "going far enough."

resort to ridicule and hyperbole. I call it a lazy debate because they try to impugn your motives rather than debating the merits of the idea, and try to win the debate by default. Lots of straw-man arguments are used . . . to try and shoot the messenger so [they] don't actually have to deal with the contents of the message."

Ryan said he emerged from the Bennett interview without giving the offending snippet a second thought, and that he was "dumbfounded" when his staff showed him Democrats' public rebukes and press releases. His takeaway? Many of conservatives' ideological foes "want to shut down debate. They would rather attack a person and their character rather than talk about ideas." He explained why so many liberals resort to emotionalist intimidation on issues like poverty. "In the poverty space, what I think is interesting is that the Left has had a political monopoly in poverty fighting for a long time. And in one area conservatives have made an incredible difference and that's really bothering the Left—that's education. I witnessed this in Milwaukee and you're seeing this in New York. Conservatives brought energy and principles to the education debate and have claimed and held on to a moral high ground, which is [standing for] the students. I think we have captured people's imagination; we have seized that moral high ground through things like choice and charter schools and vouchers. We need to bring the same kind of energy and principles to the rest of poverty fighting which is exactly what I am trying to do and I think it threatens a political monopoly. I think that people would rather not have that debate in the first place, [so they] intimidate those of us that do," he said.

"I think this is an attempt to prevent the debate from happening and to encourage conservatives to disengage." He sighed, then summarized the Left's aim bluntly: "Raise the cost of participating in the debate so that it doesn't take place." End of discussion. Ryan is quick to point out that these tactics extend far beyond racial matters, and he would know, given his scrapes and bruises from various policy fights.

We agree, which is why this book has more than three chapters, but there's a reason why our discussion on race bats leadoff in our lineup of issue-based chapters: abusing the R-word to shut opponents up is the most pernicious and effective silencing method in modern American politics. Racism is an awful thing, so the fear of being called or thought of as a racist is pervasive and logical. Silencers exploit that fear by tossing the accusation about. Their aim is to get Paul Ryan—or us, or *you*—to keep that reasonable, nonracist thought in your head to yourself because they don't want to address your actual argument.

HIGH-DOLLAR HYPOCRISY

Before we proceed to our "issue" chapters, there is one more significant theme that we have to talk about up front, because it influences everything you see, hear, read, and talk about: money.

Everyone knows that Democrats strive to reduce the "influence of money in politics," while Republicans milk their fat-cat donors to buy elections. That's why liberals caterwaul endlessly about the *Citizens United* Supreme Court decision, culminating in the president himself scolding the justices to their faces during his 2010 State of the Union address. In doing so, he grossly mischaracterized the facts of the case and the ruling's implications, prompting Justice Samuel Alito to visibly shake his head and mouth the words *not true* in response to Obama's perfidious hectoring. Various fact-checkers sided with Alito. But our former constitutional law professor in chief wasn't interested in sweating the details. His goal was to advance for public consumption the "money in politics" narrative, which is a win/win for Democrats. They get to pretend that they're against big money infesting American politics while energetically exploiting the system they "oppose," quite often outraising Republicans by substantial sums.

Throw Momma from the Cliff

R yan's fiery baptism into hysteria bombardment came when he first introduced a proposal to reform Medicare. Yes, Medicare reform is a dreadfully dry subject, but it couldn't be more relevant. If you're within spitting distance of retirement age or beyond, your path ahead is relatively stable—but for everyone else, America's largest government-run health program is going broke. Quickly. The government's own accountants project that Medicare "as we know it," a description Democrats invoke to stave off attempts to save the currently popular program, will be insolvent within the next decade and a half. And those are *optimistic* estimates that rely on unrealistic policy assumptions. Our friend Philip Klein has done yeoman's work chronicling the government's Medicare manipulations, many of which are tied into Obamacare. We recommend his stuff highly.

Without going too "CBO" on you, here's the rub: the Obama administration "double counted" cuts to Medicare as both contributing to Medicare's fiscal longevity *and* as paying for parts of Obamacare. The same "saved" dollar cannot be used in two different places to achieve two different ends. Also, Obamacare's Medicare cuts are unpopular with seniors, and seniors vote. Thus, Democrats have a strong incentive to unwind the new law's Medicare "savings." This process began ahead of the 2014 elections, when anxious Democrats began to abandon the cuts they'd voted to enact four years prior. As those spending reductions are reversed, some of Obamacare's pay-fors vanish, *and* Medicare's sustainability picture darkens. When you double-count "savings" to simulate impossible budgetary feats, you set yourself up to sustain a policy double whammy when those savings melt away under political pressure.

All of which is to say that Medicare's accountants are aware that their own 2030 expected insolvency date is Pollyannaish. The program's chief actuary issued a blunt assessment in 2014, warning that Obamacare's cuts to Medicare aren't politically viable, so they're very likely to vanish. If and when that happens, the insolvency clock will churn at a faster clip. As it stands, Medicare faces an "unfunded liability" in the neighborhood of $40 trillion. That's D.C.-speak for the simple premise

Throw Momma from the Cliff *(continued)*

that the federal government has made $40 trillion in future Medicare benefit promises that are not paid for. Even President Obama has acknowledged the long-term implications of this looming wave of red ink. Here's the appropriately dire picture he painted in a 2011 "Remarks by the President on Fiscal Policy" address:

> *By 2025, the amount of taxes we currently pay will only be enough to finance our health care programs, Social Security, and the interest we owe on our debt. That's it. Every other national priority—education, transportation, even national security—will have to be paid for with borrowed money.*

The single biggest driver of that debt bomb is Medicare, which is why Paul Ryan rolled out a plan to reform the program for future seniors. The Left went ballistic. Ryan tweaked his proposal enough over the following year that he managed to attract a prominent liberal Democrat cosponsor, in the person of Senator Ron Wyden of Oregon. Democrats promptly shoved Wyden into a closet and campaigned hard against a dishonest caricature of Ryan's idea. A left-wing group infamously ran television ads depicting a Ryan look-alike wheeling an elderly woman off a cliff. Hapless DNC chairwoman Debbie Wasserman Schultz declared that Ryan's plan would rip "like a tornado through America's nursing homes," an original and incisive variation on the calumny she'd leveled one year earlier against Ryan's previous budget: It "passes like a tornado through America's nursing homes," she said. There's an aphorism about consistency, small minds, and hobgoblins floating around out there, isn't there?

The Obama campaign and national Democrats repeated with relish a claim for which they'd earned 2011's political "lie of the year"[5] from *PolitiFact*, a left-leaning fact-checker; namely, that Republicans supported "killing Medicare." They deliberately avoided mentioning that the bipartisan Ryan-Wyden plan did not apply to anyone over

---

[5] They took home the same prize in 2013 for Obamacare's "If you like your plan, you can keep it."

the age of fifty-five, and that it was designed to prioritize assistance for sicker and needier future seniors. They could not permit a serious, substantive debate on this issue. Winning that debate would be hard. Scaring people and vilifying Paul Ryan as mean-spirited and heartless was much easier, they reasoned, and acted accordingly. The unsustainable current trajectory, not Paul Ryan, is killing Medicare. If you're young or middle-aged, the government is forcibly extracting a chunk of your every paycheck and funneling it into a program that will be defunct by the time you're eligible to benefit from it. Unless big changes occur, that is. That's not our opinion. That's math. Paul Ryan is trying to fix the problem. Democrats are not. They're trying to win the next election by punishing Ryan for having ideas that are easily lied about, all while complaining that the GOP never offers ideas or solutions. This cynical, solutions-free sentiment was most candidly expressed by former Treasury secretary Timothy Geithner. At a 2012 House Budget Committee hearing, Ryan confronted Geithner with the Obama administration's own fiscal chart, which predicted an explosion of national debt. Again, these numbers were produced by the Obama administration itself:

PUBLICLY HELD DEBT UNDER 2013 BUDGET POLICY EXTENDED

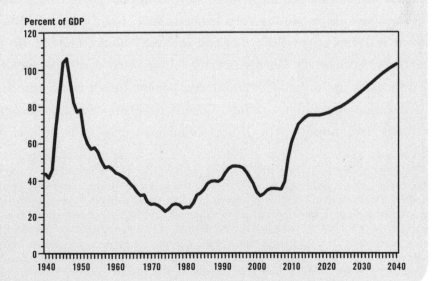

Throw Momma from the Cliff (continued)

Congressman Ryan asked Geithner which transformative reforms the White House wanted to pursue to avoid that calamity. The secretary's verbatim answer: "You are right to say we're not coming before you today to say 'we have a definitive solution to that long term problem.' What we *do* know is, we don't like yours." Geithner's boss was reelected nine months later.[6]

---

[6] Important caveat: Romney/Ryan's loss was not primarily driven by "Mediscare." Republicans effectively parried those accusations with the fact that Democrats voted to slash hundreds of billions of dollars from Medicare to pay for Obamacare, neutralizing the attack.

According to OpenSecrets.org, Barack Obama's 2008 campaign outspent John McCain's by roughly *$400 million*.[7] A *New York Times* headline published the week preceding 2010's GOP landslide read, "Democrats Outspend Republicans on Campaigns." The *Huffington Post*'s post-2012 analysis of Federal Elections Commission data revealed that the Obama camp had outspent Romney on payroll, on-air ads, online ads, polling, and total operating expenditures.

But wait, you may protest, *this only tells half the story. What about all that "outside money" we keep hearing about?* Good question. What *about* so-called super PACs, "special interest" money, and the Koch brothers? Let's briefly touch on each of those. First of all, Democrats have caught up to the GOP on outside money. Here's *Politico* in the final weeks of the 2014 campaign: "The 15 top Democrat-aligned committees have outraised the 15 top Republican ones $453 million to

---

[7] Obama was able to run up this score by abandoning "public financing," a good-governance idea enthusiastically embraced by the Left as a means to limit money in politics. Obama had specifically promised to adhere to a publicly funded campaign if his Republican opponent would do the same. John McCain agreed, then Obama peaced out. Why? There was a hell of a lot of money to be had, that's why. Faced with an opportunity to live up to supposed values, self-interest easily overwhelmed "principle," and the rest is history: Obama $730 million, McCain $330 million. Liberals tut-tutted about this, then popped the champagne with Obama and rode his epic cash wave to victory. The ends justify the means.

$289 million in the 2014 cycle, according to a *Politico* analysis of the most recent Federal Election Commission reports."

After the cycle concluded, the Associated Press reported, "For as often as Democrats attack conservative billionaires . . . for their spending on politics, it's actually the liberal-minded who shelled out the most cash in the just completed midterm elections . . . Among groups that funneled more than $100,000 to allies, the top of the list tilted overwhelmingly toward Democrats—a group favoring the GOP doesn't appear on the list until No. 14."

Second, President Obama called the rise of super PACs—independent political expenditure groups—a "threat to our democracy" in 2010.[8] Two years later, he set up his very own, um, "threat to democracy," a super PAC that ended up running a television commercial that blamed Mitt Romney for the death of a woman with cancer. (We remembered this episode when Obama lamented the state of American politics in his 2015 State of the Union Address, in which he called for less demonization and decried "constant fund-raising," without a shred of self-awareness.) Obama's campaign manager, Jim Messina, weakly defended the creation of the super PAC as a necessary evil to "balance" out the money game, invoking "oil company billionaires, investment bankers on Wall Street, Karl Rove and the Koch Brothers." In short, the devil made them do it. We'd direct Mr. Messina to this articulation of righteous principle:

> *You can't say, yesterday, you don't believe in [outside spending groups], and today, you're having three-quarters of a million dollars being spent for you [by those groups]. You can't just talk the talk. The easiest thing in the world is to talk without change during election time. Everyone talks about change during an election time. You've gotta look at how they act when it's not*

---

[8] The two most prolific super PACs of 2014 were Senate Majority PAC and House Majority PAC—both Democratic groups. And both turned out to be misnomers, given the election results.

convenient. When it's hard. And the one thing I'm proud of is my track record is strong on this. I walk the walk.

That was . . . Barack Obama at a campaign rally in 2007, taking then primary opponent John Edwards to the woodshed over campaign finance hypocrisy. If you think we're just scoring cheap points here by pointing out Obama's hypocrisy, you're more or less correct. Here's why it's important, though: Back then, Barack Obama sold himself as the very embodiment of reforming Washington's corrupt and cynical ways. That was a central element underpinning the whole "Hope and Change" mantra. If anyone was going to selflessly lead by example and clean things, it was him. But when it came time to "walk the walk," when it was "not convenient" for his own expedient interests, Obama shamelessly sprinted away from his passionately stated beliefs. The whole "money in politics" thing is an act, and anyone who still buys into it is willfully naive.[9]

On "special interest" money, Democrats often conjure images of wealthy, portly conservative white men in pinstriped suits handing each other briefcases full of cash, slapping one another on the back, and cackling. In smoke-filled rooms, of course.[10] And yes, Republican cronyism is hardly in short supply. But the Left's preferred narrative omits a mind-blowingly prolific source of special interest spending: labor unions. The *Wall Street Journal* reported in 2012 that unions, including taxpayer-funded government unions, spent roughly $4.4 billion—with a *B*—on political campaigns between 2005 and 2011, more than a billion dollars more than previously thought. From the *Journal* report:

Corporations and their employees also tend to spread their donations fairly evenly between the two major parties, unlike

---

[9] We're looking forward to lefty populist heroine *du jour* Elizabeth Warren getting an Exxon/Mobil neck tattoo if and when the political moment demands it.

[10] Smoking is not yet banned in liberal fever dreams.

unions, which overwhelmingly assist Democrats. In 2008, Dem-
ocrats received 55% of the $2 billion contributed by corporate
PACs and company employees, according to the Center for Re-
sponsive Politics. Labor unions were responsible for $75 million
in political donations, with 92% going to Democrats. Unlike
super PACs, which cannot directly support campaigns, corpo-
rate PACs give money from employees to candidates.

It's little wonder, then, that Democrats have attempted to carve out sweetheart exemptions for their union benefactors from various legislative efforts to rein in "money in politics" (see, for instance, the debate over the so-called DISCLOSE Act). Democrats aren't actually against money in politics per se; they're against *conservative* money in politics. And they loathe special interests, you see, unless they're the *right sort* of special interests—the Service Employees International Union (SEIU), Planned Parenthood, and teachers' unions, among them.

Which brings us to Charles and David Koch, two wildly successful businessmen and philanthropists who are actively in favor of gay marriage and marijuana legalization, and who've given prodigious gifts on behalf of the arts (check out the David H. Koch Theater at Lincoln Center) and medical research (see the Koch Institute for Integrative Cancer Research at MIT).[11] But no amount of humanitarian penance can atone for the Kochs' inexpiable sin: donating generously to libertarian-leaning political groups who help Republicans win elections.[12] For this

---

[11] When David Koch made a *nine-figure* donation to New York-Presbyterian Hospital to fund a new wing, a collection of left-wing activists picketed the hospital for accepting his dirty right-wing money. Those bastards! We repeat: These people *picketed a hospital.* One speaker at the rally, representing SEIU, shouted, "If there ain't gonna be no justice, there ain't gonna be no peace!" Given the setting (picketing a charitable hospital donation), her slogan was about as coherent as it was original.

[12] The *Journal's* Kimberley Strassel put the Kochs' political spending in perspective: "The Center for Responsive Politics' list of top all-time donors from 1989 to 2014 ranks Koch Industries No. 59. Above Koch were 18 unions, which collectively spent $620,873,623 more than Koch Industries ($18 million). Even factoring in undisclosed personal donations by the Koch brothers, they are a rounding error in union spending."

political activism and speech, they've been transformed into comic book villains ("Kochtopus!") by the Left. Senate Democratic leader Harry Reid has developed something of a *Fatal Attraction*-esque big-boy crush on the duo, denouncing them by name approximately eighty-seven thousand times from the Senate floor ahead of the 2014 mid-terms. In one diatribe, Reid called the brothers "about as un-American as anyone I can imagine."

By contrast, one of the finest Americans around, according to Reid, is one Tom Steyer. He's an environmentalist billionaire who's committed tens of millions to Democratic causes over the years. We hear a lot about conservative megadonors; much less attention is paid to the Left's intricate big-money network. Few people, if anyone, have done more shoe-leather reporting on the latter subject than journalist Lachlan Markay, formerly of the Heritage Foundation and now at the *Washington Free Beacon*. His indefatigable work has shed light on a secretive cabal of lefty donors, spearheaded by a little-known group called the Democracy Alliance, which is basically a secretive piggy bank for left-wing causes, funded by *über*wealthy, mostly undisclosed donors.

"A lot of the stuff [the Democracy Alliance] does is behind-the-scenes: On data, on get-out-the-vote, and on programs devoted to different ethnic groups," Markay tells us. The structure of the alliance falls into two tiers: The "aligned network," featuring roughly 20 central member organizations, and a much broader "progressive infrastructure map," of at least 153 like-minded groups. DA donors collectively pump approximately $70 million into these organizations' coffers each year, Markay estimates. Members of the aligned network include such heavy hitters as Organizing for Action, the "independent" organization that spun off of Barack Obama's 2012 reelection campaign, which operates both BarackObama.com and the @BarackObama Twitter handle. (For the bargain basement price of just $500,000, OFA donors are entitled to attend four in-person annual meetings with the president at the White House. This is literally selling access. But remember, kids, liberals staunchly oppose money in politics.)

The "progressive infrastructure map" is a much broader umbrella, including "a who's-who of liberal interest groups, causes and publications, like Rock the Vote, Harry Reid's Senate Majority PAC, [opposition research group] American Bridge, the Sierra Club, [abortion giant] Planned Parenthood, *The Nation*, and Tom Steyer's NextGen Climate," Markay says. Democracy Alliance members must give a minimum of $200,000 annually to at least one allied group. How exactly does the money flow? We don't know, by design. "They disclose nothing. Not their donors, not how much they give, and not to whom they're giving," Markay explains. "What we know is that it's quite coordinated. They decide how best money can be allocated, and how to maximize every dollar. The Democracy Alliance doesn't micromanage member organizations; it's a Darwinian process. They decide who is doing things effectively and make recommendations to their donors to give accordingly."

Based on some of the Democracy Alliance literature Markay has obtained in the process of his reporting, the network rates and classifies its groups among ten categories—one of which is called "fighting the right," denoted by a boxing glove in DA's promotional materials. This is where the outrage purveyors earn their keep. Literally. "They have a very adversarial attitude," Markay says. Rich liberals with deep pockets are funneling large amounts of money to keep organizations on hair-trigger alert to carry out steps one through three of the outrage progression we described at the outset of this chapter. It's a mini-industry unto itself, being bankrolled by extremely ideological monied interests.

Revisiting step four, with few exceptions, the mainstream media seems far less interested in any of this information than covering the comparatively puny Koch network. As someone who works the money-in-politics beat, Markay spitballs that media coverage of the Kochs versus the Democracy Alliance runs about twenty to one. "It's not just the amount of coverage. It's the tone and the depth of the coverage," he says. "If you take some money from the Koch brothers, even once, the media brands you as a 'Koch group.' Meanwhile, we have nearly 200 affiliated liberal groups splitting tens of millions of dollars, and they are not referred to as members of the Democracy Alliance in the style-books of major American newsrooms."

We can't help but suspect that if Markay's determined and thorough reporting on these matters were devoted to incrementally exposing a private web of *right*-wing cash, he'd have been nominated for a Pulitzer by now. Setting aside the Left's coruscating hypocrisy and undeserved self-righteousness on this issue, please allow us to quickly note that the Democracy Alliance crew has convinced their Democratic benefactors to actively attempt to *legislate* silencing. We're not just talking intimidation via outrage anymore; in 2014, Senate Democrats used the trumped-up "money in politics" panic as a pretext to propose a constitutional amendment aimed at . . . limiting the political speech protections of the First Amendment.[13] As Markay described it, "if enacted, the amendment would allow Congress to regulate any expenditure—even those made by individual voters—aimed at convincing others to vote a certain way."

Chuck Schumer and company knew this had zero chance of ratification, which is why they were very happy to feign ardent, principled support for the idea. They could preen and claim moral superiority without any risk of their idea actually coming to fruition, separating them from the cash they covet. But for a group that repeatedly brands their opponents as "extreme," gutting First Amendment speech protections is a truly radical step to formally propose.

Some of their rhetoric in support of the amendment candidly exposed their means-to-an-end motives. Self-described socialist Bernie Sanders, a senator from Vermont, explicitly stated that the underlying

---

[13] When Democrats brought this wretched document up for a so-called cloture vote (requiring 60 votes to proceed to debate) in September, they fully expected Republicans to block it. The script was prewritten: *These GOP obstructionists refuse to even debate because they're doing the Kochs' bidding!* But Republicans called their bluff and voted overwhelmingly to proceed to the days-long debate Democrats claimed to desire. Because the preelection floor calendar was limited, Democrats were livid that Republicans had complicated the timing of a parade of additional show votes on other matters teed up by Harry Reid. What they really wanted was *no debate* on their . . . political speech-curtailing *amendment to the First Amendment.*

purpose of "campaign finance reform" was to advance a political agenda by limiting the ability of others to influence the conversation: "If people think this is some kind of esoteric issue, not related to jobs and the economy and wages and women's rights and income and wealth inequality and healthcare and global warming, you are deadly wrong," he said at a September press conference. Shorter Sanders: *We want to use the power of government to silence opposing voices, which will make it easier for us to achieve our ideological objectives.* It's not a conspiracy theory when they're openly articulating their methods and goals.

So while the Left seeks credit for trying to curtail the scope of constitutionally protected political speech under the guise of anti-influence-peddling good governance, they're using their vast reservoir of free-flowing funds to bankroll hatchet groups like Media Matters for America and *ThinkProgress*. These organizations largely exist as platforms to dishonestly attack and smear ideological opponents, in hopes that they'll be hounded out of the arena. They're trying to *ban* money to silence conservatives, while *spending* gobs of money to silence conservatives. It's a neat discussion-ending twofer.

4

THE DOG-WHISTLE WHISPERERS

Race Baiting as a Silencing Strategy

"**B**arack Obama is from Chicago."

Did you catch the racial subtext of that sentence? *You didn't?* Nice try; claiming not to hear racially charged "dog whistles" is one of the oldest tricks in the book. For the uninitiated, let's flag the infractions: (1) referring to Obama without the word *president* in front of his surname is disrespectful and quite possibly racist,[1] and (2) the word *Chicago* is quite plainly racist—at least in the eyes of MSNBC's Chris Matthews and friends.

Political dog whistles are coded messages that are intended for a narrow, discrete audience, while passing unnoticed by everyone else. This is how literal dog whistles work; they're so high pitched that only dogs can hear them. Racially coded appeals have a long, dishonorable, and bipartisan history in U.S. politics, but that's not the point the Left seeks to make these days. The way they tell it, conservatives are currently and constantly slipping secret codes into their rhetoric as a means of conveying ugly, race-based messages about a person or subject without coming out and articulating it explicitly. By claiming to

---

[1] An NPR ombudsman felt compelled to write a column in 2011 pleading with complaining listeners to understand that declining to refer to "President Obama" on every mention was not a sign of disrespect. Shifting to "Mr. Obama" on second mention was, in fact, official NPR style, dating back many years. How many of those who objected also smirkingly referred to President Bush as "shrub," or some such witticism?

hear dog whistles at every turn, liberals use racial bullying to suppress and delegitimize political criticisms that are unhelpful to their cause.

Which brings us back to the kings of race baiting at MSNBC. During the network's coverage of the 2012 Republican National Convention, Matthews and a panel of guests spelled out the dirty business of dog whistles:

> **Eugene Robinson** (*Washington Post* columnist): It's all part of this Barack Obama as "other" sort of blanket campaign that has been waged by the Republican Party for some time now. It may be gaining some traction now, though I wonder why now, as opposed to a bit closer to election day?
>
> **Matthews:** Yeah, let me ask you about that, John. Is this constant barrage of assault . . . they keep saying "Chicago," by the way, have you noticed? They keep saying "Chicago." It sends that message, this guy's helping the poor people in the bad neighborhoods, and screwing us in the 'burbs.
>
> **John Heilemann** (*New York* magazine): There's a lot of black people in Chicago.
>
> **Matthews:** Yeah, I think that may have something to do with it.

Matthews and his crew have routinely accused the Right of hurling covert racial invective at the first African American president. The use of "Chicago" is just the beginning. A partial list of phrases lefties have identified as subtly demeaning to Obama, based on the color of his skin: "Golf" (MSNBC's Lawrence O'Donnell), "Kitchen Cabinet" (radio host Mark Thompson), "Constitution" (Fox News's Juan Williams), "professor" (er, *law professor* Charles Ogletree), and "Obamacare," which was decried as "race baiting" by columnist Michael Tomasky and equated to the N-word by MSNBC host Melissa Harris-Perry. Things became rather nuanced when the White House openly embraced the latter term, plastering it on OFA (Organizing for Action) bumper stickers. "Once it's working well, I guarantee you they will not call it Obamacare," the president himself told a crowd in Maryland, taunting the GOP just days before the law's October 2013 rollout.[2]

Dog whistles are everywhere. Writing at the *Huffington Post* in 2014, Ian Moss informed readers that employing the word *arrogant* to describe Barack Obama[3] is a new spin on *uppity*, a term with obvious racial connotations. "Recognizing the political incorrectness and well-deserved criticisms which accompany the use of 'uppity,' a more palatable, less provocative adjective was needed," Moss explained. "Enter arrogant. Arrogant is an opportune surrogate for uppity."

So scratch that one off the ever-shortening list of words you're allowed to use in describing your president. This encroachment on language is problematic unto itself. What's the next "arrogant" going to be? What word might you say tomorrow, or next week, or next year, that has suddenly been stricken from the realm of acceptability? You won't even know that you've erred until it's thrown in your face. Your denials will be sneered at. And you'll probably end up talking more "carefully" in the future, even if it's a subconscious shift. Mission accomplished.

Before being fired for declaring—in a scripted, on-air segment—that someone ought to defecate in Sarah Palin's mouth (it was supposed to sound more erudite in his clipped British accent), MSNBC's Martin Bashir thought he had the IRS targeting affair all figured out. The real scandal *wasn't* that a government agency had been abusing ideological opponents of the ruling party for years, "losing" the relevant evidence, and lying about it. No sir. "The IRS is being used in exactly the same way as they tried to use the president's birth certificate," Bashir told his handful of viewers in June 2013.

After reading a decades-old quote from former Republican strate-

---

[2] Strangely, the White House returned to calling it the "Affordable Care Act" the following month. It's unclear why. Kathleen Sebelius could not be reached for comment.

[3] Quote: "I'm a better speechwriter than my speechwriters. I know more about policies than my policy directors. And I'll tell you right now that I'm gonna think I'm a better political director than my political director."—Barack Obama, to *The New Yorker* in 2008.

gist Lee Atwater describing some *actual* racial code words from the Southern Strategy era, which included several invocations of the N-word, Bashir revved up for this big finish, in a segment entitled "Clear the Air": "So this afternoon, we welcome the latest phrase in the lexicon of Republican attacks on this president: the IRS. Three letters that sound so innocent, but *we know what you mean.*"

The "secret dog whistle" construct is an ingenious and tendentious creature: If conservatives hear the coded message, they're racist. If they say they don't hear it, or reject the premise altogether, they're covering up their racism. And the people *most* attuned to this form of encryption—liberals—are allowed to identify them around every corner with blanket immunity.

We hate to keep picking on the Lean Forward network, but they're the center ring of this perverse circus. To wit, Guy appeared on MSNBC's *The Ed Show* in July 2012, with network contributor Michael Eric Dyson filling in for the vacationing Ed Shultz.[4] Here's what went down:

> *The panel was stacked: You had the leftist guest host, the leftist MSNBC contributor Jimmy Williams, your leftist "political comedian" John Fugelsang . . . and me, the designated villain. Based on guidance provided in the production email I'd received, I was prepared to discuss Mitt Romney's record at Bain Capital in the first of a two-segment panel discussion. Instead, when the exchange began, I found myself on live television in the middle of a conspiratorial frenzy over racist Republican "dog whistles."*

---

[4] Fun fact: Once upon a time, Big Ed was a failed conservative talk-show host. He switched sides to revive his career, ultimately landing his own program on MSNBC. His nuanced commentaries include such gems as this classic pronouncement during the Obamacare debate: "Republicans lie! They want to see you dead! They'd rather make money off of your dead corpse! They kind of like it when that woman has cancer and they don't have anything for her!" Though producers told Guy that Ed was on holiday, he's always suspected that it may have been a physician-mandated regimen of bed rest, given that particular episode's proximity to Governor Scott Walker's recall election victory.

The GOP's sin in this particular case was criticizing President Obama's revealing "you didn't build that" expression of collectivism, which the MSNBC crew naturally declared to have been taken "out of context." Former New Hampshire Governor John Sununu had blasted Obama on a Romney campaign conference call, at one point straying off script, ad-libbing that the president needed to "learn how to be an American." The Obama campaign and its myriad outrage appendages went ballistic, prompting Sununu to apologize within a matter of hours. (The Obama campaign never apologized, incidentally, for falsely calling Romney a felon, but whatever.)

In spite of Sununu's mea culpa, his original comments served as "proof" that sinister Republicans were trying to "paint [Obama] as un-American," Dyson intoned. "It's code," Williams breathlessly agreed. "Ask the Birthers . . . this isn't 1963," he added, apropos of nothing. Up next was Fugelsang, whose "comedic wit" instantly lightened the mood: "The use of the word un-American is un-American in itself. Only fascist societies or fascist people use that kind of language." Charming. The conversation had achieved unanimous agreement—an MSNBC staple—until I chimed in with a simple question:

> *[Candidate] Obama called President Bush 'unpatriotic' for the debt that he racked up over eight years—which, by the way is less than this president has racked up over three-and-a-half years. Was that a dog whistle of some sort?*

The panel exploded. "That was unpatriotic!" Williams thundered, his face contorted with fury. "If you don't like deficits, you're morally obliged to unlike the Ronald Reagan administration," Fugelsang averred, again showcasing an allergy to relevant arguments. Williams wasn't quite through. He (wrongly) implied that Bush was primarily responsible for our nation's *then—$16 trillion deficit (he meant debt), obliviously doubling down on Obama's 2008 attack. "Do you like the wars that got us half those deficits? Because I actually think that was remarkably unpatriotic," he sneered.*

Let's be generous and set aside the accuracy of these "rebuttals," which no doubt merit a hefty fact-check. These guys were proving my point. *The irony was both glorious and completely lost on them. After Dyson tried to pin me down on the use of "wolf whistles" (dear God,* the dogs had grown into wolves!), *I gently tried to note for the home audience how my fellow panelists had huffed and puffed and toppled the segment's entire premise. "You guys say, 'well, Bush* was *unpatriotic for the policies that we don't like . . . but if a Republican says President Obama is 'un-American' for [his] bad policies—which they immediately retract—that's all of a sudden some sort of really nasty, insidious 'code word.'" I mistakenly thought they would see how silly they'd made themselves look. Wrong. Their surreal response:*

> **Fugelsang:** *No one was ever calling President Bush's policies un-American or unpatriotic.*
> **Williams:** *Or him! (meaning Bush personally).*
> **Me** *(visibly incredulous):* Yes. President Obama did.

Nobody ever *said those sorts of things about Bush . . . except, you know, both of them—literally* 30 seconds *earlier. Not to mention Barack Obama, whose comments I'd deliberately recapitulated for the purpose of puncturing their moronic argument. They would either take the bait or realize how hacktastic they sounded and back off. They did the former, springing the trap, blissfully unaware of what had just happened.*

Soon we were off to a commercial break, after which they turned their attention to some other outrage du jour *featuring Rep. Michele Bachmann, which was at least one of the issues I was asked to prepare for. Shockingly, Dyson was very angry at*

*Ms. Bachmann. Without a trace of self-awareness, he denounced
her as (ta-da!) "un-American."*

Behold, the Outrage Circus in full throat. Guy's MSNBC adven-
tures once again demonstrated the purpose of the "dog whistles!"
nonsense: to disqualify criticisms of President Obama as motivated
by racial animus, thus rendering them beyond the pale.[5] As we've discussed, alleging racism is one of the heaviest charges one can level in
American life, so dropping that bomb is a particularly effective way of
kneecapping a debate. Most people will do just about anything to avoid
being slapped with that designation, including keeping their mouths
shut. Inventing dog whistles and casually tossing about the "R-word" as
a means of bludgeoning political opponents and stifling debate through
intimidation hampers important and worthwhile efforts to combat real
racism, which still exists and probably always will, sadly. It cheapens
the seriousness of the subject and fosters a boy-who-cried-wolf syndrome. It jades the public's outrage palate toward genuine racism. This
is toxic.

But for the Outrage Circus, playing the race card is a hell of a substitute for engaging in a rational debate, and it almost certainly contributes to Republicans' (very real[6]) problems among nonwhite voters
at the margins. Republicans' tarnished image on race isn't entirely un-
earned, by the way, but that doesn't give critics free license to endlessly
recycle attacks that no longer apply, or never did.

---

[5] #DogWhistle

[6] Mitt Romney won the white vote by 20 percentage points, the same margin among
that group that propelled Ronald Reagan to a blowout win in 1980. But the composi-
tion of the electorate has shifted considerably since then. The 2012 Republican ticket
lost blacks (93/6), Latinos (71/27), and Asians (73/26), and the candidates were defeated by nearly four million popular votes. The party and its supporters ignore demographic trends, and their own message and rhetoric, at their peril. But that's for
another book.

"UNPRECEDENTED!"

A kissing cousin to the dog-whistle preoccupation is the Left's frequent claim that opposition to Barack Obama is somehow "unprecedented" in nature. The objective here is to establish anti-Obama sentiment as wholly unusual in our body politic and derived primarily from racial animosity, subconscious or otherwise. This tactic (which requires brushing aside Democrats' own sordid racial history) reached new lows during the 2008 campaign and has been carried on ever since, being most ruthlessly deployed against the Tea Party. The tactic's adherents are too numerous to name, so here are a handful of representative statements:

> *I'll be able to dig up some emails . . . from people who made up their mind that they don't want the [Affordable Care Act] to work because they don't like the president. Maybe he's of the wrong color, something of that sort. I've seen a lot of that and I know a lot of that to be true. It's not something you're meant to talk about in public but it's something I'm talking about in public because that is very true.* —Sen. Jay Rockefeller (D-WV)

> *I've been in Washington. I saw three presidents now. I never saw George Bush treated like this. I never saw Bill Clinton treated like this with such disrespect . . . That Mitch McConnell would have the audacity to tell the president of the United States—not the chief executive, but the commander-in-chief— that "I don't care what you come up with we're going to be against it." Now if that's not a racist statement I don't know what is.* —Rep. Bennie Thompson (D-MS)

> *[Obama] has had a very difficult opposition out there . . . who from the very beginning wanted to destroy this presidency . . .*

and some of it is ethnic, and some is good old ideology. But the way they treated this guy is unusual in our history . . . Al Gore accepted the fact, even though he won by 600,000 votes, that W. was president. And the Democrats accepted the legitimacy of George W. Bush 100 percent . . . There is an asymmetry here between the hard right and the Democratic center, there is a real asymmetry . . . There really is. And to say that they are both the same is not true. —MSNBC's Chris Matthews

These people are trying to convince you (and perhaps themselves) that opposition to this president is unlike anything the country has ever witnessed, due to the color of his skin. Period. If they can convince their audience of that premise, there is no need to address any of the specific objections, since they're presumed to be fundamentally tainted. This is a cynical, lazy cop-out of the worst kind.

Senator Rockefeller's inflammatory statement came months before he retired from public life; he bravely insulted his constituents *after* he was through needing their support. In his defense, aside from rank bigotry, why would anyone dislike Obamacare?[7] He cites as evidence undisclosed e-mails from unnamed correspondents. We're confident that Mr. Rockefeller could produce some highly unpleasant e-mails from ignorant haters. But here's why his argument is specious: virtually everyone in public life, ourselves included, receives appalling nasty-grams (also see: Twitter), but random assholes do not a movement make.[8] It's also undoubtedly true that some number of American voters explicitly oppose Obama because of his race. Some people *support* him for that

---

[7] Beyond its broken promises, individual mandate tax, rising premiums, high out-of-pocket costs, canceled policies, dropped doctors, access obstacles, economic harm, increased federal costs, shoddy implementation, massive sums wasted on failed exchanges, data security concerns, expansion of failing Medicaid, and raiding of cash-strapped Medicare, that is.

[8] Exceptions exist. Google "Bronies."

explicit reason. But Barack Obama's political fortunes aren't dictated by these small pockets of voters. To pretend as if they do gives little agency to the president himself, despite his significant, documented political skills, and gives no credit to the country for truly making racial strides from the dark and unjust elements of its past.

According to CNN's exit polls, Obama carried independent voters by eight percentage points in 2008; he essentially tied John McCain among white independents ($^{47}/_{49}$). Six years on, many of those white and/or independent voters had fled the Obama coalition. A survey of battleground states conducted by NPR ahead of the 2014 midterm elections measured Obama's job approval underwater by nearly a two-to-one margin ($^{33}/_{63}$) among independents, a growing portion of the electorate. A Fox News poll released around the same time asked whether people were glad Obamacare passed, or if they wished it had never happened. Among political independents, regret outpaced contentment by a resounding 27 percentage points. So unless these swing voters suddenly embraced racism in droves after sweeping Obama into office, Rockefeller and his ilk are going to have to try harder.

But thoughtfulness wasn't the point of his remark, was it? The point was to use the repellent specter of racism to silence people. To his credit, one of Rockefeller's Commerce Committee colleagues who was present in the hearing room for the slander (yes, Rockefeller spun his theory during formal Senate proceedings) pointedly declined to play along.

An uncharacteristically irate Senator Ron Johnson, a mild-mannered Republican businessman from Wisconsin, teed off, challenging Rockefeller's insulting premise to his face: "I didn't object to this because of the race of the president. I objected to this because it is an assault on our freedom. And Mr. Chairman . . . I found it very offensive that you would basically imply that I'm a racist because I oppose this health care law. That is outrageous," Johnson seethed. When Rockefeller denied that he'd played the race card and accused Johnson of supporting a bad-old-days health-care policy, Johnson shot back, "You are assuming the wrong thing, Mr. Chairman. You've implied that I'm a racist. Now you're saying [I want] to go back to a failed health-care system? Please don't assume. Don't make implications of what I'm thinking and what I would really support. You have no idea."

Rockefeller, evidently unaccustomed to getting called out,[9] had his dander up. "I actually do [know]. And, you know, God help you," he retorted, drawing another impassioned counterpunch from Johnson: "No, Senator, God help *you* for implying I'm a racist because I oppose this health-care [law]. I was called a racist. I think most people would lose their temper, Mr. Chairman." Indeed they would, and so he did. Bravo.

But we digress. (We do that sometimes.) The quotes from Representative Thompson and Chris Matthews are even more emblematic of the "unprecedented opposition" canard. Matthews insists that Democrats accepted Bush's legitimacy "100 percent," which he says illustrates the "asymmetry" between the "hard right" and the "Democratic center." We looked into it, and discovered that *Hardball* was, in fact, on the air during and after the 2000 election. Maybe it was a sports show or something back then, in which case Matthews might be forgiven for having no recollection of the "stolen election" hysteria, replete with hot slogans like "Not my president!" and "Selected, not elected!" Matthews is willfully suffering from political amnesia, which is the only way he can advance these arguments with a straight face.

But Mary Katharine and Guy, skeptics might say, *some liberal activists may have lodged those sorts of allegations, but not elected Democrats. There's a difference.* To which we respond, conduct a LexisNexis search and look up what congressional Democrats had to say about President Bush's victory in 2000. "Official" Democrats *still* can't let it go. Thirteen years after the fact, Vice President Joe Biden was still suggesting that

---

[9] MKH, in beast mode, slammed Rockefeller on Fox at the time: "If he were an adult and a real person instead of an entitled senator and scion of a robber baron, he would apologize."

Bush wasn't legitimately elected, introducing Al Gore as "the man who was elected president" at a Democratic fund-raiser. Jimmy Carter— who, believe it or not, was actually president of the United States for several years in the 1970s—has become a self-stylized international elections expert in his postpresidency. He was asked about Republicans cheating to win elections in a 2014 interview with left-wing radio jockey Thom Hartmann. The host overtly implied that no Republican had been legitimately elected president since Dwight Eisenhower, which may give you a sense of the tenor of this discussion. Though the ex-president didn't fully embrace Hartmann's bizarre conspiracy, he allowed, "I don't think that George W. Bush won the election in 2000 against Al Gore because I think he probably lost Florida."

Over to you, FactCheck.org: "According to a massive months-long study commissioned by eight news organizations in 2001, George W. Bush probably still would have won even if the U.S. Supreme Court had allowed a limited statewide recount to go forward as ordered by Florida's highest court. Bush also probably would have won had the state conducted the limited recount of only four heavily Democratic counties that Al Gore asked for, the study found." Sorry, guys. Mr. Matthews and friends have remarkably selective memories.

The same can be said of Congressman Thompson, who swears he can't recall Presidents Bush or Clinton ever being subjected to such shoddy treatment as has befallen our first black president. Conservative writers and bloggers have done excellent work refuting the revisionist theory that Bush was treated with dignity and respect by liberals over his eight years in office. The list of counterexamples is basically endless—from the ubiquitous BusHitler placards at antiwar protests, to Senator Harry Reid calling the president "a loser," to the acclaimed independent film depicting Bush's assassination, to the parade of Bush effigies hung and/or burned.[10] But nothing quite

---

[10] According to a glowing *New Yorker* profile, *New York Times* columnist and former Enron adviser Paul Krugman hosted a 2008 Election Night party, at which guests burned effigies of politicians they detested—including Senator John McCain.

exemplifies Democrats' febrile "Bush Derangement Syndrome"[11] like a very special game of make-believe undertaken by House Democrats in June 2005. The *Washington Post*'s Dana Milbank reported:

> *[Assembled Democrats] pretended a small conference room was the Judiciary Committee hearing room, draping white linens over folding tables to make them look like witness tables and bringing in cardboard name tags and extra flags to make the whole thing look official. Rep. John Conyers Jr. (D-MI) banged a large wooden gavel and got the other lawmakers to call him "Mr. Chairman." He liked that so much that he started calling himself "the chairman" and spouted other chairmanly phrases, such as "unanimous consent" and "without objection so ordered." The dress-up game looked realistic enough on C-SPAN, so two dozen more Democrats came downstairs to play along. The session was a mock impeachment inquiry over the Iraq war. As luck would have it, all four of the witnesses agreed that President Bush lied to the nation and was guilty of high crimes—and that a British memo on "fixed" intelligence that surfaced last month was the smoking gun equivalent to the Watergate tapes . . .*
>
> *At Democratic headquarters, where an overflow crowd watched the hearing on television, activists handed out documents repeating two accusations—that an Israeli company had warning of the Sept. 11, 2001, attacks and that there was an "insider trading scam" on 9/11—that previously has been used*

Krugman has since penned multiple shrill screeds against the Right's dangerous "climate of hate" and "eliminationist" rhetoric, to which we'll return in a later chapter.

[11] A joking psychological "condition" in which sufferers' hatred of President Bush clouded all reason and judgment, coined by the inimitable Charles Krauthammer, a trained psychiatrist. And for which his good-humored colleagues actually tried to have him expelled from the American Psychiatric Association. It seems Dr. K hit a bit too close to home with that one.

to suggest Israel was behind the attacks. The event organizer, Democrats.com, distributed stickers saying "Bush lied/100,000 people died." One man's T-shirt proclaimed, "Whether you like Bush or not, he's still an incompetent liar," while a large poster of Uncle Sam announced: "Got kids? I want yours for cannon fodder." Conyers's firm hand on the gavel could not prevent something of a free-for-all; at one point, a former State Department worker rose from the audience to propose criminal charges against Bush officials. Early in the hearing, somebody accidentally turned off the lights; later, a witness knocked down a flag. Matters were even worse at Democratic headquarters, where the C-SPAN feed ended after just an hour, causing the activists to groan and one to shout "Conspiracy!"

That's right, *dozens* of elected Democrats held fake impeachment hearings in the basement of the Capitol, while a motley crew of "9/11 truth" nutters watched the "proceedings" with rapt attention in an overflow room at DNC headquarters.

Those who cling to the "unprecedented" talking point must also have ignored the five-alarm shinola storm that took place in Wisconsin in 2011 over Governor Scott Walker's budget reform proposals.[12] Democratic senators literally fled the state and holed up in an Illinois Best Western for weeks in a futile effort to obstruct a vote by denying quorum. Indiana Democrats attempted a similar maneuver that year, as did Texas Democrats in 2003. But the media only reached for the smelling salts when a South Carolina backbencher lost his cool and shouted "You lie!" at President Obama during a health-care speech. (For the record, Obama did lie throughout that 2009 address to a joint session of Congress, but Representative Joe Wilson's outburst was still rude and wrong.)

---

[12] More in chapter 10.

Patriot Games

Dick Cheney is not a fan of Barack Obama. The feeling, we'd imagine, is mutual. When Iraq descended into deadly chaos in the spring and summer of 2014, Cheney upbraided the Obama administration in a series of media appearances for recklessly abandoning the country without a residual force, which created an opening for the ISIS savages to seize large swaths of the country. Liberal journalist Jonathan Alter couldn't abide Darth Vader's criticisms, firing off an angry Twitter pronouncement: "What kind of former VP trashes president on EVERYTHING. Total break with long tradition. Totally unpatriotic." In fewer than 140 characters, Alter achieves a rare self-unawareness trifecta. He displays an amusingly selective and short memory, clumsily plays the "unprecedented!" card, then sticks the landing with a violation of the Left's patriotism taboo. Indeed, Cheney's actions marked a distressing departure from a lengthy tradition that by our calculations dated all the way back to January 20, 2009.

Guy dispensed with Alter's premise by tweeting two video clips in response. The first excerpted a 2004 speech in which Al Gore bellowed that President Bush had "betrayed this country!" (What kind of former vice president would do such a thing?) The second featured a delicious rebuttal on patriotism, courtesy of a 2003 Hillary Clinton screed: "I am sick and tired of people who say that if you debate and you disagree with this administration, somehow you're not patriotic, and we should stand up and say, *We are Americans and we have a right to debate and*

No matter how many counterexamples we provide, the "unprecedented opposition, rooted in racism" story will persist. It's been such a lazy staple of Obama defenders' diet that it has trickled down to shield other members of his administration, as well. National Security Adviser Susan Rice's tenure at the White House has been less than stellar, punctuated by two high-profile flops on national television. She infamously repeated false administration talking points about the *disagree with any administration!"*[13] Well said, Hillary. During the Bush years, we were frequently lectured, dissent was "the highest form of patriotism." When Obama took over, dissent suddenly became the lowest form of racist anti-Americanism.

This speech-chilling "dissent" about-face descended into self parody in March 2015 when hundreds of thousands of Americans signed a petition—on the White House website, by the way—calling for the *jailing* of forty-seven Republican senators. A number of supposedly respectable pundits, including Donna Brazile, talked up the idea; Chris Matthews sputtered about "sedition." The duly-elected senators' alleged infraction: penning an open letter to Iran's regime, warning that an Obama-arranged nuclear deal would carry no legal weight after the current administration leaves office, absent congressional approval. The missive entailed a prosaic recitation of constitutional fact, and represented an entirely legitimate effort to remind both Tehran and the White House that the federal government's coequal legislative branch must have a say in the formation of United States foreign policy. This exercise was denounced as an unacceptable attempt to undermine an Obama legacy project (which richly deserved undermining, in our view), and was therefore a crime—based upon a truly ludicrous misreading of something called the Logan Act, which bars unauthorized Americans from engaging in freelance diplomacy.[14] Out: the "highest form of patriotism." In: a basis for imprisonment, you despicable traitors.

---

[13] The written word cannot adequately capture the shrillness of this tirade.

[14] An irate pro-Obama Internet commenter (who, no doubt, "loves science") informs us that merely reading this sentence is likely a violation of the Logan Act as well. Prepare for your frog march.

Benghazi attacks on all five Sunday chat shows in 2012, then declared that accused army deserter Bowe Bergdahl had served the military he'd allegedly abandoned with "honor and distinction."[15] Battling a

---

[15] An often-overlooked Susan Rice classic came during the 2008 Democratic primary. Rice, then an Obama surrogate, was dispatched to respond to Hillary Clinton's "3 a.m. phone call" attack ad, which suggested that an untested Obama would be ill-equipped to respond to an international crisis. Rice's stellar comeback, speaking of Hillary and

renewed outcry over his boss's incompetence, an aide to Rice served up this quote to *Time*'s Michael Crowley: "I'm not here to suggest it's because she's a woman or a minority . . . but other principals in the national-security team don't come under this kind of attack." Right. In that same spirit, we're not here to suggest that this anonymous aide is a craven race-baiting moron.

One last point on this: The "unprecedented!" crowd *is* aware that Republicans *impeached Bill Clinton*, yes? You know, Bill Clinton—that paunchy, white, southern dude. Why, it's almost as if acrimonious political feuds are fueled by something other than any of the major players' melanin levels. Like—and we're just brainstorming here—passionate ideological disagreements. How very . . . precedented.

NOBODY'S SAFE

Though they most frequently target conservatives with their "silence, racist!" strategy, the Left does not hesitate to eat its own when the moment demands it. Bill Clinton, once dubbed "the first black president" by adoring supporters, briefly morphed into a race-baiting neo-Klansman in 2008. His pointed criticism of Barack Obama on the campaign trail was deemed to be an unacceptable roadblock to liberals' latest ideological crush, and thus the outrage machine on which Clinton had relied for much of his political career was unleashed against him. "Give me a break. This whole thing is the biggest fairy tale I've ever seen," Clinton said of the public image Obama had cultivated. Startled by the resulting outcry, Clinton was forced to call into Al Sharpton's radio show[16] to genuflect and explain how his remarks had been taken out of context.

Obama: "They're both not ready." An epic flub. And hauntingly prescient in light of the Benghazi affair, with which she would one day be indelibly associated.

[16] Mystifyingly, instead of getting himself ejected from polite society after years of despicable conduct, Sharpton has somehow become President Obama's "go-to" man on issues of race, according to a 2014 *Politico* story.

Two months later, the former president was in hot water again. When asked about Obama's blowout victory in the South Carolina primary, Clinton uncorked a non sequitur history lesson: "Jesse Jackson won South Carolina in '84 and '88. Jackson ran a good campaign. And Obama ran a good campaign here," he said, roping Jackson into the discussion unprovoked. Furious Obama backers denounced Clinton's racial subtext,[17] prompting yet another clarification and apology. Team Clinton suffered a related blow at around the same time when former vice presidential nominee Geraldine Ferraro, a Hillary surrogate, inflamed Obama allies with a candid assessment quoted in a California newspaper:

> *"If Obama was a white man, he would not be in this position. And if he was a woman of any color, he would not be in this position. He happens to be very lucky to be who he is. And the country is caught up in the concept."*

Ferraro's untouchable status as a Democratic trailblazer was immediately discarded, as Obama backers pummeled her with the "R-word." She angrily responded to her critics in an interview with the *New York Times*. "Every time [Obama's] campaign is upset about something, they call it racist," she said. "I will not be discriminated against because I'm white. If they think they're going to shut up Geraldine Ferraro with that kind of stuff, they don't know me." Within hours of her defiant self-defense, Ferraro was put out to pasture by the Clinton campaign; she quietly stepped down from her fund-raising role. They did, in fact, "shut up Geraldine Ferraro with that kind of stuff."

Mary Katharine's weekly *O'Reilly Factor* sparring partner—aside from Bill, of course[18]—is Fox News analyst Juan Williams, who for years served as a National Public Radio host and correspondent. He is

---

[17] As far as dog whistles go, this one strikes us as more legitimate than, say, "golf."

[18] *She kids!* We're all laughing together!

Racism Rorschach

Attorney General Eric Holder—July 13, 2013: "There's a certain level of vehemence, it seems to me, that's directed at me—directed at the president. Um, you know, people talk about 'taking their country back.' There's a certain racial component to this for some people. I don't think this is a main driver, but for some, there's a racial animus."

Vice President Joe Biden—September 1, 2014: "So folks, it's time to take back America!"

a black Democrat—generally liberal, but occasionally unpredictable—who joyfully wept on-air when Barack Obama was inaugurated in 2009. He's also a bona fide scholar of the civil rights movement, author of *Eyes on the Prize: America's Civil Rights Years 1954–1965*, a companion tome to a seminal fourteen-hour PBS documentary of the same name. His employment at NPR was abruptly terminated in 2010 after he offered a bit of controversial analysis during a Fox News segment on the "clash of civilizations" between Islamists and the West. Note well his up-front admonition about the paralysis of political correctness, which proved to be demoralizingly prophetic:

> *I think political correctness can lead to some kind of paralysis where you don't address reality. I mean, look, Bill. I'm not a bigot. You know the sort of books I've written on the civil rights movement in this country. But when I get on the plane, I've got to tell you, if I see people who are in Muslim garb and I think, you know, they are identifying themselves first and foremost as Muslims, I get worried. I get nervous.*

Williams spent much of the balance of the segment arguing with Bill O'Reilly about the importance of routinely distinguishing between radical Islamists and moderate, peaceable Muslims. But his frank admission that he sometimes feels anxiety when he sees fellow airline passengers dressed in "Muslim garb" sealed his fate. Realities and personal feelings that violate liberal orthodoxy (and offend a community whose thought enforcers are particularly aggressive and litigious) are not to be addressed in public. You are not to articulate your thoughts, no matter how obvious they may seem, or how many people would agree with you.

In truth, NPR had been casting about for a pretext to expel Williams from its warm cocoon of liberalism for some time. When he made an unflattering remark about Michelle Obama on Fox in 2009, the radio network instructed him to cease associating himself with their precious brand in future Fox News appearances. NPR's ombudsperson disclosed that she'd received . . . *fifty-six* complaints from listeners about the incident. Fifty-six. That's roughly equivalent to the number of hate tweets Ted Cruz receives between two and three a.m. on any given Tuesday. Those dozens of negative comments made Williams a "lightning rod" among NPR's listeners, the ombudsperson explained, noting that she'd been inundated with 378 e-mails objecting to Williams's Fox segments in 2008 alone—or approximately one whole gripe per day. The long knives were out for Juan Williams; his politically insensitive comments about Muslims were merely the turnkey excuse to can him that the NPR brass had been waiting for.

Upon Williams's departure, NPR's president and CEO, Vivian Schiller, sniped that her erstwhile employee's feelings about Muslims should have remained between him and "his psychiatrist or his publicist—take your pick." Ellen Weiss, the executive who actually did the firing, reportedly denied Williams the courtesy of a face-to-face meeting, telling him, "There's nothing you can say that will change my mind." Ain't that the truth.

When we spoke with Williams about the incident, he said that the trend toward punishing "deviant" thoughts and crushing open debate is accelerating, and agreed that it's primarily a phenomenon of the Left:

The polarization of our politics has become a source of identity. To be a good liberal, all of a sudden, you speak this way, think this way. Previously, we had political correctness in our society, which was curse enough. But people were speaking out about that, especially conservatives, back in the '80s and '90s. But what we've got now is beyond PC. It's not, "Well, we hear you, but let's try to be polite to each other." Now we've got a situation with a lot of people just saying, "We don't want to hear you. We don't want to hear the other side."

I can open my shirt and show you scars. I've been skewered, from the Left, remember—and I would say that it was one of the shocks of my life that this knife came from the Left of me— say, "we don't want to hear what you have to say because it's unacceptable and evidence that you're a bigot."

There's something about the way these sort of people view themselves; there's a certain arrogance and self-righteousness that feeds into this intolerance. That they know what's right, and when they see somebody who challenges their orthodoxy, they aren't intellectually curious and wanting to engage. In the old days it used to be called joining the debate. Their reaction, to the contrary, is to pull out the knives to kill the messenger. They do not want anybody from the other side.

It's not the case that I am a voice of extremism in American debate. Without sounding self-aggrandizing, I think most people would say, "Yeah he makes mistakes, but I don't think that he's an insincere guy." And my background, having worked at the Washington Post *for 20 years, CNN, seven books, I could go on. I thought that people would think, "Well let's hear what he has to say." But that wasn't their response. Their response was, "This is the pretext, the opportunity we've been waiting for, to knife this son of a bitch."*

I'm sixty years old this year, and one of the biggest surprises of my life has been that intolerance for free thought, it seems to me, has now become the property of the Left, much more so than it is the property of the Right. Just think about my circumstance: I was fired by the Left—NPR—but the Right, Fox, continues to allow me to say what I want to say. They may think I'm crazy a lot of the time, but I'm there. And there's nobody telling me what to say, or sanctioning me for my thoughts.

Williams detailed the circumstances of his ouster after more than a decade at NPR in a 2011 book entitled *Muzzled: The Assault on Honest Debate*.[19]

#FIREDFORATWEET

One need not be a former vice presidential nominee or a prominent media figure to have one's life turned upside down or livelihood threatened by the knee-jerk muzzlers. One young man learned the hard way that merely commenting on a national controversy in a manner that offends a certain crowd's sensibilities can cost you your job. The hubbub in question was the Donald Sterling affair, in which the former Los Angeles Clippers owner found himself in hot water when audio emerged of a phone conversation in which Sterling insisted that his girlfriend stop "broadcast[ing] that you're associating with black people." He requested that she stop posting photos to Instagram featuring her black friends, and that she not "bring them to my games." This, for the record, is actual racism. Sterling was roundly denounced and banned for life by the NBA. We shed no tears for him. But given that his incriminating statements came in a private conversation that was surreptitiously recorded by his lover, then leaked to the media, we do harbor some concerns about how his racism was exposed to the world.

---

[19] This was going to be the title of our book until we were informed it had already been taken.

"Racist!" Shot/Reality Chaser

"Silence!" Shot, via *Gawker*: "*Crain's* reports on SketchFactor, a racist app made for avoiding 'sketchy' neighborhoods, which is the term young white people use to describe places where they don't feel safe because they watched all five seasons of *The Wire* . . . With firsthand experience living in Washington, D.C., where white terror is as ubiquitous as tucked-in polo shirts, [the] grinning Caucasian [creators] should be unstoppable in the field of smartphone race-baiting . . . But don't worry: they're not racist." [Our note: The post's title is "Smiling Young White People Make App for Avoiding Black Neighborhoods." We'll just point out that it was *Gawker*'s writer who made the leap from "sketchy" to "black" all by himself, while in the process of slamming other people's alleged racism.]

Reality Chaser, via *Raw Story*: "A District of Columbia news crew reporting on an app that identifies 'sketchy' neighborhoods had their van burglarized while they were interviewing individuals who lived in a neighborhood the app identified as 'sketchy.' . . . [the WUSA9 intern] had her iPhone stolen, but the crew was able to use the Find my iPhone application to track its location, eventually finding it—and much of the crew's other gear—in a raccoon-infested Dumpster in a different part of DC." *Racism.*

So did Josh Olin, a community manager for a gaming company. He expressed his reservations on his personal Twitter account: "Here's an unpopular opinion," he wrote. "Donald Sterling has the right as an American to be an old bigot in the security of his own home. He's a victim." This kicked up a small tempest online, and within hours, Olin's employer (Turtle Rock) tweeted out an apology, repudiating Olin's views and referring to him as a "former" employee. He'd been let go for mounting a qualified, principled defense of an unpopular figure on his own time, from his personal social media platform. After being sacked for his thoughts, he issued the following statement to the popular video-game blog *Kotaku:*

Anyone who follows me knows my tweets were not in support of Sterling's actions. Rather, they were promoting three core tenets I believe in: 1) The harm sensational media presents to society. 2) The importance and sanctity of your privacy within your own home. And 3) The right to be whatever you want to be as an American, as long as it isn't hurting anyone else. That last point not to be confused with condoning Sterling's actions, which I don't.

That said, it's disappointing to see that a select few in Turtle Rock and 2K Games management bought into this hysteria without even having a conversation with me—or even thoroughly reviewing the context of the tweets themselves. Ironically, it serves as a great example of why I hold tenet #1 above so close to heart.

He went on to encourage gamers to purchase his ex-company's product, which we confess is a classier gesture than we'd have been capable of if we were in his shoes. Turtle Rock management caved to the shouters and handed Olin his walking papers without even talking to him. In the blink of an eye, the outrage meter shot from zero to eleven, and an entirely defensible tweet about a national controversy cost a young man his job. Gaping onlookers may well have quietly wondered whether they should refrain from wading into sensitive debates in the future. That's the whole idea. We reached out to Olin, who initially entertained the possibility of talking with us, then decided against it. It turns out he's a tad mistrustful of the media. In light of what he went through, can you really blame him for going the "no comment" route?

Olin wasn't alone in his views. First Amendment attorney Marc Randazza penned a column for CNN lamenting the circumstances of Sterling's downfall, while taking care not to endorse the man himself. Randazza's conclusion: "As you applaud Stiviano [Sterling's girlfriend] for bringing the racist old man's views to light, consider if it were you speaking to a woman friend in what you thought was a private conversation. Do we now live in a world where we can trust nobody? Where there is no privacy? In this story, there are two villains. Sterling represents the bad old days. But Stiviano's behavior represents the horrifying future."

And now it's time for us to approvingly cite Bill Maher[20] for the second time in this book. (We're as surprised as anyone, trust us.) The anti-Sterling mob mentality didn't sit well with the HBO host, who devoted a protracted monologue to the subject. He asked his audience if Americans really want "to live in a world where the only privacy you have is inside your head." A few highlights from Maher's righteous rant:

> *Even at home, [do we] have to talk like a White House press spokesman? Let me get this straight: We should concede that there's no such thing anymore as a private conversation, so therefore remember to "lawyer" everything you say before you say it—and hey, speaking your mind is overrated anyway, so you won't miss it. Well, I'll miss it. I'll miss it a lot . . . Does anyone really want there to be no place where we can let our hair down and not worry if the bad angel in our head occasionally grabs the mic? . . . If I want to sit in the privacy of my living room and say, "I think the Little Mermaid is hot and I want to bang her, or I don't like watching two men kiss, or I think tattoos look terrible on black people," I should be able to. Even if you think that makes me an asshole. Now, do I really believe those things? I'm not telling you, 'cause you're not in my living room.*

If Maher sounds a bit sensitive on this subject, perhaps it's because he's been in the crosshairs himself, albeit on a subject other than race. Shortly after 9/11, Maher ignited a major controversy by making politically incorrect comments on the ABC show he hosted, called, um,

---

[20] Just add it to our RINO rap sheet.

Politically Incorrect. Maher disagreed with President Bush's characterization of the hijackers as "cowards," noting that it took real conviction and dedication to follow through on their horrific acts. He went further, suggesting that by comparison, U.S. missile strikes launched from a safe distance more closely fit Bush's description. Maher clarified that the degree of bravery or cowardice of a given act was by no means a commentary on its morality. In light of the segment's proximity to the terrorist attacks, many Americans were offended by what he said. Advertisers pulled out of the show, which was suspended by ABC and ultimately canceled, ending the discussion. *Ahem.* We say again: outrage and scalp collecting is by no means limited to the political Left; they're just more skilled practitioners of the silencing arts. Just ask Josh Olin.

ESTRADA V. SOTOMAYOR

M uch ink has been spilled on the subject of how viciously conservative minorities are attacked for daring to think critically and coming to the "wrong" political conclusions, so we won't retread much of that ground here. One telling juxtaposition, however, is worth exploring because it demonstrates the Left's capacity to both enforce pungent double standards and steer media narratives as they see fit.

On May 26, 2009, President Obama announced the nomination of Judge Sonia Sotomayor to replace retiring justice David Souter on the United States Supreme Court. We'll note just two major factors of the low-decibel confirmation fight: First, in a 2001 speech at Berkeley, Sotomayor expressed the opinion that her immutable identity—her race and womanhood—equipped her to reach legal judgments that were superior to those of white male colleagues. "I would hope that a wise Latina woman, with the richness of her experiences, would more often than not reach a better conclusion than a white male who hasn't lived that life," she told the audience. If a white male, particularly a conservative white male, had offered a similar self-assessment, that transgression alone would likely have rendered him unconfirmable. Second, as a lower court judge, Sotomayor had issued a controversial decision in a racially charged case upholding New Haven, Connecticut's decision to invalidate the results of an exam taken by firefighters seeking a promotion because too few black officers had passed. Sotomayor's decision was ultimately overturned by the Supreme Court 5–4, with her controversial reasoning being rejected 9–0.

Those flashpoints served as the backdrop to the administration's PR push on behalf of the president's nominee. Much emphasis was placed on her potential historic status as the high court's first-ever Hispanic member. CNN published a story headlined "Latinos Rejoice in Sotomayor Nomination," packed with quotes from jubilant Hispanic leaders. A Latino law student was quoted as being "almost numb" with excitement. Representative Nydia Velázquez, the Congressional Hispanic Caucus chairwoman at the time, warned Republicans against opposing Sotomayor's nomination too vociferously. Her message wasn't subtle: "The Republicans are looking at ways they can make inroads in the Latino community . . . they need to be very cautious and careful" in critiquing this "wise Latina," she said. A White House memo emphasized Sotomayor's extraordinary life story: She was raised in a public housing project in the Bronx and lost her father at the tender age of nine. She applied herself in her studies and proved to be an outstanding student, eventually earning a scholarship to Princeton. After graduating from that august institution summa cum laude, Sotomayor enrolled at Yale Law School, where she received her legal training. Her undeniably impressive résumé, coupled with heavy attention on her compelling personal narrative and a heavy dash of ethnic politics, paved the way for a smooth confirmation process. Within a few months, she was confirmed rather easily by the Senate, 68–31, and has been on the bench ever since.

Which brings us to Miguel Estrada, a man of whom most Americans have never heard, and whose name may be only vaguely familiar to even some devoted politicos. In 2001, Estrada was nominated by President Bush to the influential U.S. Court of Appeals for the District of Columbia. As CNN reported at the time Estrada stood to be "the first Hispanic to sit on that court, which sometimes serves as a stepping stone to the U.S. Supreme Court." Guy wrote a piece at *National Review Online* in 2009 that ran through the highlights of Estrada's personal and academic biography, which revealed a glaring parallel in hindsight:

> *[Estrada] was born in Honduras and moved to the United States as a teenager from a broken family who couldn't speak fluent English. Despite these obstacles, Estrada put his nose to the grindstone and managed to graduate* magna cum laude *from both Columbia University and Harvard Law. After a series of exceptional clerkships, Estrada served in the Department of Justice, including a stint as an assistant to the solicitor general under the Clinton administration.*
>
> *His story may sound familiar. Both Miguel Estrada and Sonia Sotomayor spent many of their formative years living with only one parent. Both emerged from difficult life circumstances to attend and thrive at multiple Ivy League institutions. Each developed impressive records, accumulating reams of serious—and varied—legal experience prior to their nominations. Both were deemed so talented that presidents from both parties sought their services. And, of course, both are Hispanic.*

But Mr. Estrada was the wrong sort of Hispanic because his political worldview failed to hew to liberal expectations. Some compelling personal narratives, it turns out, are more compelling than others. He was torpedoed by Senate Democrats, who used the since-jettisoned (by Senate Democrats) judicial filibuster to keep his nomination in limbo for two years.

Miguel Estrada's Latino identity, hardscrabble upbringing, and top-flight credentials meant nothing to the very same people who experienced identity politics orgasms over Sonia Sotomayor. But there was a more sinister chapter to his story: an internal strategy memo spelled out the reasons why Senate Democrats went to the mat to block Estrada's nomination, one of which was expressly racial. The document from Senator Dick Durbin's office fingered Estrada "as especially dangerous, because he has a minimal paper trail, he is Latino, and the White House seems to be grooming him for a Supreme Court appointment." That's right, they explicitly stated that the well-qualified nominee was "especially dangerous" *because* "he is Latino," and was possibly being groomed for a spot on the high court. Just imagine the five-alarm racial-political firestorm that would have exploded if the parties involved were reversed.

So despite enjoying the support of a majority of upper chamber members, Democrats' maneuvering ensured that Estrada was never afforded an up-or-down vote. Stymied, he finally withdrew his name in 2003, citing the need to make long-term plans for his family. Democrats declared victory. Senator Chuck Schumer of New York vowed to continue obstructing Bush nominees who were "beyond the mainstream," in his view, with the late Senator Ted Kennedy crowing that Estrada's withdrawal was "a victory for the Constitution." More specifically, he said, the development "reflects a clear recognition . . . that under the Constitution the Senate has shared power over judicial appointments." Just over a decade later, Senate Democrats—by then the majority party—changed the Senate rules to banish the very sort of filibuster they'd pioneered to thwart Bush.

Oh, and there actually *was* a tempest over Durbin's disgusting racial memo. Senate Democrats, rather than being humiliated by their strategy, released their well-trained outrage hounds, demanding to know how Republicans had obtained the memos in question. Kennedy spokesman David Smith angrily accused Republicans of dirty tricks. "These are thefts of Democratic memos," he said, telegraphing to the media who the true culprits were. Democrats paid no price for their racial tactics, nor was much attention paid to the revelation that they were colluding with outside left-wing groups to target and defeat judicial nominations. In a piece of political jujitsu, which required media complicity, the Left turned a humiliating exposé into a whodunit over the source of the leaked memos. They got their man: Manuel Miranda, an aide to then Senate majority leader Bill Frist.

Miranda, himself a Latino immigrant, had discovered Democrats' strategy memos were easily accessible on a shared server. He and several colleagues exploited this availability, eventually passing along some of the most incriminating details to the press. After he was fingered as the leak, Democrats insisted that Miranda lose his job and face a criminal investigation. Miranda was forced to resign in 2004, along with another staffer. He spoke with us, recalling how rapidly a story about Democrats' external coordination and racial targeting boomeranged around and took him down:

> *One of the reasons I was so interested in promoting Miguel Estrada, and why I was the leader of his nomination process for seven votes on the Senate floor, is because I am—like Miguel—an immigrant.*
>
> *As an aide to Senator Dick Durbin of Illinois put it, [Estrada's] being Hispanic was a 'negative positive' ... they knew Miguel Estrada was a prime Hispanic nominee for a Republican president. And also Janice Rogers Brown, who was an African American judge that they targeted because she was African American. And others, especially women. Women were the most hard hit by Democrats' opposition, and many women judges were opposed, delayed, and obstructed during those years.*

There was no hacking. I was never called for any criminal investigation and was certainly never charged. In fact, I was so certain that we hadn't broken any laws—that this was all a huge smoke screen by Durbin and others—that I actually filed a lawsuit in federal court asking them to get on with it. If they were going to charge me, to charge me. And of course, they didn't.

I was surprised at the media that didn't go after the real story—not how the documents were obtained, but what they said. The documents showed that the Democrat Senators on the judiciary committee were wholly owned subsidiaries of George Soros's [one of the most prominent and activist left-wing billionaires on the planet] coalition of organizations. One memo actually indicated that the organizations would get together and vote as to which nominees could go forward in the committee.

Judging Sotomayor positively because she is Hispanic was hypocritical and ludicrous considering the fact that media had not equally defended and protected and applauded Miguel Estrada—who had a much more difficult life story to tell. A man who was not only Hispanic, and poor, and an immigrant, but he also has a speech impediment, for God's sake. His is an incredible story of achievement, and it was halted and silenced by Democrats' obstruction.

Today, Sonia Sotomayor is one of the nine most powerful legal figures in the United States, who will shape American jurisprudence for generations to come. Miguel Estrada, far removed from the national spotlight, serves as a private sector attorney. He has argued before the Supreme Court on twenty-two occasions, including a handful of appearances since the political process chewed him up and spat him out. Perhaps he's stood before those nine robed justices and privately wondered what might have been. When we contacted him, Mr. Estrada politely declined to discuss his treatment by hypocritical, calculating partisans more than a decade ago. Miranda isn't surprised: "Miguel is a very quiet, unassuming man. He suffered a great deal because of that nomination; more than anyone knows. During that nomination, they had to change their home telephone numbers because they were getting so many threatening and hateful calls. It was very upsetting to his wife," he recounted. We can't quarrel with Mr. Estrada's decision to opt out of rehashing that ugly chapter in his life, in which a "wise Latino" was sidelined because he didn't think the way he was "supposed to."

The Estrada affair highlights an infuriating reality: when the Left scurrilously accuses conservatives of opposing people like Barack Obama because of his race, they rarely have to answer for what they do to people like Miguel Estrada—whom they *explicitly targeted* for defeat because of his skin color.

EVERYONE'S A LITTLE BIT RACIST

"It is undeniably the case that racist Americans are almost entirely in one political coalition and not the other," proclaimed MSNBC host Chris Hayes[21] during the 2012 election cycle. He was, in his view, stating the obvious: the center-right Republican coalition is home to most of the country's racists. The Outrage Circus seems to possess an uncanny ability to manufacture "useful truths."

To his credit, Hayes later tweeted some data that exploded his thesis. Here's what he discovered: Economist Alex Tabarrok culled a 2002 study on politics and race conducted by the University of California at Berkeley, which will never be mistaken for a conservative bastion.

---

[21] Guy here. I've been friends with Chris for years. He truly is the nicest socialist you'll ever meet. But occasionally he advances empirically unsupportable and/or intellectually lazy caricatures of conservatives, and I call him out in public. When that happens, some of my readers scold me for befriending such a person and urge me to disassociate myself with him—which is exactly the wrong solution. Living a "siloed" existence is boring and polarizing. It's exactly the sort of thing we're arguing against in this book.

More important, the survey was conducted years before Barack Obama entered the national picture. One of the questions Tabarrok flagged asked respondents whether they would hypothetically vote for a black presidential candidate.

Among self-described "strong Democrats," 92.4 percent said yes, with 7.6 percent answering in the negative. Among "strong Republicans," the breakdown was 94.7 percent to 5.3 percent. Zero partisan gap, with hard-core Republicans holding a statistically insignificant nonracist edge. Another question asked whether respondents favored laws banning interracial marriage. This, too, produced zero partisan gap, with Democrats and Republicans equally opposed. A 2013 Gallup poll showed that fully 87 percent of Americans approve of interracial marriage, including vast majorities of Republicans, Democrats, and Independents. When Gallup first began asking that question in 1958, support for mixed-race unions stood at an appalling 4 percent.

We're not perfect, and there's progress still to be made. But we've come a long way, America. Willfully ignoring all such progress for partisan gain isn't a healthy or accurate lens through which to view the news. And pretending that one side of the spectrum has a near monopoly on racism as a means of impugning all conservatives' motives isn't just a mean-spirited conversation-squelching maneuver, it's factually false.

We're especially encouraged by the trend among younger voters to downplay race and disdain affirmative action. A 2014 national poll of millennials conducted by Harvard University's Institute of Politics asked respondents to rank a series of statements on a scale of one to five—one signifying strong agreement, and five strong disagreement. Young voters were presented with this proposition: "Qualified minorities should be given special preferences in hiring and education." This was the *only* domestic policy statement against which a majority of young Republicans and Democrats stood united in disagreement. Content of character, color of skin, and so on.

WHAT NOT TO DO

Winning the long fight against the thought censors frequently entails rejecting their faulty premises and denying them even the smallest of victories. We are great admirers of our friend John Podhoretz's inimitable writing style and occasionally ornery sense of humor, but we're afraid he did precisely the opposite of what one should do when caught in the center of a phony outrage dustup. During the 2014 Gaza War, musical artist John Legend fired off a volley of anti-Israel tweets, prompting Podhoretz to tweet back, "Shut up and play the piano." This was a slight variation on the conservative "shut up and sing" meme, crystallized in Laura Ingraham's 2003 book by that title. We're not necessarily big fans of the "shut up" part of this quip, for reasons that should be made clear by glancing at the cover of this book. Nevertheless, the intended message of that phrase is less about *actually* silencing the celebrity set, and more about reminding people that entertainers are often *not experts* on the various public affairs topics about which they are wont to spout off. Yet their ignorant, sanctimonious, or loony tunes pontifications tend to attract undue attention thanks to their fame. The spirit of Podhoretz's snarky put-down of Legend was, *Dude, you're a singer—you don't know what the hell you're talking about, so stick with singing.*

The Left decided that J-Pod, as he's affectionately known, had committed an act of racism because Legend is black. The tone and ferocity of this pop-up furor made it seem as if Podhoretz had used the N-word while telling a slave to go pick some more cotton. It was ridiculous. The Democracy Alliance hit squad at *ThinkProgress* wrote the incident up in a blog post, which quickly zoomed around the lefty Twitterverse. "Angry" liberals flooded into J-Pod's timeline, spitting profane invective and calling him a racist. No one bothered to check that "shut up and sing" is a long-established phrase that's been directed at lily white entertainers like Susan Sarandon, Alec Baldwin, and the Dixie

Chicks. The calculus was simpleminded: white conservative + black liberal singer + terse online tell-off = RACISM.

The point of this rigged firestorm was to cow Podhoretz into silence. It worked. Panicked about being called a racist over a color-blind insult, Podhoretz disappeared from Twitter for hours, going so far as to delete his account. The mob did virtual victory cartwheels. The fact that he restored his account and resumed tweeting within twenty-four hours was lost in the shuffle—the Outrage Circus had already skipped town, in search of its next victim. Podhoretz was successfully bullied, and his overreactive retreat was interpreted as a tacit admission of guilt. With due respect to John, the correct response in this situation is to straight-up reject the premise of the attack. *No, that tweet was not racial in any way, shape, or form. No, I won't slink away because of your faux outrage. Yes, you are bad people for trying to racialize this.* Flip them the bird. And let others have your back, too. Many of us strongly defended him on Twitter in his absence (which made it harder), leading *ThinkProgress*'s original character assassin to mock the push-back with a self-unaware, racialized follow-up tweet. Guy was rather pleased with this retort:

@guypbenson: Tweets area white dude/racism expert RT @ JuddLegum: BREAKING: Conservative white dudes on Twitter are experts on what is and is not racist

---

Voter ID Edition

"I always use the word extreme."
—Senator Chuck Schumer (D-NY)

I t was spring 2011, and Republicans and Democrats were already jockeying for position ahead of a bruising budget battle that would eventually culminate in the Kafkaesque "Budget Control Act"—which formed the failed "Supercommittee," which, in turn, triggered sequestration.[1] In advance of a conference call with reporters, Senate Democrats' messaging quarterback, Charles Schumer of New York, offered his colleagues a refresher on their talking points. When all else fails, he reminded them, just label the opposition as radicals. "I always use the word 'extreme,'" Schumer explained. "That is what the caucus instructed me to use this week." As it turns out, and unbeknownst to the assembled senators, several reporters were already dialed in for Schumer's tutorial. They heard everything, and subsequently reported on it. *Awk-ward!* When the call officially went live, all five Democrats on the line carried out their marching orders with great aplomb. Schumer laid the "extreme" on thick, with Senators Barbara Boxer (D-CA), Ben Cardin (D-MD), Tom Carper (D-DE), and Richard Blumenthal[2] (D-isgraced) dutifully following suit.

---

[1] This word soup of dysfunction is best filed under "reasons why normal people hate politics."

[2] Blumenthal, it should be noted whenever possible, spent his entire adult life brazenly lying about having served in Vietnam. He did not. This fact came to light during the 2010 campaign, when Blumenthal was seeking an open Senate seat. The people of Connecticut learned this information, then proceeded to elect him by a double-digit

What Republicans were seeking at the time was to take a small bite out of the ever-expanding federal spending pie. In 2011, the U.S. government spent $1.3 trillion more than it took in.[3] The "extremists" ultimately secured $21 billion in spending reductions, out of $3.54 trillion in total FY 2012 outlays. That's a fraction of a drop in the bucket. And thus ends our insipid budget rant.

The larger point is that the word *extreme* is routinely used as a means to marginalize opposing viewpoints. Much like the cultural flop, pounding the table about "extremism" is also a tactic to work the refs and shape Beltway conventional wisdom, even when—or especially when—the characterization does not actually apply. *They keep calling this extreme*, lazy journalists with liberal-leaning instincts think to themselves, *so there must be something to it*. It can be maddeningly effective and can even start to insidiously cloud the judgment of conservatives.

Senator Rand Paul, a Tea Party favorite and presidential hopeful, spoke with the *New York Times* in May 2014 and expressed his conviction that Republicans need to "lay off" voter ID laws because the issue is "offending people." Many on the left nodded vigorously, having spent years casting the issue as an extreeeeeeeeeme attempt by racist Republicans to "suppress" minority voters. The hyperpolitical Obama Justice Department has filed lawsuits to block such legislative efforts, which Attorney General Eric Holder has likened to a modern-day poll tax. Literally all of that is unsupportable nonsense, yet Paul seemed to be taken in by the Outrage Circus's kabuki theater.

The Supreme Court rejected the "poll tax" analogy in *Crawford v. Marion County Election Board*, a 2008 decision that upheld Indiana's strict voter ID law 6–3, with liberal justice John Paul Stevens authoring

---

margin. He was assigned to both the Senate Veterans' Affairs and Armed Services Committees. Really.

[3] That annual shortfall receded to "only" half a trillion in 2014 but is projected by the nonpartisan Congressional Budget Office to track upward again, topping $1 trillion by the end of the current budget window, absent reform.

the decision. "Voter ID laws = voter suppression!" hasn't panned out either. To wit, the *Atlanta Journal-Constitution* reported that since Georgia's ID measure went into effect (despite hysterical protests from opponents and a slew of failed legal challenges), minority turnout markedly *increased* in successive election cycles—including the 2010 midterm elections: "Turnout among black and Hispanic voters increased from 2006 to 2010, dramatically outpacing population growth for those groups over the same period," the story explained.

The standard narrative is that voter ID laws are the sole province of Republicans and their shadowy Kochtopus/ALEC/Voldemort overlords. But they're not. Rhode Island's heavily Democratic legislature passed a robust voter identification law in 2011; its lead sponsor was Senator Harold Metts, a black Democrat. Another key supporter was Representative Anastasia Williams (also a black Democrat, for the identity politics scorekeepers at home), who testified in hearings that someone had voted under her name in 2006, and that she'd once personally witnessed a man vote twice at her polling place. They had good reason to advocate for the bill. A 2014 *Providence Journal* investigation found 180,000 potentially problematic voter registrations in the state. Twenty of thirty-nine Rhode Island municipalities boasted more people registered than voting-age people who lived in them, prompting the editorial board to back voter ID laws as "reasonable precautions to make sure that voting is on the level." Did the Koch brothers get to these African American liberal Democrats in this one-party state, too? *My God, they're everywhere!*

Last but not least, voter ID laws are not, in fact, "offending people"— professionally aggrieved interest groups notwithstanding. A 2012 *Washington Post* poll posed this straightforward question to a representative sample of American adults: "In your view, should voters in the United States be required to show official, government-issued photo identification—such as a driver's license—when they cast ballots on Election Day, or shouldn't they have to do this?" Seventy-four percent of respondents said yes, including 67 percent of nonwhites. The results of a 2013 McClatchy/Marist survey were even more lopsided, with 83 percent of respondents supporting voter ID laws. Seventy-two percent of Democrats and 83 percent of nonwhite voters joined the overwhelming national majority in favor of these commonsense laws. That's a rather unlikely coalition of pro–vote suppression "extremists." And yet a bright and well-meaning conservative like Rand Paul managed to be browbeaten into a defensive posture on a $75/25$ issue. The "extreme" criers are relentless and effective.

Our editor recommended that we end this minichapter here, as venturing further into the weeds on voter integrity policy is *slightly* beyond the scope of our thesis. We replied to this (accurate and astute) note by paraphrasing Boon from *Animal House*: Forget it, we're rolling. Two more points on voter ID laws, then we're done. We promise.

First, opponents of these measures often warn that certain eligible voters may not be able to procure proper identification and could therefore be disenfranchised. There's a solution to this objection that doesn't involve compromising the integrity of the American electoral system: providing IDs to all eligible citizens who want one, at taxpayer expense. This is a proper government function if there ever was one. Ironically, those who are most likely to reject this proposal as infeasible also happen to be the same people who support the full nationalization of our health-care system. In their minds, the government's sphere of influence is boundless . . . except when it comes to the rudimentary task of figuring out which of its citizens need IDs to vote. Strange, isn't it?

Second, we've grown accustomed to the tired refrain that voter ID laws are "a solution in search of a problem." If voter fraud is a figment of the Far Right's imagination, it would follow that any suggested remedy to a nonexistent problem must be rooted in some dark ulterior motive. We don't subscribe to the conspiratorial view that voter fraud is a widespread and systemic crisis that regularly infects elections and poisons outcomes. But the facts demonstrate that it isn't a made-up problem, either. Voter ID laws and robust efforts to clean up and synchronize voter rolls across jurisdictions are both popular and appropriate. Five recent examples help illustrate our point, four of which come from swing states:

Florida: A 2012 investigative report from WBBH-TV in Ft. Myers identified dozens of local residents who were both (a) noncitizens and (b) registered to vote. Correspondent Andy Pierrotti took it upon himself to painstakingly cross-reference a list of people who'd checked a box on a government form declining to serve on a jury because they weren't citizens with the state's voter rolls. When he tracked a number of these individuals down, they openly admitted to having voted in recent elections. "I vote every year!" one woman boasted. In his own backyard, using this extremely narrow method, he found 94 illegal voters. That may not seem like a significant number at first blush, but keep in mind that those are only the people he personally located through this very limited procedure. Even so, if you extrapolate Lee County's dozens of ineligible voters across the state's 67 counties, the sum comes to nearly 6,300 potential illegal voters.[4] In 2000, the presidency of the United States was decided by a margin of 537 Florida votes. How many illegal votes are anti-ID crusaders willing to accept? They should have to answer that question.

North Carolina: WNCN-TV reported in 2014 (emphasis ours):

"State election officials are looking into thousands of cases where registered voters may have voted in two states or after their reported death. A report presented Wednesday by Elections Director Kim Strach to the Joint Legislative Elections Oversight Committee **said 81 voters have a voter history later than the date of their death.** The audit further identified 13,416 deceased voters on voter rolls in Oct. 2013. The audit showed 155,692 registered North Carolina voters whose first and last names, dates of birth and last four digits of their Social Security number match those of voters registered in other states, but who most recently registered or voted elsewhere. **A total of**

---

[4] Lee County is Florida's eighth most populous jurisdiction, so our back-of-the-envelope extrapolation may be slightly inflated. After adjusting for that factor, however, the total is still in the thousands.

35,750 voters with matching first and last names and date of birth were registered in North Carolina and another state, and voted in both states in the 2012 general election. Another 765 voters with an exact match of first and last name, date of birth and last four digits of their Social Security number were registered and voted in the 2012 general election in North Carolina and another state . . . **A total of 28 states participated in the crosscheck, leaving data missing from 22 other states.**"

Close to 36,000 potential double votes in one state, and that's *without* cross-check data from 44 percent of U.S. states. Voter fraud deniers contend that there could be innocent explanations for some of these disparities, such as people with common names who happened to be born on the same day in the same year, as well as clerical errors. Let's be generous and chalk up half of the apparent double votes to aboveboard mistakes. That leaves 17,875 questionable Tar Heel State ballots cast in the most recent presidential election. Barack Obama carried North Carolina by fewer than 15,000 tallies in 2008. Again we ask, how much voter fraud is "acceptable"?

Virginia: The *Washington Post* reported in late 2014: "Tens of thousands of voters were registered to cast ballots in both Virginia and Maryland during the 2012 presidential election—and more than 150 appear to have voted twice . . . Seventeen of those alleged instances were in Fairfax County, where election officials found the evidence so compelling that they have turned the information over to law enforcement." Democrats dismissed these concerns, denouncing a Republican "witch hunt." We do not think they know what that term means.

California: Democratic state senator Roderick Wright was convicted of eight felonies in early 2014, including five counts of fraudulent voting for illegally casting ballots in a district where he didn't reside.[5] We now present an excerpt from a *Los Angeles Times* article:

---

[5] The month after his *eight felony convictions*, California Democrats heroically blocked a Republican attempt to expel Wright from the Senate.

"Asked why he didn't decide to voluntarily forgo pay during his [post-conviction] leave of absence, Wright said: 'Why would I do that? If I were a police officer and I shot someone, I wouldn't be asked to do that. There are no other state employees that would be asked to do that. Why should I be treated differently than someone who works at the highway patrol or the DMV?'" Public. Servant. By the way, in September 2014, a Democratic state representative from Connecticut was arrested on nineteen charges of voter fraud, including fabricating evidence.

Ohio: At a Cincinnati rally against voter ID laws in 2014 keynoted by (who else?) Al Sharpton and cosponsored by the Ohio Democratic Party, a very special guest was honored onstage. That guest was Melowese Richardson, a local woman who beamed and waved to the crowd as she was greeted by an ovation and embraced by Sharpton. What had Ms. Richardson, a former Ohio poll worker, done to earn such adulation? She'd gotten herself convicted on four counts of illegal voting in 2012, that's what. Just before the event, her jail sentence had been reduced to probation, so she was there to bask in the glory of a martyr's welcome from her fellow fraud enthusiasts. The *Cincinnati Enquirer* recapitulated some of this charmer's greatest hits in their story about her controversial appearance at the rally: "Richardson was previously convicted of threatening to kill a witness in a criminal case against her brother; of stealing; of drunken driving; and of beating someone in a bar fight." And *then* she became an elections worker. That inspires confidence. State Democrats murmured a few notes of disapproval of this spectacle (translation: *not helping*, guys), then hastily moved on.

Pro tip: If you're holding an indignant political rally in opposition to "racist" laws designed to address the "myth" of voter fraud, don't openly celebrate someone who was, you know, *convicted of engaging in the exact sort of criminal activity you're claiming doesn't exist.*

5

SPEECH POLICE ACADEMY

Orthodoxy Enforcement on Campus

The Outrage Circus has set up permanent camp at many of America's colleges and universities, where the silencing mob's worst instincts are routinely indulged, if not encouraged. The academy is where the outrage arts are taught, where the craziest outrage rules and trends take shape, and where, perversely, the values of free speech and free thought are valued least. Even if students aren't active participants in the insanity, they marinate in this milieu for approximately four formative years of their lives. Professors and other circus ringmasters work diligently to ensure that the proper lessons are learned, even if by some form of social osmosis. If you ever find yourself surveying the state of our national discourse and quietly wonder how things got so bad, look no further than the ivy-covered buildings and manicured quads that dot our map from coast to coast.

Decrying the speech-stymieing madness that too often prevails on American college campuses may be well-trod ground, but it is more fertile ground than ever. Many others have chronicled the existence and enforcement of highly restrictive speech codes on campus, the serial disruption of "offensive" speakers' remarks, the mistreatment of nonleftist groups and students, and the freezing out of ideologically unenlightened faculty. We are not inclined to recapitulate these countless, endless battles. They're alternatively enraging and depressing. We do, however, salute liberty-minded organizations who voluntarily wade into these skirmishes on a daily basis—perhaps the most prominent, indispensable, and indefatigable of which is the Foundation for Individual Rights in Education, or FIRE. The group's YouTube page features a video exhorting students, "Don't shut up—*stand* up for speech." How subversive.

Columnist and eminent public intellectual George F. Will aptly describes the toxic anti-intellectual culture the Academy has wrought for itself: "It [has] made campuses, which should be islands of intellectual curiosity and free expression and vigorous debate, into islands instead of wary people walking on eggshells, eager not to offend the constantly shifting standards of what is, and is not, discussable."

In the name of diversity and tolerance, diversity of thought will not be tolerated. *"End of discussion!"* bellows the "safe space" faculty liaison. *"You shouldn't be thinking those thoughts, let alone expressing them."* Many colleges may be gun-free zones, but the campus speech and thought police are armed to the teeth with regulations, tools of intellectual intimidation, and an ever-expanding glossary of speech-squelching terms. Three examples spring to mind.

Privilege: In short, your "privilege" is any form of status you may hold (race, gender, upbringing, sexuality) that confers a historic social advantage on your group, and is therefore an inborn advantage for you. The first thing you need to know about privilege is that you almost certainly have it, and it must be "checked" at all times. Before one weighs in on any issue, or engages in a conversation with a coworker, or orders lunch at a deli, one owes it to society to reflect on the panoply of privileged statuses bestowed upon one by the circumstances of one's birth. This is important for anyone who is *not*, say, a differently abled,[1] genderqueer Pacific Islander who was raised by wolves in a rain forest devastated by climate change. It is uniquely important for white heterosexual males, who achieve the trifecta of coveted privileges. If

---

[1] Disabled.

you are a white heterosexual male, you are to *very seriously* consider anything you might say or think pertaining to people who are different from you. When in doubt, don't speak.

Those who may be unsure about the level of guilt they ought to feel by virtue of their existence may consider logging on to a cheeky website called CheckMyPrivilege.com.[2] It features a short and handy privilege quiz, featuring questions such as, *What is your gender?* Possible answers: trans, genderqueer, cis,[3] or trans (passable). The most progressive among us may notice that these options are nowhere near comprehensive. Facebook recently added *dozens* of choices beyond "male" and "female" to its gender category. Offerings include "gender-fluid" and "intersex." If you're even slightly confused by this nomenclature, you'd best check your privilege. And remember, the most effective way to check your privilege is to remain silent on any number of political and cultural questions because you and your type have already had your say—unless, that is, your privilege requires you to "speak out." The rules are complicated. Consult your local safe-space faculty liaison for details, and be sure to ask for the current month's guidelines.

A University of Albany website describes a common college diversity activity called the "Privilege Walk," in which students start shoulder to shoulder in a line and are told to step forward or backward depending on their life experience. For instance, "If you are a white male, step forward," "If you attended grade school with people you felt were like yourself, take one step forward," and "If you've ever felt unsafe walking alone at night, take one step backward." At the end of the activity, the physical distance you've created between yourself and your classmates is supposed to merely encourage "reflection and realizations" not "blame" or "isolation." Make no mistake, though, those at the front are meant to experience shame and guilt.

---

[2] Guy's score: 25. Ruling: "Advantaged." Also, we are 95 percent sure this website is satire.

[3] You, dear reader, are almost guaranteed to be this.

Triggers: Words, phrases, or topics that may offend an observer's sensibilities (the more delicate, the more socially responsible!), thus "triggering" an upsetting and/or hurtful response. Triggers are ubiquitous, leading to the creation of crucial "trigger warnings," designed to alert potential offendees that an imminent subject of discussion may cause them to have a sad. (Common problematic topics include race, sex, sexual assault, sexual abuse, violence, and mental illness.)

The liberal *New Republic* covered this issue in March 2014, after the student government at the University of California at Santa Barbara passed a "Resolution to Mandate Warnings for Triggering Content in Academic Settings," including disclaimers on course syllabi—literally bowdlerizing curricula. Writer Jenny Jarvie cites a number of primary sources and articles in her piece, including a document produced by Oberlin College's Office of Equity Concerns.[4] It urges faculty to:

Be aware of racism, classism, sexism, heterosexism, cissexism, ableism, and other issues of privilege and oppression, to remove triggering material when it doesn't "directly" contribute to learning goals and "strongly consider" developing a policy to make "triggering material" optional.

For a look at how this works in practice, consider an opinion column penned by Rutgers student Philip Wythe, who writes that a syllabus that included *The Great Gatsby*—an infamously traumatic novel cruelly assigned to American high school sophomores—should include the following content advisory, TW: "suicide," "domestic abuse," and "graphic violence."

This trend proves to be a bit too much for even the Obama-endorsing editors of the *Los Angeles Times*, who published a house editorial on the subject of triggering. Its headline read, "Warning: College Students, This Editorial May Upset You." Its conclusion:

---

[4] Oberlin's policy has been tabled. For now.

As psychologists point out, a post-traumatic response is just as likely to be triggered by something that has nothing to do with subject matter: a glimpse of the same blue-colored clothing that was visible during a traumatic event, or a certain scent that was in the air that day. Colleges cannot bubble-wrap students against everything that might be frightening or offensive to them.

We're shocked and dismayed that even at a paper like the *Los Angeles Times*, it seems as though many editors' privilege remains worrisomely unchecked.

Microaggressions: Writing at the American Psychological Association's website, a writer named Tori DeAngelis describes racial microaggressions as "racism . . . so subtle that neither victim nor perpetrator may entirely understand what is going on." So be on the lookout for that. DeAngelis and other sources credit Harvard psychologist Chester M. Pierce with coining the term in the 1970s; his successors have been refining the concept ever since. The *New York Times* reports in a March 21, 2014, article by Tanzina Vega that a "recent surge in popularity" in microaggression-related hypersensitivity can be traced to a 2007 essay by Columbia University professor Derald W. Sue.

Vega notes that Sue "broke down microaggressions into microassaults, microinsults and microinvalidations," authoring a book on the subject entitled *Microaggressions in Everyday Life: Race, Gender, and Sexual Orientation*. It's no doubt a white-knuckle[5] thrill ride of a read. In his writings, Sue laments that microaggressions are often perpetrated by "well-meaning white people." Tread carefully, friends. Your good intentions are no excuse.

This chapter, we can safely assume, amounts to a straight-up aggression (macroaggression?), but any of its sentences or turns of phrase may qualify as microaggressions—also known as virtually anything

---

[5] We regret this racial microaggression.

that offends anyone for any reason. Because individuals' thresholds for offense are varied, microaggressions are literally everywhere.

White guilt alone isn't enough to absolve you from these sometimes-imperceptible sins. Brown University's Micro/Aggressions Community Facebook page has attracted roughly 900 "likes," equivalent to 15 percent of the school's undergraduate population. Established in 2013, the page serves as a clearinghouse for students to anonymously submit (unverifiable) examples of microaggressions suffered at the hands of fellow students and faculty. The group's administrators include this request in the "about" section: "So that people who have 'liked' this page are better able to take care of themselves (especially if they have been affected by similar situations), if people could submit TRIGGER WARNINGS associated with their stories, it might make for a safer page environment." ("Safe" = "not being exposed to ideas or thoughts that disrupt one's coddled worldview.") This site is not parody. A tasting menu of actual submissions:

> *As a genderqueer person, every time someone complains that gender-neutral pronouns are "too weird" or "not grammatically correct" it disappoints me (not to mention triggers). Is obeying antiquated grammar rules really more important than the feelings and identities of your friends and loved ones?*
>
> *I have been struggling recently with upper-class white people who use their queerness to "access" and then speak for my oppression as a working-class person of color.*
>
> *A white man recently told me he is "tired of so many people telling" him that he is entitled for sharing his opinions about oppression. First of all, why do you think that's an okay thing to say to a person of color? Please tell me more about how tired you are. It must be truly tiring when the world ceases to act as a private platform for the dissemination of your thoughts and opinions. It must have been difficult to face a lifetime of people not listening to your opinions because of your entitlement. Now, I'm*

not gonna say that your opinions should always be discounted.
They are welcome in the right time and in the right way . . .

Your opinion counts, bro, as long as it's stated at the "right time," and in the "right way." At least one contributor to the forum was able to cut through the absurdity: "As a white, cisgendered male from a middle class family . . . never mind." Administrators, who approve all posts, may not have realized that may have been a sly critique of their premise. So sly and subtle, in fact, that it might qualify as a micro-aggression. Or even a nanoaggression (working definition: an insult so slight that literally no one perceives it, yet it exists nonetheless, and must be guarded against).

Now that we've concluded our primer on the lexicon of speech-stifling grievance mongering, kindly allow us to make three important points: First, our disdain for the privilege police shouldn't be confused with blind denial that some races and classes of Americans *have* enjoyed supremely privileged statuses over the history of our nation. To ignore that reality would be ahistorical and idiotic. Nevertheless, past and current disparities are not legitimate excuses for stoking the fires of resentment, nor do they justify the shutting down of ideas and speech via guilt-based manipulation. One's position at the end of the "Privilege Walk" ought to have minuscule bearing on the value of one's opinions.

By demonizing groups of people on racial, gender, and socioeconomic grounds, the privilege obsessives are in fact constructing their own privilege structure, wherein the only "legitimate" and "authentic" voices belong to the traditionally nonprivileged. The goal of this is not to "give voice to the voiceless," or whatever feel-good slogan they're spouting; it's to subordinate and disqualify political and social views that don't hew to a certain ideological program. If a white man patronizingly informing a black woman that her opinions are only "welcome at the right time, and in the right way" shouldn't fly (and it shouldn't), then neither should the reverse dynamic.

Second, our ridicule of the "trigger warning" club is not a dismissal of the very real condition known as posttraumatic stress disorder (PTSD), suffered by some soldiers returning from the battlefield, and survivors of scarring episodes of abuse or assault, to cite two common examples. Triggers can be real and traumatizing. We reject "trigger warning" hysteria *because* we believe PTSD to be so serious. Trivializing a genuine psychological phenomenon as a means of ensuring that "progressive" college undergraduates never endure the horror of hearing something that might upset them is an insult. It diminishes and cheapens the real thing.

Finally, our ostentatious eye-rolling over "microaggressions" is not an endorsement of rudeness or insensitivity. We'd be a happier, better nation if more people made more of an effort to treat others with kindness and respect. And we'd be a happier, better nation if others chose to forgive or shrug off unintentional or perceived slights from well-meaning fellow citizens. If only there were some sort of "rule," if you will, that captured the essence of this spirit of mutual respect and empathy. Distilling such a sentiment down to a single sentence[6] would be golden. Someone could probably sell a lot of books.

Back to our recurring theme: the purpose of triggers and privilege checking and "microaggressions" is to create a culture in which uncomfortable conversations do not happen. Where difficult thoughts are not explored. Where anodyne political correctness is the default setting, and where violators will be punished. This would be terrible anywhere. It's especially terrible at college, where young people are theoretically supposed to feel free to find themselves, to expose themselves to new ideas, and to develop critical thinking skills.

---

[6] Matthew 7:12

GEORGE WILL AND "SYNTHETIC OUTRAGE"

As the debunked *Rolling Stone*/gang rape imbroglio of December 2014 demonstrated, sexual assault on college campuses is a hot, emotionally fraught topic these days. So George Will knowingly and bravely stepped into a minefield when he penned a nationally syndicated column earlier that year that dared to question the terms of the debate on this subject. "When [campuses] make victimhood a coveted status that confers privileges, victims proliferate," Will wrote. "Academia is learning that its attempts to create victim-free campuses—by making everyone hypersensitive, even delusional, about victimizations—brings increasing supervision by the regulatory state that progressivism celebrates." Will was sharply critiquing an Obama administration effort to discourage sexual assault (a worthy goal if there ever was one) that featured what he argued was an overbroad affront to due process, justified by highly suspect statistics. His core argument:

> Now the Obama administration is riding to the rescue of "sexual assault" victims. It vows to excavate equities from the ambiguities of the hookup culture, this cocktail of hormones, alcohol and the faux sophistication of today's prolonged adolescence of especially privileged young adults.
>
> The administration's crucial and contradictory statistics are validated the usual way, by official repetition; Joe Biden has been heard from. The statistics are: One in five women is sexually assaulted while in college, and only 12 percent of assaults are reported. Simple arithmetic demonstrates that if the 12 percent reporting rate is correct, the 20 percent assault rate is preposterous. Mark Perry of the American Enterprise Institute notes, for example, that in the four years 2009 to 2012 there were 98 reported sexual assaults at Ohio State. That would be 12 percent of 817 total out of a female student population of

approximately 28,000, for a sexual assault rate of approximately 2.9 percent—too high but nowhere near 20 percent.

Education Department lawyers disregard pesky arithmetic and elementary due process. Threatening to withdraw federal funding, the department mandates adoption of a minimal "preponderance of the evidence" standard when adjudicating sexual assault charges between males and the female "survivors"— note the language of prejudgment. Combine this with capacious definitions of sexual assault that can include not only forcible sexual penetration but also nonconsensual touching.

In taking on a sacred cow, Will invited a firestorm of criticism that echoed beyond the reflexively close-minded precincts of the academy. Team Outrage instantly sprang into action. Four Democratic senators[7] fired off a letter to the *Washington Post*, Will's flagship newspaper, airing their grievances against the column:

Your thesis and statistics fly in the face of everything we know about this issue. More egregiously, you trivialize the scourge of sexual assault, putting the phrase in scare quotes and treating this crime as a socially acceptable phenomenon . . . Your column reiterates ancient beliefs about sexual assault that are inconsistent with the reality of victims' experiences, based on what we have heard directly from survivors. Your words contribute to the exact culture that discourages reporting and forces victims into hiding and away from much-needed services . . . There is no acceptable number of sexual assaults; anything more than zero is unacceptable.

By questioning the way sexual assaults are calculated and dealt with, Will was fueling "rape culture." So *shut up, George*, they explained. The *Post* published Will's retort (emphasis ours):

---

[7]Dianne Feinstein (D-CA), Robert Casey (D-PA), Tammy Baldwin (D-WI), Richard Blumenthal (D-bunked Vietnam War veteran).

I have received your letter of June 12, and I am puzzled. You say my statistics "fly in the face of everything we know about this issue." You do not mention which statistics, but those I used come from the Obama administration, and from simple arithmetic involving publicly available reports on campus sexual assaults. **The administration asserts that only 12 percent of college sexual assaults are reported. Note well: I did not question this statistic. Rather, I used it.**

I cited one of the calculations based on it that Mark Perry of the American Enterprise Institute has performed. So, I think your complaint is with the conclusion that arithmetic dictates, based on the administration's statistic. The inescapable conclusion is that another administration statistic that one in five women is sexually assaulted while in college is insupportable and might call for tempering your rhetoric about "the scourge of sexual assault."

As for what you call my "ancient beliefs," which you think derive from an "antiquated" and "counterintuitive" culture, allow me to tell you something really counterintuitive: **I think I take sexual assault much more seriously than you do. Which is why I worry about definitions of that category of crime that might, by their breadth, tend to trivialize it. And why I think sexual assault is a felony that should be dealt with by the criminal justice system, and not be adjudicated by improvised campus processes.**

It requires an aggressive form of ignorance, not terribly uncommon in the United States Senate, to dispute Will's math or warp his thesis into a downplaying of the seriousness of sexual assault. Will's eloquent rebuttal did little to satiate the political bloodlust of the professionally outraged. To the Outrage Circus, his actual arguments were secondary at best. His status as a "rape denier," or whatever, was an opportunity to shut him up more broadly.

The National Organization for Women (NOW) called for his firing, and a group called UltraViolet took out ads urging newspapers to drop Will's column. Only one paper, the *St. Louis Post-Dispatch*, did so—and its opinion editor was subsequently embarrassed by radio host Hugh Hewitt. The editor, having run out of intellectual runway, hung up on Hewitt midinterview. UltraViolet also collected nearly ninety thousand signatures demanding that Will lose his job for employing "hate speech" and—ta-da!—"dog whistles." According to the *Weekly Standard*'s Mark Hemingway, the group's cofounder is a woman named Nita Chaudhary, who is married to Jesse Lee, a senior Obama White House official.[8]

The InstaMob wasn't limited to shrieking anonymous Internet commenters or Twitter users. It included four senators, NOW, and a deeply connected spouse of an influential administration official. Will stood firm and prevailed—and a great deal of credit is owed to the hundreds of editors who chose not to capitulate. In a discussion with us, Will reflected on the episode without regrets:

I've written well over 4,000 columns. I write about books, I write about electoral outcomes, I write about issues like the Ex-Im bank, I write about court rulings, and I think those are all interesting and important to write about. And I try to do so conscientiously. But every once in a while, you have to do something that is terribly important. This subject was one of those. When the federal government uses its vast megaphone for propaganda, and does so for the purpose of disseminating spurious statistics, and does that for the purpose of arousing passions, and tries to arouse passions for the purpose of sweeping away

---

[8] Some liberals on Twitter decided that the *Standard*'s reference to Ms. Chaudhary as the "Wife of White House Media Director" in its headline was sexism unto itself, for diminishing her individual accomplishments. A cursory search reveals the *Standard* also referred to astronaut Mark Kelly, who has quite the career and identity of his own, as "[Gabrielle] Giffords' husband," because it's common practice to refer to a spouse using his/her relationship to the public-figure spouse in question.

*due process protections surrounding criminal accusations, it's
at that point that a columnist actually earns his keep. You have
to take a stand against the manufactured hysteria of a government engaged in conscienceless propaganda. The synthetic hysteria, which is probably the biggest manufacturing product in
our economy these days, just indicated to me that I had struck
a target worth striking.*

He's taken the firestorm in stride, defending his premise and delivering deliciously George Willian insults to his elected critics:

*The four senators wrote a singularly unconvincing letter, which
I think I had no particular trouble refuting. Remember, they're
senators. They probably didn't read my column, they probably
didn't write the letter—that was done by some staffer who put
it in front of them, and they signed it. Senators are too busy to
be knowledgeable, and they pass on to their next grandstanding
episode.*

    *My assertion was that if you really take sexual assault seri-
ously, as our criminal justice system does and as we as a society
do because we have established rape as second only perhaps to
murder among serious felonies, then you say that as soon as
rape is charged, you should turn this over to the criminal justice
system. Now what you hear from campuses is that it takes too
long. Well, yes, that's called due process. There are always people
with a kind of lynch mob spirit who say "We're all for due process
except when we're not, and we're in a hurry, and delays amount
to justice denied." Can't be done. That's what I meant when I
said that if you really take rape seriously, and if you continue
to use rape and "sexual assault" as interchangeable synonyms,
then you ought to be all the more determined that those who are
accused should be subjected to the criminal justice system, not to
some jerry-built, improvised campus process.*

On the subject of *our* thesis, Will said he isn't quite as concerned about unhealthy societal trends toward silencing as we are. He agrees that "there certainly is an increase in name-calling as a substitute for reasoning, and invective as a substitute for evidence, on the part of some people." He chalks some of this up to the "democratization" of the public discourse: "Thanks to modern technology, [more people] can in some sense be participants in the public forum. By lowering all barriers to entry to the public forum, by democratizing access to the public forum—which is a very good thing—the Internet has made it so that the inability to read, write or think is no longer a barrier to entry. So you have an awful lot of ignorant and hysterical people who I think *know* they're ignorant, and whose hysteria is meant to cover up that fact. They shout at the margins of public discourse. We should view this with a bemused disdain because they're making a ruckus, perhaps noted by people of similar persuasions, but I don't think they're having many consequences."

In the realm of campus life, however, Will is on board, full stop. "Here, I think you're entirely right. Colleges are designating one percent of campuses a 'free-speech zone,' neglecting the fact that James Madison designated the United States of America a free-speech zone in the First Amendment," he said. "It's unfortunate that we've come to expect this, but campuses often have the lowest possible standards of due process and intellectual integrity."

One of the reasons Will says he doesn't share our concerns about the state of the national conversation is how this specific episode was resolved. "The *St. Louis Post-Dispatch* dropped my column, and a couple weeks later, another paper in the St. Louis area picked it up," he explained. "So I had 476 newspapers carrying my column before I wrote that one, and I have 476 today. So I think the bark of these people is much louder than their bite. I'm not hurting right now. This doesn't bother me. This is part of doing my job." (A few weeks after our interview with him, Scripps College pulled the plug on a planned event with Will. The speech was to have been part of "a program designed to promote conservative views on campus," according to the *Claremont Independent*.)

Though we applaud his attitude, and celebrate this defeat of the Outrage Circus, we can't endorse his conclusion. George F. Will is a man with an extraordinary media platform at his disposal, a strong public reputation, a first-class intellect, and a support network gathered and fortified across decades of public life. He emerged from this demagoguery cyclone unscathed, but others haven't been so fortunate. Many, if not most, people lack the resources and wherewithal (and sometimes even the opportunity) to resist the outrage inertia. So it is with no small amount of irony that we respectfully suggest that Mr. Will, um, *check his privilege*. This is awkward.

BLURRED LINES

What if you're not a superstar columnist, but an average working stiff who runs afoul of this insanity? We give you the maddening tale of a North Carolina disc jockey who was sent packing due to his alleged contribution to "rape culture."[9]

The Wire reports that in April 2014 a University of North Carolina student named Liz Hawryluk was minding her own business, enjoying a Saturday night out with friends at a local Irish pub, when her world came crashing down around her. The venue's DJ played Robin Thicke's "Blurred Lines,"[10] which peaked at number one on the American pop charts. A scandalized Hawryluk sprang into action:

---

[9] We loathe this term; much more to come in chapter 6. "Rape culture" is the idea that communities writ large, and not just the perpetrators themselves, are responsible for those awful crimes. If you're interested in reading about something that might truly qualify as rape culture, google "Rotherham."

[10] Let the record reflect that Guy detests this seemingly interminable song. Mary Katharine thinks it's pretty catchy. Valuable writing time was wasted debating this point.

Hawryluk asked the DJ . . . to stop playing [the song] because it "triggers" victims of sexual assault. After Hawryluk spoke out about the incident on social media, Fitzgerald's fired the DJ . . . "Fundamentally, all I was aiming to do is to create a safe space in the Carolina community," she explains. "In a lot of ways, violent or graphic images that allude to sexual violence are triggers."

After she left the bar, Hawryluk "took to her Facebook" to complain, and some sympathetic students posted an "open letter" to Fitzgerald's manager Kyle Bartosiewicz in a UNC online magazine, The Siren. *Fitzgerald's spokeswoman Lauren Shoaf then issued an apology and assured the public that the offending DJ would never spin at Fitzgerald's again.*

Bear in mind that this Tar Heel *bien-pensant* wasn't claiming that *she* was triggered by the song, only that a victim *might* be triggered by it. All she was trying to do, "fundamentally," was to create a "safe space" in which a number-one hit could be banned at a college bar, and in which a DJ could be fired for committing the grievous offense of playing it. The resulting open letter featured the Twitter hashtag #KeepUNCSafe and included, naturally, a trigger warning "for violent, threatening language and perpetuation of rape myths" at its outset. The screed concluded with a call for a boycott of the establishment until its manager was "held accountable for harassing Liz" and "not taking the safety of our community seriously." In case readers hadn't gotten the point, it states in bold font that **"rape culture exists everywhere."**

Yes, "Blurred Lines" is highly sexually suggestive, and no, we probably wouldn't write a song that included the lyric "I know you want it." Then again, we also wouldn't show our faces in public if we'd subjected the music-listening public to this masterful poetry:

You wanna hug me . . .
What rhymes with hug me?

Charming. A 2013 *Daily Beast* column denounced the song as "kind of rapey," and the tune ended up being formally prohibited at a number of British universities.[11] Out of curiosity, how many of the people who were aghast at reports that Sarah Palin had attempted to ban books in Wasilla, Alaska (she hadn't), are also enthusiastic members of the itchy-"trigger"-finger-ban brigade? We'd imagine the overlap is significant.

We don't object to a debate about "Blurred Lines." What we object to is preemptively declaring your opponent too insensitive to engage. Olivia Lubbock, Zoe Ellwood, and Adelaide Dunn of the University of Aukland law school took a different tack than Liz Hawryluk, registering their distaste with a perfect mirror image of the original video, campily objectifying their male counterparts and rewriting the original song with feminist lyrics.

We ain't good girls/
We are scholastic / Smart and sarcastic / Not fucking plastic.
Listen mankind!
If you wanna get nasty / Just don't harass me / You can't just
*   grab me.*
That's a sex crime!

More speech, more effective, more fun.

Returning to Chapel Hill, let's consider the plight of the DJ. He got canned for playing a wildly popular song—which was quite literally his job. Correction: He got canned because the bar's management was disoriented and frightened by aggressive agitators accusing them

---

[11] Hectorers Without Borders.

of encouraging rape. They figured that the easiest way to make the problem disappear was to issue a groveling apology and offer up a sacrificial lamb to appease the mob. After all, all they're trying to do is sell some beer. They need a "rape" boycott like they need an ID raid from the local cops. As a result, some dude who was just trying to pay his bills by spinning records ended up needing to check his bank account in addition to his privilege. None of the news stories we encountered included the DJ's name, and our attempts to find him came up empty. Given everything that went down, we strongly suspect this person is perfectly content to remain anonymous. Is this the type of country we want to live in?

It is the kind of country one Trevor Dougherty wants to live in. Dougherty, who performs as a DJ under the name Good Ratio (of course he does), is on board for firing other DJs who violate the unwritten UNC code of art sensitivity. "I just think it's totally unacceptable for DJs in a college town—or anywhere—to play it," Dougherty told the *Daily Tar Heel*. "As a good DJ you can do better than playing a track that is so overplayed and so insensitive." Who does Trevor think should decide which tracks get a DJ fired, one wonders? Perhaps Trevor himself? After all, the best, *ahem*, ratio for him would presumably be one mediocre but assiduously socially acceptable DJ for all the parties. Hire DJ Good Ratio today! Ugh.

COMMENCEMENT REGRESSION

E very year, some conservative outfit is bound to release a study demonstrating that right-leaning college commencement speakers were outnumbered by their left-leaning counterparts by a margin of 716-to-1, or whatever. We know we're supposed to be outrageously outraged by this, but our general attitude is *meh*. It is what it is: insular, self-selective, limiting, and boring. We wish things weren't this

Marquetiquette

I n the fall of 2014, a philosophy instructor at Marquette University named Cheryl Abbate informed her undergraduate students that bigoted opinions would "not be tolerated" in her classroom. This policy evidently entailed a strict ban on "homophobic comments," including any expression of opposition to same-sex marriage. When a student in her Theory of Ethics course pushed back against Abbate's speech-stifling decree, she shot back that dissatisfied parties would be well advised to drop the class. The student complied.

That undergraduate, in turn, wrote an e-mail to a political science professor at the school, describing what had just happened. Professor John McAdams was appalled by the story and wrote an online post blasting Abbate's actions. McAdams was promptly suspended from teaching and thrown off campus by administrators, pending an investigation into his conduct. In a statement to the *Washington Post,* a Marquette spokesperson explained that by criticizing Abbate, McAdams had failed to live up to the university's "values" of respecting all community members' "value and worth." (What about the undergraduate's "value and worth"? Never mind.)

Eugene Volokh, a UCLA law professor and a blogger for the *Post,* noted with dismay that Marquette's official handbook indicates that merely stating one's opposition to same-sex marriage as a matter of public policy could be deemed highly offensive by other community members and could amount to "*unlawful* harassment" (emphasis ours). He concluded:

> Universities, it seems to me, shouldn't just take the most liability-avoiding, speech-restrictive position in such situations—if they want to continue being taken seriously as places where people are free to investigate, debate and challenge orthodox views. A professor at Marquette (not Prof. McAdams) tells me: "[T]he new harassment training, which McAdams mentions on his blog and which we as faculty all had to go through this fall, has a chilling quality to it . . . basically urging people, when in doubt, to refrain from expression." A sad thing to see at a university.

Sad, but hardly atypical.

way,[12] but we just don't have the bandwidth to be angry about it. We're more interested in the increasing number of commencement speakers and honorary degree recipients who are disinvited from speaking, withdraw from ceremonies amid controversy, or are stripped of their honors. We wondered if these sorts of incidents were, in fact, rising in frequency, or if we were falling prey to some blend of confirmation and recency bias. ("Things are worse than ever! Which has to be true because we believe it!") A May 15, 2014, *USA Today* column by our Fox News colleague and liberal-leaning commentator Kirsten Powers confirmed our sense of things:

> *According to the Foundation for Individual Rights in Education, this trend is growing. In the 21 years leading up to 2009, there were 21 incidents of an invited guest not speaking because of protests. Yet, in the past five-and-a-half years, there have been 39 cancellations.*

Capitulations to howling mobs beget more capitulations to howling mobs.[13] Powers, whose intellectual honesty and heterodox brand of liberalism is refreshing, penned her piece toward the tail end of 2014's tumultuous graduation season—during which the Outrage Circus rousted three accomplished women from ceremonies they'd been invited to address.

To get a sense of just how much things have changed, and not just by the numbers, travel back with us to a time known as 1990. It was a time when Wilson Phillips was "Hold[ing] On" and *90210* just debuted.

---

[12] We'd be very happy to help even things out. We charge very reasonable, very un-Hillaryesque speaking fees.

[13] We should point out that conservatives have occasionally gotten in on this act, too. Some successfully targeted Michelle Obama's commencement address at a Kansas high school, while others pressured Notre Dame to rescind its offer to President Obama to deliver the school's 2009 commencement address.

It was also a time of greater openness to intellectual diversity on campus, as illustrated by a debate over First Lady Barbara Bush's invitation to give Wellesley College's commencement speech. A group of 150 students objected to the invitation, notably not because of Bush's politics, but because they claimed it "honor[ed] a woman who has gained recognition through the achievements of her husband, which contravenes what we have been taught over the last four years at Wellesley."[14]

The president and first lady responded graciously to the students' concerns, arguing for Bush's perspective as valuable to women of a younger generation, and faculty members acknowledged the complaints but did not fold to them. Perhaps most striking, "[t]he petition protesting Mrs. Bush's invitation did not demand that it be withdrawn, and Mrs. Bush is expected to attend the ceremony on June 1," the *New York Times* reported contemporaneously.

What enlightened times! Fast-forward to present day, and let's see how things are "progressing":

Condoleezza Rice—Let's start by smushing in[15] some context: in 2011, Rutgers University (the state university of New Jersey) extracted $32,000 from its mandatory student activity fee fund for the privilege of welcoming MTV's "Snooki" to campus. According to a *Star-Ledger* account of the ensuing production, the *Jersey Shore* star's appearance was punctuated by sage and original advice ("study hard, but party harder"), hair product tips ("it smells good and stays in good"), and all manner of hijinks: "Snooki . . . brought eight students on stage to teach them the 'Jersey Shore' fist pump and her signature 'tree branch' dance. [She] also judged a 'Situation' contest to see which of five male students had the best abs." When a student asked about inspiration in her life, Snooki courageously offered a glimpse into her soul: "Being

---

[14] A strange complaint considering Wellesley boasts perhaps the most famous alumna to have ever "gained recognition through the achievements of her husband," Hillary Clinton.

[15] If you don't already get this reference, you don't want to know.

tan. When you're tan, you feel better about yourself." She departed with an unforgettable *au revoir* to the sold-out audience: "I love you, bitches!"

Three years hence, loud and relentless protests prevented America's first female African American secretary of state[16] from delivering Rutgers's commencement address. Dr. Rice's sin was being a member of the infernal Bush administration. The school's student newspaper, the *Daily Targum*, described the atmosphere on campus leading up to the speech: "More than 100 students interrupted a senate meeting yesterday to talk to [University president Robert] Barchi after he failed to show up when more than 50 protesters staged a sit-in last Monday, occupying his office in the Old Queens building." One hundred students, egged on by left-wing faculty members, disrupted a student senate meeting to valiantly defend the core human right never to be subjected to the views of speakers with whom one disagrees. That's in the Constitution. And the Bible.[17] Anti-Rice agitators carried signs reading WAR CRIMINALS OUT, chanting, "Cancel Condi!" In a telling juxtaposition, the Rutgers–New Brunswick faculty council passed a resolution urging the administration to rescind Rice's invitation to speak, whereas the elected *student* assembly "voted 25–17 to welcome Rice to the campus," according to the *Christian Science Monitor*. Small-minded professors remain the vanguard of campus intolerance. Perhaps some of the Rutgers faculty were simply manifesting their base fear of "the other"—the "other" being a highly accomplished intellectual powerhouse.

Nevertheless, the cacophony from a tiny band of left-wing students—and a larger group of anti-intellectual "intellectuals"—caused enough of a stir to convince Rice to back out of the speech. *National Review* broke the story, quoting Rice's gracious public statement on her decision:

---

[16] President George W. Bush appointed the first two black secretaries of state in American history. A clever ploy, no doubt, to distract from his more telling racist dog whistles.
[17] Citations not found.

Commencement should be a time of joyous celebration for the graduates and their families. Rutgers' invitation to me to speak has become a distraction for the university community at this very special time.

I am honored to have served my country. I have defended America's belief in free speech and the exchange of ideas. These values are essential to the health of our democracy. But that is not what is at issue here. As a Professor for thirty years at Stanford University and as its former Provost and Chief academic officer, I understand and embrace the purpose of the commencement ceremony and I am simply unwilling to detract from it in any way.

Good luck to the graduates and congratulations to the families, friends and loved ones who will gather to honor them.

Heaven forbid a "distraction" impede on anyone's "joy." The jackals quickly declared victory. An anti-Rice student ringleader told the *Daily Targum* he was "happy that all our actions and pressure as the University community have led to our ultimate goal which was to not have a war criminal speak at our commencement." The self-appointed "university community" of *at most* 150 active student protesters achieved their "ultimate goal," allegedly on behalf of the school's 45,000 undergraduates, thousands of whom were denied the opportunity to hear from a woman whose life journey has been nothing short of extraordinary. One of the few genuinely electric moments of the 2012 Republican National Convention was Secretary Rice's goose bumps–raising ode to the American dream. This passage in particular drew a thunderous and sustained standing ovation from the packed arena:

On a personal note, a little girl grows up in Jim Crow Birmingham. The segregated city of the South where her parents cannot take her to a movie theater or to restaurants, but they have convinced her that even if she cannot have a hamburger at

Woolworth's, she can be the president of the United States if she wanted to be, and she becomes the secretary of state.

Thank goodness Rutgers graduates were spared the ordeal of hearing from *that* woman. Rice's withdrawal prompted a backlash from some of America's less totalitarian precincts, including from a number of appalled liberals. But the perpetually enraged raged on. Their mindless indignation was captured in an *Esquire* blog post written by University of Virginia media studies professor Siva Vaidhyanathan. He congratulated those intrepid few students for "refusing to forget" Rice's actions, which "dishonored herself and her country." He accused her of "lying" America into an "illegal" war, and allowing 9/11 to happen by "ignoring clear warnings." Such a "disgrace" has "no business pretending [to] have the moral authority to preside over a graduation ceremony at a great American university," he fumed.

Fortunately, Stanford—which has employed Ms. Rice in several prestigious capacities, and which is listed exactly 64 slots ahead of Rutgers and 19 slots ahead of UVA in *US News & World Report*'s 2014 rankings[18] of national universities—never received that memo.

Christine Lagarde—Smith College is an elite, private, all-female institution in central Massachusetts. The school's recent fund-raising campaign was dubbed "women for the world." One worldly woman, however, was deemed unworthy of being listened to by the school's 2014 graduates. Christine Lagarde is among the most influential and powerful women on planet Earth. She began her career as a successful labor and antitrust attorney, becoming the first female chairman of her firm's global executive committee in 1999. Between 2005 and

---

[18] Yes, we're aware. These rankings aren't necessarily comprehensive or reflective of educational quality because the formula on which they rely isn't blah, blah, blah . . . Also, Mary Katharine proudly attended one of those "best-value" state schools that has yet to become sophisticated enough to hound prestigious speakers off of campus. Go Dawgs.

2011, she served in the French government, attaining the important role of finance minister in 2007. She was the first woman to hold that position in any G7 country, according to her official biography. Midway through 2011, Lagarde was named the managing director of the International Monetary Fund (IMF). Only eleven people have ever held that title, of whom she is the only woman.

It may have come as a surprise, therefore, when her selection as Smith's commencement speaker was met with an anonymous online petition to dump her for such crimes as contributing to "imperialist and patriarchal systems that oppress and abuse women worldwide." Again, she is a *French labor attorney* who broke the glass ceiling at one of the world's most powerful organizations. The document's short statement allows that Lagarde's biography is impressive, but concludes that more than five hundred signatories "do not want to be represented by someone whose work directly contributes to many of the systems that we are taught to fight against. By having her speak at our commencement, we would be publicly supporting and acknowledging her, and thus the IMF." In a letter to Smith's president, Lagarde wrote:

> *In the last few days, it has become evident that a number of students and faculty members would not welcome me as a commencement speaker . . . I respect their views, and I understand the vital importance of academic freedom. However, to preserve the celebratory spirit of commencement day, I believe it is best to withdraw my participation.*

And thus, an entire campus's "celebratory spirit" was dictated by a squealing few, and a female titan of achievement was silenced—a devastating blow to the "patriarchy" if there ever was one. *Girl power.* Many students and faculty rushed to express their dismay at this development, but the damage was done. In a curiously titled[19] local

---

[19] "Let's agree to disagree at college commencements." Agreeing to disagree generally involves . . . not hounding away the person with whom you disagree.

newspaper column, Smith associate professor Elisabeth Armstrong defended the students and faculty who objected to Lagarde's invitation and created the climate that led to her withdrawal. "Commencement is a celebration. It celebrates the development of hard-won knowledge and thoughtful ethics, tested by arguments and counter-arguments, in a rigorous and diverse learning environment," she wrote. "Dissent over who should hold the honor of giving the commencement speech is deeply linked to the celebration in this ceremony." Yes, and loaded, cartoonish attacks against fantastically qualified speakers is "deeply linked" to their decisions not to be harangued by self-righteous assholes. Armstrong asserted that Lagarde *chose* to allow her speech to be stifled, which is her fault, not the fault of those whose actions precipitated that decision. Believe it or not, we half agree with this sentiment; she shouldn't have given in. That said, the active refusal to politely sit and listen to a richly accomplished speaker betrays a juvenile self-importance that is neither bold nor "celebratory." It's rigidity and rudeness dressed up as "principle," and it's cheered on by smug lefties like Professor Armstrong. *Quelle surprise.*

Ayaan Hirsi Ali—A tireless advocate for women's rights and an unremitting critic of Islam, Ms. Ali possesses *real* courage in an era in which that word is frequently and ludicrously defined down. A native of Somalia, Ali was subjected to genital mutilation as a child, before fleeing to the West to escape a forced marriage arranged by her family. A piece in the *Economist* traces her political journey in the Netherlands, where her activism drifted "steadily rightward," culminating in her election to parliament as a member of the center-right Liberals. She wrote the screenplay for a controversial and provocative 2004 film, *Submission*, which was harshly critical of Islam's subjugation of women.

The man with whom she collaborated on the project was an outspoken, brash filmmaker and writer named Theo van Gogh. After the film's release, Van Gogh was murdered in broad daylight by a radical

Muslim on the streets of Amsterdam. The assailant repeatedly shot Van Gogh, who witnesses say begged for mercy as he lay bleeding on the street. His last words, reportedly, were "Can't we talk about this?" They could not. A particularly grisly end of discussion. The jihadist attempted to decapitate Van Gogh before pinning a five-page letter to his corpse. The letter was addressed to Ali and included an explicit death threat. Her ordeal and life story is powerfully catalogued in a lengthy 2007 *UK Independent* profile entitled "My Life Under a Fatwa," as well as her book, *Infidel*.

Though we don't share all of Ali's views on Islam and believe some of her condemnations to be overly broad and counterproductively abrasive, her opinions are rooted in her own experiences. She, more than most, has truly earned the right to speak out—and she's done just that, in breathtakingly brave defiance of those who've vowed to snuff her out for doing so. We would therefore have been eager to attend her scheduled speech at Brandeis University's commencement ceremony, at which she was to receive an honorary degree. But the speech never happened, and the degree was never awarded. The *New York Times* summarized the outrage industry's impact on this turn of events in an April 8, 2014, article by Richard Pérez-Peña and Tanzina Vega:

> At first, it was bloggers who noted and criticized the plan to honor Ms. Hirsi Ali, a visiting fellow at the American Enterprise Institute. Within a few days, a Brandeis student started an online petition against the decision at Change.org, *drawing thousands of signatures. The Council on American-Islamic Relations, a civil rights and advocacy group, took note, contacting its members through email and social media, and urging them to complain to the university.

The controversy jumped from a handful of blogs to a major online petition, to a full-court press from the Council on American-Islamic Relations (CAIR), the activist group that works relentlessly to silence critics of Islam.[20] The group fired off a letter denouncing Ali as a "notorious Islamophobe." Phobias, Ali might retort, are typically defined as *irrational* fears. But regardless of whether the fear of bad press, demonstrations, and angry letters is irrational, Brandeis's administration succumbed to it. In a statement, the university revoked its offer of an honorary degree, inviting Ali to visit the campus at an undetermined future date to "engage in a dialogue."

A few days later, Ali published a truncated version of her prepared remarks in the *Wall Street Journal*. Her comments invoked the Boston Marathon bombing and 9/11, and condemned the surge in antiwoman violence in Islamist-controlled regions. Without further comment, here is a portion of her undelivered speech (emphasis ours):

> *When there is injustice, we need to speak out, not simply with condemnation, but with concrete actions.*
>
> *One of the best places to do that is in our institutions of higher learning.* **We need to make our universities temples not of dogmatic orthodoxy, but of truly critical thinking, where all ideas are welcome and where civil debate is encouraged. I'm used to being shouted down on campuses, so I am grateful for the opportunity to address you today. I do not expect all of you to agree with me, but I very much appreciate your willingness to listen.**
>
> *. . . The connection between violence, particularly violence against women, and Islam is too clear to be ignored. We do no favors to students, faculty, nonbelievers and people of faith when we shut our eyes to this link, when we excuse rather than reflect. So I ask: Is the concept of holy war compatible with our ideal of religious toleration? Is it blasphemy—punishable by*

---

[20] See: Juan Williams, chapter 4. We thought you may be interested to know that CAIR was listed as an unindicted coconspirator in the infamous Holy Land Foundation terrorism financing trial, which resulted in the 2008 conviction of five leaders of a Texas-based Muslim "charity" organization.

death—to question the applicability of certain seventh-century doctrines to our own era? Both Christianity and Judaism have had their eras of reform. **I would argue that the time has come for a Muslim Reformation . . . Is such an argument inadmissible?** *It surely should not be at a university that was founded in the wake of the Holocaust, at a time when many American universities still imposed quotas on Jews.* **The motto of Brandeis University is "Truth even unto its innermost parts." That is my motto too.**

Oof. Ali's exhortations for free exchange and critical thinking, rather than the prevailing paralysis of "dogmatic orthodoxy," didn't fall on deaf ears. They fell on no ears, for the very reasons she intended to caution graduates against. The Yale Muslim Students Association also protested Ali's 2014 appearance on campus, sending off a furious letter to event organizers condemning her "hate speech." They pronounced themselves "highly disrespected," complaining that Ms. Ali lacked the "credentials" to discuss Islam, and warning that listening to her words would be "uncomfortable" for members of the "community." We wouldn't want that, would we? Though we wonder: Would it be more or less uncomfortable than the process of genital mutilation?

At Brandeis and elsewhere, the task of piercing swaddled, privileged twenty-two-year-olds' "safe space" cocoon was left to others. And to their credit, certain others accepted that gauntlet. Following this spate of graduation kerfuffles, Michael Bloomberg—the billionaire former mayor of New York City whose heroic efforts to ban large soft drinks has earned him deserved scorn—did something important. He used the high-profile platform of Harvard University's 2014 commencement address to repudiate the one strain of intolerance that is aggressively enshrined and administered on many college campuses.

"Today, I'd like to talk with you about how important it is for that freedom to exist for everyone, no matter how strongly we may disagree with another's viewpoint," he said. "Tolerance for other people's ideas, and the freedom to express your own, are inseparable values at great universities. Joined together, they form a sacred trust that holds the basis of our democratic society. But that trust is perpetually vulnerable to the tyrannical tendencies of monarchs, mobs, and majorities. And lately, we have seen those tendencies manifest themselves too often, both on college campuses and in our society."

He went out of his way to highlight the pronounced ideological homogeneity among elite university faculties, citing the Federal Election Commission statistic that fully 96 percent of 2012 presidential campaign contributions from Ivy League faculty and employees went to Barack Obama. He joked that more disagreement existed within the old Soviet Politburo, warning that the 96 percent figure "should give us pause." He averred that universities cannot be great with a faculty that marches in ideological or partisan lockstep, warning that such a hive-mind culture deprives students of a "diversity of views." He then confronted the commencement purges head-on, and in no uncertain terms (again, emphasis ours):

> *Requiring scholars—and commencement speakers, for that matter—to conform to certain political standards undermines the whole purpose of a university. This spring, it has been disturbing to see a number of college commencement speakers withdraw—or have their invitations rescinded—after protests from students and—to me, shockingly—from senior faculty and administrators who should know better. It happened at Brandeis, Haverford, Rutgers, and Smith. Last year, it happened at Swarthmore and Johns Hopkins, I'm sorry to say.* **In each case, liberals silenced a voice—and denied an honorary degree—to individuals they deemed politically objectionable. That is an outrage and we must not let it continue.** *If a university thinks twice before inviting a commencement speaker because of his or her politics, censorship, and conformity—the mortal enemies of freedom—win out.*

And sadly, it is not just commencement season when speakers are censored. Last fall, when I was still in City Hall, our Police Commissioner was invited to deliver a lecture at another Ivy League institution—but he was unable to do so because students shouted him down.

Please excuse us as we pick ourselves off the floor. For a guy whose values-imposing priorities as mayor were so often confounding and vexing to conservative critics, he cleared away the nonsense and homed in on perhaps the single most important message a speaker in that setting could have championed. And he did so aggressively and eloquently. Bravo. Encouragingly, his commentary was interrupted with several bouts of applause, even as some in the audience—and especially on the dais—squirmed noticeably. But clapping for the *idea* of diversity of thought is much easier than standing up to the silencers, particularly when you share their worldview.

Were it not so sad, we would relish the irony that the voices of three women, two of them women of color who had overcome tremendous odds to get to their positions, were the voices liberal college campuses felt should be most urgently shunned. The data on college commencement speakers shows not only a dearth of ideological diversity, but also a lack of the racial and gender diversity about which campus leftists are usually so concerned. A 2013 survey of such speakers by American Enterprise Institute scholar Kevin Hassett found only 23 percent were women, and a vanishingly small proportion of those were minority women. In 2014, campus liberals did more than any white patriarchy could ever have hoped to keep those numbers down. We're all worse off for it.

You may have noticed that Bloomberg mentioned another 2014 example beyond the trio we've already relayed: Haverford College. That instance is worth touching on briefly because of how it turned out. By way of background, Haverford's invited commencement speaker, Robert J. Birgeneau, withdrew from participating after a few dozen students and faculty raised a stink over an episode that had occurred at UC Berkeley during Birgeneau's tenure as chancellor. (Campus police had used force against a student protest in 2011.) The outrage clique wrote a letter to Birgeneau, insisting that he "meet nine conditions, including publicly apologizing, supporting reparations for the victims, and writing a letter" explaining himself to the Haverford "community," as reported by the *Philadelphia Inquirer*. Birgeneau took a pass. The school's replacement speaker, former Princeton president William Bowen, devoted his address to an upbraiding of the noisy pack that had driven Birgeneau away. He chided them as "arrogant" and "immature," rejecting one agitator's assessment that Birgeneau's withdrawal represented a victory. "It represents nothing of the kind," Bowen intoned. "In keeping with the views of many others in higher education, I regard this outcome as a defeat, pure and simple, for Haverford—no victory for anyone who believes, as I think most of us do, in both openness to many points of view, and mutual respect."

As we established earlier, George Will agrees that "most of us" still believe in open dialogue and mutual respect. We *want* to agree, and mostly do. But you wouldn't have this book in your hands if we weren't concerned about the direction things are heading.

TALE OF TEARS

Let's take a few moments to examine the curious case of Senator Elizabeth Warren, who has replaced Barack Obama as the Left's hottest political crush. Warren has ruled out a 2016 presidential run on several occasions thus far, but that hasn't dampened the spirits of "Ready for Warren" grassroots supporters, who've printed up posters, placards, and sundry swag. They've also produced a painfully bad unofficial campaign music video, which we'd suggest looking up on YouTube if we didn't like you so much. (Sample lyric: "We need a leader who will stand for all the corporate bullies, political cronies—run, run,

run; run, Liz, run!" Also, we think they meant "*stand up to*," but it's an understandable Freudian slip in the Obama era.)[21]

Warren's views are predictably doctrinaire in their leftism. One of her primary contributions to the national conversation was pioneering the "you didn't build that" argument on wealth and "fairness." An online viral clip depicts Warren passionately promoting class warfare at a 2012 private event, gesticulating sharply as she informs her entranced audience that "there is nobody in this country who got rich on his own. Nobody." Warming to the task and raising her voice to a low shout, Warren explains how entrepreneurs and businesspeople "moved [their] goods to market on roads the rest of us paid for," and that they hired workers whom "the rest of us paid to educate." Her point is that all American success is due to the efforts of the collective, which is why "the rich," who it must be noted pay for roads just like the rest of us, owe everyone else a fair (read: larger) share of the fruits of their labor. President Obama later reprised a very similar sentiment on the campaign trail.

Warren and Obama invert the truth. The government exists to serve the people, not the other way around. Without private-sector wealth, earned by individuals and groups of individuals, the government literally could not exist. Americans have entered a social compact in which we've agreed that the government should take responsibility for maintaining the commons and enforcing the rules *in order to allow individuals to strive and flourish*. We surrender our hard-earned money in the form of taxation in order to fund those core resources. To claim that nobody's success is truly their own because they've benefited from basic services for which they've already paid is a gross

---

[21] The folksy guitar strumming melody plays over a collection of soundless clips of Warren's rousing speech at a left-wing conference, which spelled out progressivism's "eleven commandments." That confab, Netroots Nation, was held, appropriately enough, in Detroit, whose leaders have scrupulously followed a number of those commandments down a path into unprecedented bankruptcy and dysfunction. Gushed one attendee after the address, "I think I just became pro-dictatorship!" Out: Impeach the imperialist war criminal, BusHitler! In: #Warren4Dictator4Lyf!

distortion of the American system and a frontal attack on merit and achievement.

Side rant: The primary villains of Warren's backward morality tale, naturally, are the wealthy, who already pay the lion's share of taxes in this country. According to the federal government's own figures, the top 1 percent of U.S. wage earners were responsible for 68 percent of all federal tax receipts in 2011. Not just federal income tax,[22] mind you, *all* federal taxes. Beyond the major tax increases President Obama has managed to put into place, he has packed recent budget proposals with every soak-the-rich taxation gimmick imaginable, yet they've all fallen massively short of achieving balance. Former Vermont governor and presidential candidate Howard Dean is one of the few progressives who's been willing to spill a dirty little secret on this subject. In order to glide along Democrats' preferred path to a European-style social democracy welfare state, he said on MSNBC's *Morning Joe* in December 2012, *"everybody* needs to pay more taxes, not just the rich . . . we're not going to get out of this deficit problem unless we raise taxes across the board." His fellow panelists, we should note, nodded along in agreement. Let's see if that useful reality check finds its way into future Warren harangues. Frankly, her message could apply to average working stiffs just as much as it does to "millionaires and billionaires." *Look, middle-class worker, congrats on your $52,000 annual household income, but let's face it: you couldn't get to your office without government roads, and you couldn't type up those invoices without government schools saving you from illiteracy, so you're going to have to cough up some more cash for Uncle Sam. You owe it to the rest of us.*

In any case, we didn't bring Ms. Warren up to bore you with tax policy. We brought her up as an ideal bookend to this chapter, which began with a discussion of the politics of "privilege." At a crucial moment in her career as an academic, Elizabeth Warren formally

---

[22] The Tax Foundation reports that in 2011, the top 1 percent paid just over 35 percent of the nation's federal income tax bill, more than the bottom 90 percent of wage earners combined.

self-identified as a Native American. Problem: based on all available evidence, Elizabeth Warren is not a Native American. When this uncomfortable complication became an issue in her 2012 Senate campaign against Scott Brown, Warren unleashed a dizzying—and at times, surreal—array of excuses and explanations, including that she'd always been told she was Cherokee. Her "papaw" (grandfather) had "high cheekbones, like all the Indians do" (actual verbatim quote). We have both, at times, hesitated to use Warren's own words in public appearances addressing this matter lest we be accused of racism for merely *repeating* her gauche assessment of Native American physical markers—"high cheekbones"—and dumb puns.

A genealogist stepped forward and stated Warren was one-thirty-second Cherokee, a claim that was subsequently downgraded to unproven. A *Washington Post* fact-checker stated that "Cherokee groups have demanded documentation of her professed ancestry"—there are actual rules and standards for these sorts of claims—"but she hasn't delivered." She *did*, however, point out that she'd contributed recipes to a Native American–themed cookbook called *Pow Wow Chow* (we swear we are not making any of this up), several of which were later alleged to have been plagiarized.[23]

The issue is that Warren didn't merely tell a few friends about her family folklore after a few glasses of Chardonnay—she used that dubious folklore to officially list herself as a highly sought-after racial minority at several major junctures in her professional career. Upon graduating from Rutgers law school and teaching at a series of lower-tier institutions, Warren catapulted into the Ivy League when the University of Pennsylvania hired her in 1987. Just over a decade later, she reached the pinnacle of her profession when she was invited to join the faculty at Harvard Law. What changed? She listed herself as "white" and declined

---

[23] One of the red-flagged recipes called for "imported mustard," Worcestershire sauce, cognac, and fresh crabmeat, prompting our blogger colleague Allahpundit to quip that those ingredients were "all presumably readily available to a, er, 19th-century agrarian Cherokee settlement in Oklahoma." It's okay to laugh.

minority status at places like Rutgers and the University of Texas, but began listing herself as a Native American in professional directories at an opportune moment. Back to the *Post* story:

> *Warren first listed herself as a minority in the Association of American Law Schools Directory of Faculty in 1986, the year before she joined the faculty of the University of Pennsylvania Law School. She continued to list herself as a minority until 1995, the year she accepted a tenured position at Harvard Law School.*

What a coincidence! To recap, this white woman decided that she'd start claiming Native American lineage just prior to making a blockbuster career jump into the Ivies, and continued to "check that box," so to speak, until she was safely ensconced as a tenured professor at the nation's most prestigious law school—at which point she decided to drop the designation. She and her defenders have insisted that her (unverified, at best) status as a minority played no role whatsoever in her advancement, but that doesn't pass the laugh test.

Both Harvard and Penn touted her as a treasured minority faculty member in official literature. Harvard did so amid heavy criticism over its lack of diversity. In some sense, this arrangement was a win/win. The universities got someone they could parade in front of the "celebrate diversity" police, and Warren was rewarded with cushy, high-paying jobs oozing with prestige and opportunities for networking and advancement—which could come in handy for, say, an eventual U.S. Senate run. But if she *didn't* suddenly begin exploiting family rumors to classify herself as a Native American for cynical self-serving purposes, why did she do it? Her answer, via the *Boston Herald:*

> *I listed myself in the directory in the hopes that it might mean that **I would be invited to a luncheon, a group something that might happen with people who are like I am.** Nothing*

like that ever happened, that was clearly not the use for it and so I stopped checking it off.

Ah. She self-listed as a Native American for the better part of a decade in hopes of getting invited to a luncheon by, um, "fellow" Native Americans, then finally abandoned the dream after she received tenure at Harvard. Since she was so keen on rubbing elbows with "people who are like I am," Warren must have been an active participant in Harvard's Native American program, right? Wrong. Harvard Law graduate and conservative writer Joel Pollack tracked down the executive director of Harvard's Native American Program (HUNAP), who told him that "Warren had not, to her knowledge, participated in the program's events while Warren was a professor at Harvard." Raise your hand if you're shocked by this. Anybody? *Bueller?*[24] Trivia nugget: According to the standard presented in the Warren case, Mary Katharine is a Native American political commentator and writer. There is a relatively unsubstantiated rumor in her family that she has a distant Cherokee relative. She looks forward to commenting on the issues important to her community and any luncheons or promotions that should happen to come her way.

In her 2014 book, *A Fighting Chance*, Warren reflects on the controversy with self-pity. She says she was "stunned" by the attacks, accusing Republicans of "attacking my dead parents," and saying of the flap, "I was hurt, and I was angry." Indeed, one can only endure so many microaggressions. Spare us the crocodile tears,[25] Senator. As far as the evidence is concerned, Elizabeth Warren appears to be a white person who pulled off an effective racial fraud for her own benefit. She's "stunned, hurt, and angry" because people finally connected the dots. None of this ended up derailing her campaign, of course, be-

---

[24] Trigger warning: Truancy, violent home invasion, exposure to Charlie Sheen.

[25] Add crocodile tears to the aforementioned crab recipe for a delectable taste enhancement!

cause northeastern liberals aren't especially bothered by lying frauds who flout the rules of privilege checking, so long as they're sufficiently liberal (see: Blumenthal, Richard). But a national audience may not be quite as forgiving. Incidentally, the next time you bump into some smug hipster tut-tutting about privilege checking, politely ask his opinion of Ms. Warren. She is, after all, a white woman who not only failed to check her privilege; she actually invented and asserted reverse-privilege status, parlaying it into great personal and financial gain. She should, in theory, be anathema to the privilege police. Let us know how that conversation turns out.

Once again, the convoluted rules apply to conservatives, not people like Liz Warren. Because the rules aren't intended to be meted out consistently. They're meant to enforce an ideological orthodoxy. Tough luck, conservatives. If you want to avoid these headaches and aspersions, just get with The Program.

In Their Own Words

Sometimes the silencers don't even attempt to camouflage their contempt for free speech and disdain for average people. Michael Yaki is one of four congressionally appointed members on the U.S. Commission on Civil Rights and a former senior adviser to Nancy Pelosi. At a July 2014 USCCR hearing exploring the propriety and constitutionality of university speech codes, Mr. Yaki advanced a theory that young adults shouldn't be entitled to the same First Amendment rights as everyone else because their brains are still developing (via law professor Eugene Volokh):

> *Certain factors in how the juvenile or adolescent or young adult brain processes information is vastly different from the way that we adults do. So when we sit back and talk about what is right or wrong in terms of First Amendment jurisprudence from a reasonable person's standpoint, we are really not looking into the*

In Their Own Words (continued)

same referential viewpoint of these people, of an adolescent or young adult, including those in universities," he said. Later in the proceedings, Yaki wondered aloud how opponents of restrictive speech codes could possibly apply their free speech advocacy, "in the atmosphere of colleges and universities as you have a population of young people, who for lack of a better word, don't process in the same way that we do when we're in our late 20s and 30s.

Professor Volokh, who testified at the hearing, dissented against Yaki's view on his *Washington Post*–hosted blog, *Volokh Conspiracy* (July 30, 2014): "This strikes me as quite misguided: While no doubt young adults are different from older adults—whether in their brain functioning as such, or in their experience, emotional maturity, and the like—that hardly justifies restricting their right to speak, or restricting speech that can be heard by them, especially when they are old enough to vote." This wasn't some fringe figure arguing that free speech shouldn't exist in any traditional sense on college campuses, Volokh pointed out; this was the position of "a political figure who holds a significant position in the federal civil rights establishment."

We wonder whether young adults—aged eighteen through "late twenties"—might resent the implication that their still-developing brains are unable to properly "process" potentially offensive forms of speech and expression. How far would Mr. Yaki and his ilk be willing to take their hypothetical First Amendment loophole? And since he evidently believes that these young people may not be sufficiently mature or mentally stable to handle the whole free speech thing, would Mr. Yaki also advocate pushing the voting age back to thirty? He presumably wouldn't want immature, undeveloped brains deciding elections, would he? Yaki defended himself in an interview with *Campus Reform*, asserting that he was simply asking questions, designed to help him "understand the challenges of this issue." He said the "million dollar question" is how to protect the "mental and physical security" of students in a manner that "doesn't require" stomping all over their constitutional rights. Yaki added that for much of his life, he's considered himself a "First Amendment absolutist." You keep using those words; I don't think they mean what you think they mean, Professor.

CAMPUS MADNESS:
"HUMP DAY," BUMPED

G EICO insurance has a knack for producing memorable spokesmen—
from the aggrieved cavemen to the sophisticated Gecko. "Fifteen
minutes . . ." One popular TV spot featured a camel in an office setting,
excitedly informing his coworkers that it was "hump day" (i.e., Wednesday). Mindless, amusing fun. How it had anything to do with insurance, we have no idea . . . but we remember the spot, so it achieved
its goal. Capitalizing on the campaign, a student group at Minnesota's
St. Thomas University organized an on-campus event called "Hump
Daaaaaaaay!" For two hours on a Wednesday afternoon, students could
come to the quad and have their photo taken with a real, live camel.
According to *Campus Reform*, the camel was "owned by a local vendor,
and trained for special events." But the ever-vigilant sensitivity squad
couldn't countenance this innocent fun. A handful of students took to
Facebook to complain that the presence of a camel on campus could be
"racially insensitive to Middle Eastern cultures."

A *Minneapolis Star Tribune* article on the flare-up dryly noted that
the university had previously brought a live reindeer to campus without kicking up any hue and cry (way to drop the ball, Scandinavian
Students Society), and that nobody seemed to take issue with a me-
chanical bull featured at a "Southern hospitality" event a few weeks
earlier. But a handful of joyless do-gooders decided that the mere presence of a camel might be interpreted as racist.[26] If you're not sensitive
to this egregious microaggression, it may be time to check your damn
privilege. By the way, good luck with beach day at the lake next year,
guys. Beach → Sand → Desert → Arabia → Muslims → BANNED.

---

[26] No word on whether any students of Middle Eastern descent were actually offended.
We also can't help but wonder how many of them were even around to potentially
claim umbrage at this . . . *Catholic* university in *Minnesota*.

CAMPUS MADNESS II:
COMMEMORATING "THE DIALOGUE"

L ech Walesa endured years of persecution at the hands of Communist authorities in his native Poland as he toiled to overthrow an oppressive, Kremlin-controlled regime. For his human rights advocacy and remarkable courage as the leader of the Solidarity movement, Walesa earned a Nobel Peace Prize in 1983. He was elected by his fellow countrymen less than a decade later as Poland's first president of the post-Communism era. Chicagoland's Northeastern Illinois University named a building in Walesa's honor in 2009, "tout[ing] the university's connection to the Polish community, including its student exchange programs with universities in Poland," according to the *College Fix*.

But things went sideways in 2013, when Walesa erased his life's work with a demeaning comment about gay members of Poland's parliament. A gay student at NEIU raced to demand that Lech Walesa Hall be immediately renamed, warning that its continued existence "could potentially lead to an increase in suicides by gay students." And that's not all. Lech Walesa's name emblazoned on the side of a building was tantamount to a burning cross or a swastika, this young man argued, adding that the administration was effectively endorsing the equivalent of a "Hitler Hall" on campus.[27] A CNN article about the controversy is paired with a photograph of eight protesters holding rainbow flags outside the offending edifice, one carrying a placard that reads INJURY TO ONE IS INJURY TO ALL. Such profundity. Its potential applications are literally endless.

Eventually, more than four hundred signatures were gathered on a petition to have Walesa's name stricken from the building—which brings us to our exciting conclusion, which truly defies satire. The university declined to accede to the mob's demands, but also sought to

---

[27] Professor Godwin, call your office.

convey how deeply seriously their grievances were being taken. They proposed a formal Dialogue (every mention of this forum by the university featured a capital *D*) regarding Walesa's comments, at which various "stakeholders" could have their say. The meeting's minutes were placed into the university archives, and the school *commissioned a piece of art* to "memorialize the Dialogue" in a "permanent display." Other Outcomes (again with the dramatic capitalization) included the establishment of a LGBTQA[28] resource center, plus "an optional question regarding sexual orientation" has been added to NEIU undergraduate and graduate applications. Roughly one year after the momentous Dialogue, the Executive Advisor Council passed a resolution calling for the renaming of Lech Walesa Hall anyway. University president Sharon Hahs responded with a four-page letter that declined their recommendation "with regret" and reminded the vaunted "community" about the Dialogue and its Outcomes. As of last year, the piece of art was "still in process." We won't keep you posted.

---

[28] This stands for "Lesbian, Gay, Bisexual, Transgender, Queer/Questioning, Asexual/ Allies." Quick story: When the University of Colorado's "visiting scholar of conservative thought"—let that title marinate for a moment—poked fun at this expanding alphabet soup jumble by referring to it as "LGBTQRSTUW (or whatever letters have been added lately)" in an online column, the chairman of the school's faculty assembly accused him of using language "bordering on what most people would say is hate speech." *Most people. Hate speech.* Silence! Imported, token conservatives are to be seen and not heard.

6

THE VAGINA DEMAGOGUES

Feminism and the "War on Women"

It has come to this. *The Vagina Monologues* is no longer progressive enough for feminists. At elite women's college Mount Holyoke, Eve Ensler's classic play has been canceled because it is "inherently reductionist and exclusive." This play, this personification of vaginas hailed by feminists as liberation from our societal fear of the female anatomy, this ultimate form of modern campus progressivism, is literally a play in which women perform soliloquies as vaginas. It even inspired a nationwide day of activism—V-Day to supplant the Valentine's Day of the patriarchy, February 14—on which women's groups perform the play to raise money for combating violence against women.

The Vagina Monologues is now, improbably, part of the war on women, because it is insufficiently inclusive of women without vaginas.

If you find this confusing, you're not alone.

You put your "ladyparts" in. You put your ladyparts out. You do the hokey pokey of womanhood, and you turn yourself around. *That's* what it's all about.

It's not that catchy as a party game ditty, but it's how many women feel.[1] From the Mommy Wars to work-life balance, from parenting advice to Pinterest envy, the task of being a thoroughly modern, liber-

---

[1] MKH here. For reasons that are hopefully clear, I'm going to be taking the lead on this chapter, for the most part. Guy says he knows his place.

ated woman can feel like a precarious balancing act of its own. It can feel like everyone and their momma (literally) has an idea about how you should live your life. Are you unwittingly enabling the patriarchy by making Angry Birds cupcakes for your kid's birthday? Is staying at home with your kids or working part-time a betrayal of those who fought for your rights in the workplace? Is buying an iPhone 6, with its giant display designed for man hands, a sexist act? Is giving your child a toy soldier or a princess or a gingerbread man at Christmas sentencing him or her to a life of horrifying gender conformity?[2]

There seems to be some confusion at the heart of all this regarding the F-word. No, not the fun one. *Feminist*. What does it mean? Who is one? What does it take to be one? And, who the hell makes the rules? The standards, of course, are capricious, ever changing, frequently contradictory, and controlled by a cadre of self-appointed commentators who adjudicate the degree of your liberation and loyalty to womanhood in blog posts and MSNBC interviews. Seemingly the only thing these Pharisees of feminism agree on for certain is that any woman who holds conservative views cannot simultaneously be liberated or modern.

When it comes to defining feminism, there are clichés aplenty that simplify into disingenuous sound bites a political movement that is on its fourth (fifth? Ask five feminists and you'll get five different answers) wave of bitterly infighting generations.

"Feminism is the radical notion that women are human beings." Sure, you'd be daft to disagree with that! "Feminist: a person who believes in the social, political, and economic equality of the sexes." We wish it were that simple. If it were, there'd be no large group of women gathering online because they feel excluded by feminism.

In the fall of 2014, an online movement emerged that represented those women and irked the Pharisees of feminism. A Tumblr page called "Women Against Feminism" collected statements from such

---

[2] Katherine Timpf of *National Review* and *Campus Reform* keeps a running tally of the unending and ridiculous list of things feminists declare sexist. Several of these are among them.

women, mostly in the form of selfies holding pieces of paper with their sentiments on them.

Some of the contributions to Women Against Feminism were silly or incoherent, as is to be expected with any movement based on aggregated selfies. But the movement was not defined by a retrograde desire for homebound careerless women and unequal protection under the law. Rather, as a blogger named AstrokidNJ found in surveying a week's worth of contributions to the Tumblr page, "46 percent were egalitarian, 19 percent endorsed men's issues, and 12 percent criticized feminist intolerance toward dissent. Only 23 percent reflected traditionalist views such as support for distinct sex roles, chivalry, or full-time motherhood," as reported by columnist Cathy Young in the *Boston Globe*.

The thrust of most of the women's complaints was this: Modern feminism does not welcome me. It does not reflect my life as a woman or accurately portray the men who love, respect, and support me in that life. In fact, it makes me feel like I can't qualify as a woman if I don't agree with a very specific slate of policy preferences and political positions, and make public pronouncements accordingly.

The backlash of the gatekeepers of feminism against these women was swift, merciless, incredulous, and biting.

"These women are slandering the movement that enabled their freedom," wrote Nina Burleigh in the *New York Observer*.

Rebecca Brink satirized the movement with her own collection of mocking sign selfies, including "I don't need feminism because I want boys to like me."

Burleigh and prominent feminist writer Amanda Marcotte each wrote that the women in the pictures were probably just expressing what their boyfriends and husbands told them to, because as feminists in good standing, they respect the agency and intellect of women, unless those women disagree with them.

"I'd lay odds that the young Women Against Feminism anti-feminists are the girlfriends and wives of these frustrated young men," because "their men (are) under-employed, bitter, and yes, bitching husbands and boyfriends," Burleigh wrote in a 2014 column in the *New York Observer.*

"Indeed, unseen husbands holding cameras while their wife gives them 'I won't ever be one of those dirty feminists who wants equality' eyes at them is a common theme here," Marcotte wrote at *Raw Story.*

But a general disaffection with the cultural understanding of "feminism" is reflected in polling. A 2013 Huffington Post/YouGov poll showed only 20 percent of Americans call themselves "feminist," though more than 70 percent in every demographic believe in social, economic, and political equality for the sexes.

Feminism, Americans say, *it's not me. It's you.*

FEMINISM IN THE BEYONCÉIC ERA

It's not just regular women who feel the constraints that feminism foists upon them. A steady stream of young starlets who, despite their success and seeming independence, fail to embrace the term *feminist* fully and are castigated for their hesitance. Pop star Katy Perry sinned in 2012, as she accepted the Billboard Woman of the Year Award no less, saying, "I am not a feminist, but I do believe in the strength of women." Kelly Clarkson and Carrie Underwood, a pair of powerful pop/country crossovers, both have misgivings about the word. "No, I wouldn't say feminist—that's too strong," Clarkson said. "I think when people hear feminist, it's like, 'Get out of my way, I don't need anyone.' I love that I'm being taken care of and I have a man that's a leader. I'm not a feminist in that sense." Taylor Swift, Zooey Deschanel, and Shailene Woodley have also been found guilty of similar transgressions.

In the end, what all these powerful, famous young women seem to want is not just equality, but the freedom to shape that equality into exactly what they see fit. They recognize our society's continuing problems with sexism but feel liberated and wish to live in a liberated fashion. Why isn't the powerful way in which they choose to lead their lives the very symbol of feminism? They own businesses, they run brands, they have families, and they are international forces on their own terms. Is it any wonder they rankle at the notion of being required to dub themselves one thing? If the patriarchy and its expectations were confining and predictable, the demands of the Pharisees of feminism are confining and arbitrary.

If feminism were as simple as the purveyors of clichés about feminism proclaim, perhaps the most universally acclaimed woman currently on the planet might have had an easier time embracing feminism and being embraced by feminists. Yes, any discussion of modern womanhood must include an examination of Beyoncé. Because when historians look back on this era, they will call it Beyoncéic in the same way that there was an Edwardian or Mesozoic era before her reign.[3]

In the spotlight since the age of fifteen, she is truly a talent, a tour de force of preternatural pipes and stems, a stunning combination of bodacious body and businesswoman. The beautiful figure she presents has become a sort of symbol of perfect, modern womanhood. She is fierce, honey-haired, happily married, both *GQ* cover girl and happy young mother. She regularly inspires such awe that she's inspired a parody of the awe she inspires.

In a fake movie trailer for "The Beygency," on *Saturday Night Live*, a band of supersecret agents abduct and detain Americans who would dare speak in tones less than admiring of Beyoncé. "Everything she does is perfect," coos one man at a typical American dinner party before another friend violates the number-one rule of the Beyoncéic era. "She is so good. I'm not a huge fan of that one 'Drunk in Love' song, though," he confesses to gasps from his friends and wife.

The lights go out, black helicopters swoop in, and the violator is told to *run*.

Maybe everything she touches really *is* perfect.

---

[3] Though not strictly a monarchy in the geopolitical understanding of the term, the reign of Queen Bey is far-reaching, powerful, and not to be questioned lightly.

But it hasn't always been that way. She was taken to task in 2013 for telling Oprah while talking about her marriage to Jay Z, "I would not be the woman I am if I did not go home to that man," and for calling her tour the Mrs. Carter tour after her marriage to Shawn Carter. Both of them changed their names to Knowles-Carter, in a quite progressive-approved and gender-neutral nod to equal partnership, but that mattered not in the pronunciations of the Pharisees.

In 2013, Beyoncé was among those young starlets who squirmed at the application of the term "feminist." "That word can be very extreme," she told British *Vogue*. "But I guess I am a modern-day feminist. I do believe in equality. Why do you have to choose what type of woman you are? Why do you have to label yourself anything? I'm just a woman and I love being a woman." She went on: "I do believe in equality and that we have a way to go and it's something that's pushed aside and something that we have been conditioned to accept . . . But I'm happily married. I love my husband."

Feminists scoffed that Beyoncé just didn't understand feminism properly if she thought it precluded loving her husband and expressing that openly. The problem is these are the same people who groused at her for declaring her love for her husband and putting her married name on her tour bus.

But in the fall of 2014, Beyoncé gave what will likely go down in pop history as one of the iconic performances in Video Music Awards history on MTV. As silly as it sounds—and the VMAs are indeed silly— such performances are a cultural barometer, the *feel* of an era, for better or worse. Madonna's stage-rolling "Like a Virgin," Eminem's marching clones, Britney Spears's all-grown-up boa constrictor embrace in the '90s, and yes, the over-the-top sexual clarion call/cry for help of another Disney kid in Miley Cyrus's twerking spectacle alongside Robin Thicke in 2013.

Beyoncé's 2014 performance felt like an attempt to reclaim the hypersexuality of a VMA performance as somehow meaningful, albeit with a level of subtlety worthy of the VMAs. She did so by performing sans pants, singing about oral sex and masturbation, with a sprinkling of sexual violence, surrounded by anonymous male and female dancers in bondage gear and painted like gold statuettes, and humping a fainting couch (a Beyoncéic-era nod to the Victorian era).

All of that is utterly routine on the VMA stage. But Beyoncé slapped a giant, neon sign reading FEMINIST behind her. And the world bowed down, bitches. The response to the display of the word, glowing white on a black background, with the powerfully posed Beyoncé's silhouette in the foreground, stirred the American commentariat to such gushing testimonials as, "I *cannot* with this perfection."

Vox explained, "How Beyoncé stole the show at the VMAs and made you forget anyone else was even there." Beyoncé gave the Pharisees of feminism what they so ardently desired—a pop figure willing to stand up and embrace the word *feminist*.

So that's what it takes to be woman enough for them.

Just be the most universally acclaimed woman on the planet and literally stand in front of a giant neon sign that proclaims simply FEMINIST. No wonder the rest of us feel like we don't measure up.

What does a feminist look like? Not even *they* know. What it takes to be feminist enough is entirely fluid, controlled by a cabal of self-righteous priestesses, and the consequences of crossing them are dire—even for fellow members of their movement, as Michelle Goldberg found out when reporting on "Feminism's Toxic Twitter Wars" for the *Nation*: "[E]ven as online feminism has proved itself a real force for change, many of the most avid digital feminists will tell you that it's become toxic. Indeed, there's a nascent genre of essays by people who feel emotionally savaged by their involvement in it—not because of sexist trolls, but because of the slashing righteousness of other feminists." Again, it's little wonder the average woman feels she can't live up to the standard.[4] Goldberg went on:

---

[4] MKH here. My grandmother was born in the 1930s in rural Virginia. She went to college, played basketball on an organized team, and was a Navy WAVE during World War II, working in intelligence in Washington, D.C., as a single woman before

"On January 3, for example, Katherine Cross, a Puerto Rican trans woman[5] working on a PhD at the CUNY Graduate Center, wrote about how often she hesitates to publish articles or blog posts out of fear of inadvertently stepping on an ideological land mine and bringing down the wrath of the online enforcers."

Cross told the *Nation*: "I fear being cast suddenly as one of the 'bad guys' for being insufficiently radical, too nuanced or too forgiving, or for simply writing something whose offensive dimensions would be unknown to me at the time of publication." Welcome to our world, Katherine.

Eve Ensler, Beyoncé, ardent feminist activists. If even they are not pro-woman enough to avoid bans and boycotts, none of us stands a chance.

GETTING PAID AND LEANING IN

The scope of opinions liberal feminism has approved as "pro-woman" within mainstream cultural and political discussion is so narrow as to exclude many women and many ideas that might help them. One of the areas in which this reveals itself most clearly is the debate about women's pay and careers, where the national discussion rarely reflects the needs and desires of regular women.

Instead, just as the language police demand you use only one label to define your modernity—*feminist*—the national conversation

---

marrying her childhood sweetheart postwar. She raised three kids, sometimes single-handedly moving their household all over the country and world depending on where my grandfather was stationed. She later became a community leader and town councilwoman. By any measure, she was a woman who believed in the equality and immense capability of women, and illustrated it every day of her life. Her politics were also mostly conservative for most of her life. No modern feminist fighting microaggressions can reasonably argue her life wasn't a credit to the progress of women, and if I stand on the shoulders of anyone who came before me, they are hers.

[5] What's all this "trans" stuff about anyway, you ask? "Shame on you for your ignorance and bigotry" is the official answer, but we'll take a stab at it in chapter 8.

demands you create only one kind of success, defined ironically by the dated patriarch-inspired goals feminism once wished to slough off. In the battle to gain parity with men, especially in the workplace, modern feminism has often ignored the actual goals of working women. Instead, it embraces the career goals and challenges of a tiny number of tech CEOs like Sheryl Sandberg and Marissa Mayer. Women all must want a corner office, CEO pay, and careers programming video games and designing bridges, according to the feminist movement.

While it is inarguably good to encourage smart young women to strive for leadership positions, demand equal treatment, and participate in male-dominated fields, it's limiting to assume that "success" for women looks exactly like success for men. Young women of a new generation chafe at the confinement that comes with the "liberation" of feminist-defined success.

In a 2012 episode of the CBS law procedural *The Good Wife*, this generational split manifested itself in the resignation of promising young lawyer Caitlin D'arcy, played by Anna Camp. Having proved herself despite being hired thanks to her uncle's influence at the show's fictional Chicago law firm, D'arcy announced her intention to quit upon getting engaged and finding out she was pregnant. The women of the generation before her evinced shock at her decision. D'arcy serenely offered, "I like the law, but I don't have anything to prove. I'm in love. I want to be a mom."

Diane Lockhart, played by Christine Baranski, and the show's titular character, Alicia Florrick, played by Julianna Margulies, reflected on D'arcy's decision. "I don't think this is what we broke the glass ceiling for," Lockhart said. "I think maybe it is," Alicia replied. Women's liberation was supposed to be about choice. D'arcy made hers. Just because that choice was not confined to the second- or third-trimester "choice" for which feminists are always so ardently fighting doesn't mean it's not liberating.

Zosia Mamet, a young actress who rose to fame playing powerful countercultural characters on *Mad Men* and *Girls*, spoke to the need for flexibility in our definitions of success in a 2014 edition of *Glamour*. The current paradigm doesn't allow for a lot of options.

> *We are so obsessed with "making it" these days we've lost sight of what it means to be successful on our own terms. As women we have internalized the idea that every morning we wake up, we have to go for the f—king gold. You can't just jog; you have to run a triathlon. Having a cup of coffee, reading the paper, and heading to work isn't enough—that's settling, that's giving in, that's letting* them *win. You have to wake up, have a cup of coffee, conquer France, bake a perfect cake, take a boxing class, and figure out how you are going to get that corner office or become district supervisor, while also looking damn sexy—but not too sexy, because cleavage is degrading—all before lunchtime. Who in her right mind would want to do that? And who would even be able to?*
>
> *I think, unfortunately, some of our need to succeed professionally is a by-product of a good thing: feminism. Feminism was meant to empower us as women, to build us up for fighting on male-dominated battlefields. It did that, but it did some other things as well. It gave us female role models like Hillary and Oprah and Beyoncé, and in the process implied that mogulhood should be every woman's goal. We kept the old male ideas of success:* power *and* money. We need new ones!
>
> *. . . I hate that we look at women who choose not to run a country as having given up. I get angry that when a woman decides to hold off on gunning for a promotion because she wants to have a baby, other women whisper that she's throwing away her potential. That is when we're not supporting our own. Who are we to put such a limited definition on success?*

Amen. Mamet is expressing what many women feel, and not just the conservative among us—a societal pressure that prevents many from voicing their real preferences about work-life balance and ideas of success for fear of being shunned as traitors to our sex.

Unfortunately, the Obama White House, Democratic politicians, and liberal activists find the appeal of the quest for "equal pay" too alluring to allow for the nuance of women's different choices and outcomes. Instead, President Obama spent two election cycles harping on the issue of "equal pay" until his own White House was finally subjected to the same standard to which it holds the rest of us.

It started with then–White House press secretary Jay Carney on Equal Pay Day 2014, when reporters started using the administration's own metric for "workplace fairness" against the White House by asking about government data showing the "women working at Obama's White House earn 12 percent less than men on average," or 88 cents on the dollar. Carney offered this explanation (April 7, 2014, White-House.gov press briefing transcript):

> *What I can tell you is that we have, as an institution here, have aggressively addressed this challenge, and obviously, though, at the 88 cents that you cite, that is not a hundred, but it is better than the national average. And when it comes to the bottom line that women who do the same work as men have to be paid the same, there is no question that that is happening here at the White House at every level.*

When it comes to White House men and women in the same job, the ratio is actually 100:91, but let's be charitable and give him that. If Carney contends it's unfair to judge the White House's commitment to gender equality by averaging salaries of male and female workers in a range of different positions and deeming all the difference between them to be a result of discrimination, he's right. It is unfair. But the Left trots out that precise unfair statistic[6] whenever it needs to claim

---

[6] Several 2014 Democratic Senate candidates were offended when their Republican

Democrats are going to fix the problem with a piece of federal legislation or a wave of the regulatory wand. The statistic is bunk, as economist Betsey Stevenson, a member of Obama's Council of Economic Advisers, acknowledged when pressed about it.

> *"They're stuck at 77 cents on the dollar, and that gender wage gap is seen very persistently across the income distribution, within occupations, across occupations, and we see it when men and women are working side by side doing identical work." But "as soon as Stevenson was actually questioned about the statistic by McClatchy reporter Lindsay Wise, the White House adviser crumbled, admitting her earlier comments were inaccurate,"* the Washington Examiner's *Ashe Schow reported.*
>
> *"If I said 77 cents was equal pay for equal work, then I completely misspoke," Stevenson said. "So let me just apologize and say that I certainly wouldn't have meant to say that . . .*
>
> *"Seventy-seven cents captures the annual earnings of full-time, full-year women divided by the annual earnings of full-time, full-year men," Stevenson clarified. "There are a lot of things that go into that 77-cents figure, there are a lot of things that contribute and no one's trying to say that it's all about discrimination, but I don't think there's a better figure."*

The problem, of course, with President Obama and the Left's entire pitch for every iteration of his plan to boost women's salaries (each of which is an admission the last one[7] didn't work) is that discrimination is the root.

---

opponents held them to their own party's standard on this issue. Incumbent Colorado senator Mark Udall was rendered practically speechless on the issue by challenger Representative Cory Gardner, who noted that not only did Udall pay women less (using Democrats' preferred crude calculus) than men in his Senate office, Gardner paid women *more* than men in his House office. Yet Udall was the one yelling about equal pay in his television commercials.

[7] Like, for instance, The Lilly Ledbetter Fair Pay Act, signed by President Obama in 2009.

Yes, there are differences in men's and women's salaries sometimes. Yes, discrimination exists. But most of the much-ballyhooed pay gap comes from the fact that women make different employment choices. They take less dangerous jobs with more flexible hours, they leave the workforce or cut back when having and raising children. To acknowledge this is not "blaming the victim." For many women, these choices are made with open eyes.

"[A]mong all mothers with children under 18, just a quarter say they would choose full-time work if money were no object and they were free to do whatever they wanted, according to a recent New York Times/CBS News poll," the *New York Times* reported in a rare article ("Coveting Not a Corner Office, but Time at Home," by Catherine Rampell) addressing the gap between the one-dimensional national political rhetoric on women's career desires and their actual desires.

But the Left's goal in constantly raising this issue is to create a useful fictional workplace wherein women can exercise no choice and can exert no agency. With that fiction, the government must step in to help rectify the situation. Of course, it makes little sense to outsource such problem solving to the federal government, which—even if you have perfect faith in its intentions—is a clumsy vehicle for getting things done. This is perhaps best illustrated by the *biannual federal bill Obama announces to solve the exact same problem.*

Now, one place women really can take more control is in asking for more money. Even Stevenson, again of Obama's Council of Economic Advisers, admitted that on the Freakonomics Radio program "Women Are Not Men": "[T]here is this other thing, which I think I should mention, which is that often women are underpaid. And they're underpaid because they simply don't ask. They don't ask for the raise they should get. And there's really compelling research on this, that women tend to not negotiate as hard, tend to be less likely to ask for a raise. And so, if you could be earning more doing the exact same job you're doing, I think you'd be better off. So you should go out there and ask for that raise."

Yet when Texas GOP chairwoman Beth Cubriel made this point in 2014, she was lambasted by liberals and national media. She was insensitive, according to them. She was sexist, a symbol of the GOP's women problem, alleged NBC's Chuck Todd. She was also correct. Cubriel knew the research when she made her remarks, and was surprised by the backlash to a notion she'd heard feminists and women's advocates push for years.

She told us she was so surprised, her first instinct was to ignore the dustup because she didn't want to give the story legs.

"It had legs of its own. I was really surprised," she told us, acknowledging she still gets Google alerts about the kerfuffle, which amounted to two weeks of national news stories. "In hindsight, I should have responded immediately," she said.

Cubriel was understandably caught off-guard by a national firestorm. It wasn't that what she said was offensive. It's that her political opponents found it convenient to be offended that *she* said it. The notion was uncontroversial as long as it wasn't a conservative expressing it, at which point it became politically useful to deem it insensitive insanity.

For many people, negotiating is not fun. It's scary, it's uncomfortable. And yes, it might be fraught with more peril for an assertive woman than an assertive man, depending on one's boss. But getting a negotiating coach, daring to ask, being frank about what your time and talents are worth—these are skills we should encourage women to hone. Women can be trusted with methods for fighting unfairness. When the Left leaves out all nuance in discussing equal pay to pitch yet another tired legislative solution, it leaves out the best part—the part where women have power and can learn to become more powerful. What's the word for that? Oh yes, *empowerment*.

SURE, YOU BASICALLY CURED BREAST CANCER, BUT WHAT HAVE YOU DONE FOR WOMEN LATELY?

S usan G. Komen for the Cure has been raising awareness and al- most $2 billion for breast cancer research, patient and survivor support, and treatment for more than thirty years. Formed in 1982 as Nancy Goodman Brinker's fulfillment of her sister Susan's dying wish, the organization has given more money to breast cancer research than any other entity over a period of time during which survival rates in- creased by 30 percent and five-year survival rates hit 99 percent in America. A diagnosis that was a sure death sentence for women when Komen passed away tragically at age thirty-six in 1980 has become something much different in the face of one of the most aggressive and fruitful awareness and research campaigns in history.

Komen for the Cure is certainly not exempt from criticism. Like any large organization, it regularly faces charges of mission creep, prizing pink P.R. over tangible progress, or bureaucratization that hurts those it's meant to help. What it can't plausibly be accused of is being antiwoman. And yet, in 2012, that was the assertion of the Democratic Party, the entire liberal activist community, and much of the media.

Thirty years after a mourning woman formed this organization to honor her sister, Susan G. Komen for the Cure found out it was *anti- woman*. Why? Because this titan of fund-raising, this template for grassroots activism, this trailblazer for encouraging successful medi- cal research into an inscrutable disease affecting mostly women had the audacity to end a seven-year partnership with Planned Parenthood.

It turns out utter fealty to the cause of abortion rights is truly the metric on which the Left measures being "pro-woman," even though half of the country's women are pro-life.

That January, Komen decided to end a partnership with Planned Parenthood affiliates, which they had been gifting since 2005. The grants amounted to a little over half a million dollars per year in 2010 and 2011, distributed among about twenty Planned Parenthood affiliates, and were meant for breast cancer screenings and other breast health services.

Komen gave several reasons for its decision. First, according to internal memos leaked to the *Atlantic*, the organization had decided to eliminate from grant consideration anyone "under formal investigation for financial or administrative improprieties by local, state or federal authorities." Such an organization could regain consideration after the conclusion of the investigation if it was cleared of "financial and/or administrative improprieties," which were another disqualifier in updated grant requirements.[8]

Second, Komen expressed a desire to eliminate "pass-through" grants to organizations that did not provide direct care. Planned Parenthood was one such organization, offering in-office manual breast exams but only referrals to mammogram services. At the time of the controversy and now, Planned Parenthood's own website, under a section entitled "Where can I get a mammogram?," answered thusly: "Ask your health care provider, health department, or staff at your local Planned Parenthood health center about where you can get a mammogram in your area."

Komen founder Brinker told CBS News, " 'I don't know very much about that investigation, frankly.' Brinker said that under the new standards, 'we like to be able to direct a person to proper training and diagnosis, and we don't like to do pass-through grants anymore.' "

Planned Parenthood's own numbers for breast exams, which it publicized during the controversy, suggest perhaps it was not giving Komen much bang for its many bucks. Komen claimed in its literature to have performed 170,000 breast exams with this money and produced about 6,400 referrals to other breast health services. That

---

[8] Why, yes, Planned Parenthood was indeed the focus of a Government Accountability Office investigation over the use of its funds—a separate issue from Live Action's ongoing probe into Planned Parenthood on malfeasance ranging from illegal abortion practices to covering up statutory rape and sex trafficking. *Champions of women!*

amounts to more than $3,000 per manual breast exam or referral to a mammogram, which seems inordinately high.

But Planned Parenthood supporters, including much of the media, were convinced a decision to remove any Planned Parenthood affiliate from grant funding was politically motivated, spurred by an investigation by former Republican representative Cliff Stearns (R-FL) and the hiring of one vocally pro-life employee to work on policy for Komen.

Karen Handel, a 2010 conservative candidate for governor of Georgia, was senior vice president for policy at the time of the grant restructuring decision. She had been hired after a stint as a contractor for the organization, during which she designed plans for convincing governments to maintain grant levels for Komen during a downturn that called for belt tightening.

But it wasn't the millions she saved for breast cancer research through her efforts that attracted coverage. Instead, Planned Parenthood's roughly $600,000 yearly grant—less than 1 percent of Komen's $100 million annual grant-making budget—became the center of news coverage for a tumultuous three-day period during a presidential election year. The ensuing circus left Komen publicly bruised and seemingly bewildered, and Planned Parenthood the Hotel California of grants and donations. Turns out Komen was more than welcome to check in with their hundreds of thousands of dollars anytime they liked, but they could never leave.

Komen failed to anticipate this firestorm, allowing opponents to break and shape the announcement, staying silent as controversy built around them, and naively assuming thirty years of work to defeat a scourge of women's health might have earned them enough goodwill not to be crucified as agents *against* women's health for declining to continue one grant among its two thousand. Handel later wrote in her book about the controversy, *Planned Bullyhood*, that Komen leaders believed they "had made a 'gentle ladies' pact, agreeing to part ways amicably and acknowledging that a media firestorm was in no one's best interest."

But opponents of the Komen decision had a powerful political motivation of their own, and a blueprint for fighting to a win. They had lost one such fight before, in 1990, when AT&T pulled its funding for Planned Parenthood after twenty-five years, squeamish about the organization's increasingly vocal role in abortion politics. Despite an onslaught of full-page ads in national newspapers declaring, "Caving in to extremists, AT&T hangs up on Planned Parenthood," AT&T stuck by its decision. I bet the telecom giant is glad it checked out when it had the chance.

A firestorm was in the best interests of the Left, which desired to draw as stark a contrast as possible between Democrats and Republicans in an election year, particularly on any issue—real or trumped up—that could conceivably touch on women or women's health. They caught Komen off-guard with a well-planned, coordinated political attack. "I think it was clearly orchestrated. It was so much ado about nothing," Handel said in an interview with us. "The reality is [Planned Parenthood is] a political machine working on behalf of the Left."

The fight over Komen's grant-making procedures happened against a backdrop of a public fight the Obama administration (and by extension the Obama campaign) was waging with Catholic and other conservative and religious groups over a regulation in the Affordable Care Act. The so-called birth control mandate forced these groups to fund contraception and abortifacients that violate their religious beliefs and consciences. The rule was not in the original law, but regulators added it to Obama's signature, partisan attempt to rewrite the health-care system in 2012. Jonathan Last explained the rule's provenance in a *Weekly Standard* article entitled "Obamacare vs. the Catholics" in February of that year:

> *The beginnings of this confrontation lay in an obscure provision of Obama's Patient Protection and Affordable Care Act, which stated that all insurers will be required to provide "preventive health services." When the law was passed, "preventive" was not defined but left to be determined at a later date.*

This past August, Health and Human Services secretary Kathleen Sebelius finally got around to explaining the administration's interpretation of the phrase. Based on a recommendation from the Institute of Medicine, the administration would define "preventive health services" to include contraceptives, morning-after pills, and female sterilization. And they would interpret the "all insurers" section to include religious organizations, whatever their beliefs.

Much as Komen's officials thought they had an agreement to respect a quiet parting of ways, liberal Catholic leaders[9] thought they had an agreement with the Obama administration that its "preventive health services" final rule wouldn't trample the conscience rights of the Church. They were wrong. Last, again:

While Catholics were blindsided by the January decision, the left had been paying close attention to the subject for months. In November, several leftist and feminist blogs began beating the war drums, warning Obama not to "cave" (their word) to the bishops. They were joined by the Nation, Salon, *the* Huffington Post, *and the usual suspects. (Sample headline: "The Men Behind the War on Women.") At the same time, Planned Parenthood and NARAL launched grassroots lobbying efforts and delivered petitions with 100,000 and 135,000 signatures*

---

[9] In March 2010, Bart Stupak, a former Michigan congressman, was one of the final persuadable Obamacare holdouts among Nancy Pelosi's caucus. She needed his vote, along with a small band of pro-life-leaning Democrats who were standing with him. Stupak was eventually won over by assurances from the White House and an executive order signed by President Obama that ostensibly ensured that no taxpayer funding would flow to abortion via the new law. Conscience protections were also part of the deal. Once the law was implemented, those aforementioned assurances were discarded, and the antiabortion executive order was being habitually ignored, according to a nonpartisan Government Accountability Office review. Four years later, Stupak penned a *USA Today* column announcing that his fellow Democrats' "ironclad commitments" on conscience rights had been betrayed.

respectively to the White House urging Obama to uphold the policy and not compromise.

By October, the two-front fight combined in President Obama's talking points in the second presidential debate:

"Governor Romney says that we should eliminate funding for Planned Parenthood," Obama said. "There are millions of women all across the country who rely on Planned Parenthood for not just contraceptive care. They rely on it for mammograms, for cervical cancer screenings." Nonpartisan fact-checker FactCheck.org noted the next day, "Actually, mammograms are not performed at the clinics; Planned Parenthood doctors and nurses conduct breast exams and refer patients to other facilities for mammograms."

Planned Parenthood president Cecile Richards had also been caught misrepresenting what the organization offers, speaking to Joy Behar on CNN's *Headline News* in 2011 about a proposal to pull federal funds from Planned Parenthood. "If this bill ever becomes law, millions of women in this country are gonna lose their healthcare access—not to abortion services—to basic family planning, you know, mammograms."

In a move of creepy, statist solidarity, twenty-six Democratic senators signed onto a letter sternly asking Komen—again, a private breast cancer charity—to reconsider its decision to pull .6 percent of its grant-making budget from an organization that doesn't offer mammograms. "We earnestly hope that you will put women's health before partisan politics and reconsider this decision for the sake of the women who depend on both your organizations for access to the health care they need," wrote the twenty-six partisans.

Nice charity you have there. Shame if anything should happen to it. Here we have a clear example of the Left putting an immense cost on dissent, as the force of the United States Senate is brought to bear on a private charity's freedom of association and minuscule grants.

OF NERDS, NAIL POLISH, NAYSAYERS, AND NINJUTSU

A former beauty queen is standing against a bar in a crowded club. She's approached by a man who gives her an instant and intense case of the creeps. It's not just the popped collar, but an intuited sense of danger that turns her off. As he turns to order a drink for himself, he jostles her drink for just a moment. Acting on her gut, the woman dunks a purple nail into her drink. When the nail polish emerges streaked in green, a sure sign of foul play, the woman knows she must act. She has two hobbies—competing in beauty pageants and kicking ass, and she doesn't see a crown in this club, bitches. So she promptly roundhouses her would-be attacker, calls the police, and enjoys a non-roofied cosmo with her friends.

Would you say this scene is an empowering study in modern womanhood and a shattering of a stereotype of the delicate, deferential pageant queen, with a James Bondian gadget twist? Or would you call this woman a feminist's nightmare? Turns out, for modern feminists, it's the latter.

In the fall of 2014, four men studying engineering and materials science at North Carolina State University came up with an innovation in nail polish, of all things. Billing themselves as the "The First Fashion Company Empowering Women to Prevent Sexual Assault," the founders of Undercover Colors created a line of polishes that would react if dipped into a drink spiked with a date-rape drug such as GHB (gamma hydroxybutyrate), or Rohypnol. The invention would give women in clubs or college parties a way to test their drinks easily, giving them one more tool to ward off perpetrators of assault. "Our goal is to invent technologies that empower women to protect themselves from this heinous and quietly pervasive crime," the team wrote on their Facebook page.

A few months before this nail lacquer made the news, the eventual winner of the Miss USA pageant, Nia Sanchez of Nevada, was asked a question in competition about sexual assault on college campuses being "swept under the rug." Here is her answer, as quoted in the *Washington Post*'s coverage of the pageant:

> *"I believe that some colleges may potentially be afraid of having a bad reputation and that would be a reason it could be swept under the rug, because they don't want that to come out into the public," Sanchez said. "But I think more awareness is very important so women can learn how to protect themselves. Myself, as a fourth-degree black belt, I learned from a young age that you need to be confident and be able to defend yourself. And I think that's something that we should start to really implement for a lot of women."*

For most who encountered either of these stories, the immediate reaction was something akin to "Wow, that's neat. Technology and technical training as tools to limit the power of rapists." Who could object to a new product that could potentially curb the use of drugs like roofies? Who's offended by a pageant-queen pile driver that could potentially strike fear into the hearts of the criminals?

But we live in a society where creating a nail polish that might help women prevent rape is objectionable. We live in a society where Sanchez's idea of arming herself is met with incredulity and ridicule. Sanchez was called "sick," an "idiot." Her answer "icky," "awful and offensive."

Why? Because of something called "rape culture." Rape culture is the idea that our society, in its very fiber, is set up to give license to and make excuses for rapists. Such a society normalizes nonconsent, blames victims for attacks, and creates socially approved roles for women and men in sexual relationships that facilitate male control. The idea of rape culture moves blame for rape and sexual assault from individuals to a more societal, collective guilt.

For a less dense, academic description, with a taste of just how expansive this concept can get in mainstream feminist thought, here's a treatise, titled "Rape Culture 101," posted October 9, 2009, by feminist blogger Melissa McEwan on *Shakesville*. Aside from a couple of the more absurd suggestions and the last line, this sounds like a list of basic precautions that women—nay, human beings, in general—should consider when living life in an unpredictable and sometimes dangerous world.

> *Rape culture is telling girls and women to be careful about what you wear, how you wear it, how you carry yourself, where you walk, when you walk there, with whom you walk, whom you trust, what you do, where you do it, with whom you do it, what you drink, how much you drink, whether you make eye contact, if you're alone, if you're with a stranger, if you're in a group, if you're in a group of strangers, if it's dark, if the area is unfamiliar, if you're carrying something, how you carry it, what kind of shoes you're wearing in case you have to run, what kind of purse you carry, what jewelry you wear, what time it is, what street it is, what environment it is, how many people you sleep with, what kind of people you sleep with, who your friends are, to whom you give your number, who's around when the delivery guy comes, to get an apartment where you can see who's at the door before they can see you, to check before you open the door to the delivery guy, to own a dog or a dog-sound-making machine, to get a roommate, to take self-defense, to always be alert always pay attention always watch your back always be aware of your surroundings and never let your guard down for a moment lest you be sexually assaulted and if you are and didn't follow all the rules* it's your fault.

For those who believe the United States is a "rape culture," giving women a new technology or skills that could potentially protect them from rape somehow empowers *rapists*. The idea is the very existence of the nail polish or ninjutsu assumes the presence of rapists and implies a woman's responsibility to protect herself from them. "Prevention tips or products that focus on what women do or wear aren't just ineffective, they leave room for victim-blaming when those steps aren't taken," posted Jessica Valenti, another prominent online feminist, in an August 26, 2014, *Guardian* article whose headline offered the false choice—"Why is it easier to invent anti-rape nail polish than find a way to stop rapists?" Why not do both?

The mere existence of a nail polish a woman might choose to wear to protect herself against a certain kind of sexual assault is tantamount to suggesting she asked for it by wearing a short skirt, according to some feminists. And, thus, literal empowerment of women is declared antiwoman. A protest of the nail polish—yes, a protest of antirape nail polish—by the Centre for Gender Advocacy of Concordia University in Montreal featured MANicures for protesters emblazoned with the words *DON'T RAPE* and *ASK FIRST*.

The objection is that the availability of any method of prevention somehow puts the onus on women to "not get raped" instead of teaching men "don't rape." Ashe Schow, who covers the feminist movement and its rhetorical and political crusades for the *Washington Examiner*, wondered, "What if we applied feminist logic to other crimes?" with absurd results:

> *We should be teaching people not to steal, not telling people to lock their doors and windows . . .*

> *I don't want to live in a world where I can't jog down deserted streets at night. I shouldn't have to change my normal behavior because someone wants to attack me or steal my iPod.*

> *Telling me to be aware of my surroundings perpetuates "burglary culture" where it is somehow my fault that I got mugged.*

> *People need to be taught not to abduct children; children shouldn't be told not to talk to strangers.*

But the fight over who is responsible is precisely why the Rape, Abuse & Incest National Network recently critiqued the term *rape culture*, much to the chagrin of adherents to the philosophy. In March 2014, RAINN's president and vice president said in a letter to the White House Task Force to Protect Students from Sexual Assault:

> *In the last few years, there has been an unfortunate trend towards blaming "rape culture" for the extensive problem of sexual violence on campuses. While it is helpful to point out the systemic barriers to addressing the problem, it is important to not lose sight of a simple fact: Rape is caused not by cultural factors but by the conscious decisions, of a small percentage of the community, to commit a violent crime.*

Giving women tools other than a mantra of "don't rape" doesn't change the fact that rape exists and those who perpetrate this heinous crime should be punished. Access to such tools as a complement to the idea of "don't rape" seems rather reasonable, even laudable. But the idea is to declare anyone who disagrees with the liberal view on this issue a part of "rape culture." Smearing one's opponents as rape abettors for their mere words is pretty much the definition of ending the discussion.

GOING FULL FALLOPIAN

It was January of 2012 when ABC anchor and former Democratic campaign strategist George Stephanopoulos opened a new front in a culture war conservatives had no idea existed. Referring to a 1965 Supreme Court ruling, Stephanopoulos asked candidate Mitt Romney, a noncombatant in this nonexistent culture war, the following question during a Republican primary debate:

> *Governor Romney, I want to go straight to you. Senator Santorum has been very clear in his belief that the Supreme Court was wrong when it decided that a right to privacy was embedded*

Explaining "Mansplaining"

M ansplain (verb): When a man talks down to a woman, explaining a subject matter she knows perfectly well or even better than the man in question, out of an ingrained, outdated, and sexist assumption that she needs things spoonfed to her because she is a woman.

Or that's how they might define it, at least. This term is frequently used for one purpose: shutting down a conversation. For instance:

Man: "Actually, those equal pay statistics are misleading because . . ."

Liberal woman: "Oh good! I was hoping someone would MANSPLAIN away the unfair gender gap for me!"

Man: *(slinks away)*

When the nation was debating late-term abortion in the wake of Texas state senator Wendy Davis's infamous filibuster of a popular legal restriction (more polling details to come), Guy tweeted some friendly messaging advice for fellow pro-lifers. Rather than calling the legislation a ban at "20 weeks," he suggested, it might be more effective and impactful to describe the proposed limitations in terms of months. "Abortion in the sixth month of pregnancy" offers context that people can intuitively understand, whereas referring to "weeks" sounds more clinical. Democratic rapid-response specialist Lis Smith, formerly of the Obama campaign, swooped in and derided Guy for "mansplaining" the issue. She wasn't disputing any of his facts. Indeed, as part of Democrats' messaging apparatus, she likely knew that he was making an effective point. So she dropped a "mansplain" to try to instill doubt ("as a man, should I really be talking about these issues at all?") and shush him.

in the Constitution. And following from that, he believes that states have the right to ban contraception. Now, I should add that he's said that he's not recommending that states do that . . . But I do want to get that core question. Governor Romney, do you believe that states have the right to ban contraception? Or is that trumped by a constitutional right to privacy?

Romney's half-confused, half-bemused answer pretty much sums up the reaction of conservatives, who had not in any conceivable sense considered such bans, let alone pushed for them:

George, this is an unusual topic that you're raising. States have a right to ban contraception? I can't imagine a state banning contraception. I can't imagine the circumstances where a state would want to do so, and if I were governor of a state or a legislator of a state, I would totally and completely oppose any effort to ban contraception. So you're asking, given the fact that there's no state that wants to do so, and I don't know of any candidate that wants to do so, you're asking: Could it constitutionally be done? We can ask our constitutionalist here. (Laughter as Romney turns to Ron Paul) . . .

George, I don't know whether the states have a right to ban contraception. No state wants to. I mean, the idea of you putting forward things that states might want to do that no state wants to do and asking me whether they could do it or not, is kind of a silly thing, I think. (Applause)

When Stephanopoulos pressed Romney further, the exasperated candidate slammed the door shut. "Contraception? It's working just fine. Let's leave it alone." The hall packed with Republicans burst into laughter and applause. Issue resolved, right? Wrong, as we'll soon discover.

Side fact: Three liberal mayors of major American cities threatened to use their government power to actually ban Chick-fil-A from establishing new franchises inside their cities because they disagreed with its leadership's political views on gay marriage. Exactly zero conservative or Republican politicians have attempted to ban birth control anywhere in the United States of America.

The question seemed to come out of left field at the time, both in a figurative and in an ideological sense. Again, Romney's reaction mirrored the reaction of the rest of the Right, which knew it didn't want to ban birth control and didn't think anyone else would believe they did. Stephanopoulos—who *Politico* reported in 2009 participated in daily conference calls with then White House chief of staff Rahm Emanuel, and fellow Clintonistas James Carville and Paul Begala—set the stage for the Democratic Party's incessant, frantic, and false messaging for the next three years with one question. He has denied that this was an act of collusion with the party, claiming he was inspired by comments Santorum made in an interview earlier that week with Jake Tapper, who then worked for ABC News. But even Santorum himself, while supporting the right of states to theoretically ban contraception, didn't support the idea, calling such a move a "dumb thing" in the interview with Tapper.

Regardless of Santorum's explanation, there was no pressing need to know Romney's position on the "issue," as he'd never even hinted at any desire to prohibit birth control in the past. The premise of the question was fabricated, as even the most outspoken social conservative in the race literally called the idea "dumb." Yet, Romney was asked the question four times in a prime-time debate. Conservatives, your writers included, figured this bizarre Stephanopoulos tangent would blow over by the end of the debate. Instead, it constituted approximately 75 percent of the Democratic Party's messaging from that day forward.

Three weeks after Stephanopoulos's seemingly bizarre question, the Obama administration announced a regulation that required every employer in the United States to provide birth control, free of charge, to all employees, regardless of the religious convictions of the employers. Its insertion into Obamacare, and conservatives' resulting religious liberty concerns about it, kicked an incessant, frantic, and false narrative into high gear. The "war on women" was born.

By February, Stephanopoulos's question and the Obamacare regulation had conveniently dovetailed to thrust birth control into the forefront of American political conversation, despite the fact that 85 percent of employer-based health-care plans already covered contraception, according to the Kaiser Family Foundation. Moreover, "[t]he federal government already paid for Medicaid recipients' contraception and spent another $300 million each year on contraception for lower-income and uninsured Americans through the Title X program," according to reporting by the *Weekly Standard*'s John McCormack.

It's almost as if this threat had been concocted as a political battle cry, instead of serving an authentic need. In three short weeks, birth control had gone from a readily available and relatively cheap medicine used commonly and without issue by American women to a human right for which one should never have to pay, and which was suddenly in grave, grave danger of disappearing if Republicans got their way.

This was, and is, completely ridiculous. It sounded ridiculous when Stephanopoulos first asked the question, and it remains ridiculous in a post–Hobby Lobby[10] world, which hasn't even "turned back the clock" on women to the dark days of, like, seven minutes ago.[11] McCormack again in "Hobby Lobby Hysteria":

> *The Court didn't even turn back the clock to the supposedly scary time when middle-class and wealthy citizens might have had to shell out $9 a month for birth control. It ruled that the government could achieve its goal of co-pay-free birth control for all without forcing conscientious objectors to violate their sincerely held religious beliefs. The federal government, which intends to spend $2 trillion on Obamacare over the next decade, could scrounge up the change to pay directly for contraceptives*

---

[10] The scope of the Supreme Court's laudable 2014 decision on religious liberty is likely more narrow than conservatives would hope, and less drastic than many liberals have been led to believe.

[11] Isn't it unconscionable the president "denied women access" (to use their preposterous parlance) to birth control for the first half of his presidency? *The horror.* We can't believe Democrats didn't address this historic injustice legislatively immediately upon gaining filibuster-proof majorities in both houses of Congress.

or abortifacients not covered by conscientious objectors' health plans, for example.

The Obama administration has been fighting a group of nuns[12] in court to force them to pay for birth control. That is a thing that's happening in real life. Because . . . war on women.

The "vote with your ladyparts!" crowd will insist that women who don't self-identify in a narrowly tailored way don't really count as full women. They'll intone that Republicans actively oppose pay equality and harbor a secret desire to grab your Yaz. And they'll try to shut people up with discussion-ending epithets like "rape culture" and "mansplaining." We're smarter than this, ladies. Liberation includes the freedom to think for ourselves.

AKIN, FILNER, AND THE "EMBLEMATIC" GAME

Two rules of thumb: First, the term "legitimate rape" should be stricken from politicians' lexicon. Period. Nothing good can come of stringing those two words together. Second, if you're a man running for office, and you're asked about abortion policy in the rare circumstance of pregnancies resulting from rape, you'd better have a rock-solid answer prepared. And it must never, ever include ignorant theorizing about the female body's magical ability to shut off its reproductive functions during a sexual assault. Congressman Todd Akin violated both of those guidelines in epic fashion in 2012, pissing away a Senate race in which Democrat Claire McCaskill's seat was ripe for the picking. McCaskill helped hand-select her gaffe-prone opponent by meddling in the GOP primary, and her strategy paid off.

But Akin's idiocy heard 'round the country illustrates a maddening

---

[12] The Little Sisters of the Poor offer care to thirteen thousand indigent elderly around the world and would like the right, as nuns, not to pay for birth control that violates their religious beliefs.

double standard, wherein virtually every Republican in America is asked to denounce any offensive or controversial statement made by a member of the party. Mitt Romney was asked on several occasions about Akin's foot-in-mouth moment, forcing him to repeatedly reject the comments and clarify his own position. Similar scenes played out in down-ticket races from coast to coast. Everyone from Senate nominees to candidates for dogcatcher were compelled to weigh in, so long as they had an *R* next to their last name. The instantly congealed conventional wisdom determined that Akin's indefensible comments were "emblematic" of Republicans' problems with women. One skirmish in the war on women was nationalized, and the party took a real hit.

Bob Filner, in contrast, is a Democrat. He served in Congress for the better part of two decades before getting elected mayor of San Diego. In 2013, he was accused of sexual misconduct, an allegation that merely opened the floodgates. Before all was said and done, at least eighteen accusers came forward to point the finger at Filner. This group included a great-grandmother and several *survivors of sexual assault* in the military, whom Filner met in his capacity as then chairman of the House Committee on Veterans' Affairs. One member of the National Women Veterans of America told CNN, "[Filner] went to dinners, asked women out to dinners, grabbed breasts, buttocks. The full gamut. Everything that is complete violation of what we stand for . . . He's a sexual predator. And he used this organization for his own personal agenda." Other women described "the Filner dance," in which the lecherous pol would corner female subordinates in a room and make sexual advances, sometimes going so far as to put women in headlocks.

When this scandal finally detonated on the serial misogynist at a July 11 press conference, national Democrats remained curiously mum for weeks. More than a week later, with victims coming out of the woodwork, former House Speaker Nancy Pelosi was asked whether Filner— her longtime House colleague—should step down as mayor of a major city in her home state. "What goes on in San Diego is up to the people of San Diego. I'm not here to make any judgments," she said. Can you *imagine* the shitstorm that would have been unleashed if Mitt Romney had said of Todd Akin, "Look, what happens in Missouri stays in Missouri. Get lost"? Senator Dianne Feinstein, who represents Filner's state, finally got around to calling for his resignation on July 28, after nearly three weeks of hedging. Senator Barbara Boxer, California's other U.S. senator and a hardened gender warrior, waited until August 9 to do the same. Her open letter was peppered with praise for Filner's work on issues "from creating jobs to protecting the environment to helping our veterans." She urged him to "get the help you need."

Appearing on CNN in late July, Democratic strategist Hilary Rosen made an unusual confession: "I had dinner over the weekend with some female [House] members and former members who said that this guy has kinda been this way all along," she said of Filner. "Everybody thought that he was a little creepy." More than a dozen alleged victims don't just appear overnight; logic dictated that Filner's reign of harassment must have spanned years. Rosen's comment indicated that his actions were an open secret among D.C.-based Democrats, who evidently shrugged off his conduct as a "creepy" peccadillo for years. Aside from naked partisanship, what can possibly explain the fact that Pelosi, Feinstein, and Boxer—grand defenders of women, all—were so reluctant to speak up? Even if we assume they knew nothing of his behavior while he was on the Hill with them, how long would it have taken after accusations started flying to race to a microphone if Filner sat across the aisle?

Filner eventually stepped down, but his habitually abusive *behavior* was treated as far less important, relevant, and urgent than Akin's *words*. Akin was emblematic; Filner was . . . an unfortunate sideshow, halfheartedly defended before being cut loose. Who really cares if Filner grabbed everything that moved for his entire political career? What really mattered was his support for abortion and birth control "access."

In another stark example, a Republican Hill staffer named Elizabeth Lauten became the subject of several days of blanket, national news coverage for writing a critical post on her personal Facebook page about the outfits and attitudes of the Obama daughters at the 2014 Turkey Pardon with the president.

The same week that Lauten was resigning from the backlash, a Democratic staffer pleaded guilty to sexual assault of two women, one a colleague whom he'd drugged and raped. Despite being an admitted rapist, Donny Ray Williams Jr., aide to then senators Mary Landrieu and Herb Kohl and prominent Democratic representatives Elijah Cummings and Jan Schakowsky, never made it onto the evening news.

The evidence is pretty clear that a *D* beside one's name and a record of voting liberal is a get-out-of-assault-free card. Often the guilty individual isn't made to pay much of a price, and his party gets little if any blowback; Democrats effortlessly shake it off and go along their merry way accusing others of warring against women.

"EXTREME" MAKEOVER
Abortion Edition

"I always use the word extreme."
—Senator Chuck Schumer (D-NY)

Shortly after the 2012 presidential election, Guy was chatting with a Democratic pollster, who shall remain nameless, about public opinion trends. The messaging guru raised Republicans' much-discussed "gender gap" struggles, arguing over and over again that the GOP is out of touch on "women's health issues" and "birth control." When Guy explicitly brought the word *abortion* into the discussion, the pollster put his index finger to his lips, shushing Guy. "Women's health," he corrected. "But most women don't agree that abortion is women's health," Guy countered, at which point he was interrupted with another *shhhhhh*. The pollster, without saying so, was conceding an important point—that the public doesn't necessarily lump abortion in with the Left's broader, sanitized category of "women's health"—the evidence for which we'll get to shortly.

One of the laziest pieces of political analysis you'll hear—and we hear it *a lot*—is that it's imperative for Republicans to abandon the "social issues" in order to attract more voters. This advice is typically supplied by people who already consider themselves social moderates or liberals ("ditch these issues I don't care about!"), and who are not referring to gun control, capital punishment, or any number of issues that might fall under the "social" umbrella. Let's face it, *social issues* is shorthand for *gay marriage and abortion*. Unless the GOP moderates significantly on this issue pairing, we're told, it'll doom itself with future generations of voters.

This quick-fix solution fails on two levels: First, it glosses over the serious political conundrum of how the party could hypothetically cut loose a massive portion of its core base and still cobble together a victory coalition for national elections, particularly in the short to medium term. Second, and more important, this faulty analysis assumes that the two issues come as a package deal in voters' minds. They demonstrably do not. We'll discuss our views on gay rights in a future chapter, but here's a thumbnail sketch of public polling on the issue: support for same-sex marriage has skyrocketed (an overused term that actually applies in this case) in recent years to a majority stance. Among young voters, including millennial Republicans and Christians, the trend is even more pronounced.

Abortion is a different ball game. While the anti-gay/pro–traditional marriage position is hemorrhaging support, the pro-life cause has made fairly extraordinary gains, bouncing back from its polling nadir in the 1990s. Polling on the issue can be all over the map due to question wording and misperceptions. For example, a majority of Americans say they oppose overturning *Roe v. Wade*, the 1973 Supreme Court decision that conjured the "right" to abortion out of whole cloth. But significant majorities also support a raft of abortion restrictions that run afoul of *Roe* and its radical companion ruling, *Doe v. Bolton*.

Doe established that the so-called right to abortion applied broadly through all nine months of pregnancy and precluded most meaningful limitations.[1]

Many people mistakenly believe that overturning *Roe* would instantly criminalize all abortion, full stop, nationwide. It would not. The fall of *Roe* (which even some prominent pro-choice legal scholars admit was a poorly decided power grab) would return the difficult policy questions surrounding abortion to the people and their elected representatives. The resulting patchwork of state-by-state legal regimes

---

[1] That, well, *extreme* precedent has been incrementally uprooted by subsequent decisions, including 1992's *Planned Parenthood v. Casey*.

would feature highly permissive laws in places like California and New York, and more restrictive laws in places like Louisiana and South Dakota. Abortion policy would be determined by the battle over hearts and minds and would often require compromise. It would not be dictated by black-robed lawyers imposing a top-down framework rooted in an invented right.

When Americans are asked what the country's abortion laws should look like, overwhelming majorities embrace limitations and protections for the unborn. A Marist poll released in early 2014 showed supermajority support for laws that: require that a mother be shown an ultrasound image of her child prior to making a final abortion choice (58 percent support), mandate that abortion procedures be performed by medical doctors only[2] (62 percent), implement a one-day waiting period prior to having an abortion (79 percent), and bar minor girls from obtaining an abortion without parental notification (80 percent). On the broader question of abortion's legality, the national survey found that just 44 percent of Americans embraced one of three pro-choice-leaning positions—including the option of "abortion should be allowed only in the first three months of pregnancy." Fifty-six percent responded that legal abortion should be restricted to extremely rare circumstances (rape, incest, and to save the life of the mother), or prohibited entirely. A substantial majority (61 percent) of respondents selected the two options closest to the "middle" of the spectrum, if you will: first trimester only, or "rape/incest/life of mother." These Marist figures aren't outliers:

An April 2013 NBC/Wall Street Journal poll found that 52 percent of Americans said abortion should be "illegal" with either limited or no exceptions, while 45 percent said it should be legal "always" or "most of the time."

A May survey from Gallup that same year produced a major prolife advantage, with fully 58 percent opposing legal abortion

---

[2] California passed a law allowing *nondoctors* to perform abortions in 2013.

in "all" or "most circumstances," (this included 57 percent of women and young voters) with just 39 percent espousing pro-choice opinions.

CNN's March 2014 poll replicated Gallup's findings, nearly to the exact percentage breakdown. Fifty-eight percent of respondents selected pro-life responses, with 40 percent leaning the other direction.

Democrats and liberals in the media[3] discuss mainstream pro-life sentiment as if it's a fringe viewpoint, limited to a shrinking segment of the Republican base. The statistics above prove that a wide array of antiabortion policies appeal to Americans far beyond traditional "socially conservative" precincts. Abortion opposition isn't the exclusive province of rosary-praying Catholics and Bible-thumpin' Evangelicals, yet that's the way this issue is routinely covered. Back to that Marist poll. If you add the "legal in the first three months" group to those who embraced one of the pro-life options, you've got 84 percent of Americans who at least believe that abortion should be illegal in almost all circumstances in the second and third trimesters. Only an extremist could cast that entire opinion range as "extreme."

The numbers are even starker on late-term abortion, in the sixth month of pregnancy and beyond. We have quite a lot of polling on that specific question to examine thanks to the news media commissioning a string of surveys on the issue after Texas state senator Wendy Davis (later a failed gubernatorial candidate) launched a filibuster against a 2013 bill to outlaw almost all abortions after the twenty-week mark. Davis was hailed as a hero by the abortion-supporting Left and

---

[3] Numerous surveys of American journalists conducted since the mid-1980s have consistently found that reporters and editors are much, much more likely to support abortion rights than average Americans. It comes as no surprise, therefore, that the media tends to uncritically parrot Democrats' definition of abortion "extremism." Elite media opinions on abortion are acutely out of step with public opinion, more so than on most other issues. The Media Research Center has a raft of data to this effect on its website.

became an instant media darling.[4] Think about that. This woman became famous by blocking a bill to recognize and protect the humanity of babies in the *sixth month* of gestation. Many in the press thought this was heroic.

Her supporters in Texas stormed the Capitol and disrupted the vote with deafening chants that ground the legislative session to a halt. (That discussion-blocking mob action alone could easily merit its own chapter in this book.) When the bill finally passed in a subsequent special session, pro-choice protesters comported themselves in cartoonishly horrible ways, including chanting "Hail Satan!" to interrupt a pro-life vigil, and holding placards featuring charming messages such as "If I wanted the government in my womb, I'd f*** a Senator!"[5] That one was held by a girl who couldn't have been older than ten, based on a photo that made the rounds at the time. Classy stuff, adults who gave her that sign to hold. These are the people who'd label all pro-lifers extremists.

A *Huffington Post* poll found that Americans supported the bill by roughly a 30-point margin, while a Quinnipiac survey pegged the gap at 25 points. In the Q-poll, women were far more likely to support the abortion restriction than men (go ahead and reread that, if you'd like), favoring the late-term ban by 35 points. Only one-quarter of American women surveyed opposed this "extreme" abortion restriction.

Let us repeat: abortion and gay marriage are not linked in the public's mind, except, apparently, among the pundit class. This holds true with younger voters, too. While the millennial generation—born between the early '80s and '00s—has swung hard to the left on gay

---

[4] Our friend and *Weekly Standard* reporter John McCormack noted that in a fawning interview on ABC News's *This Week*, Davis was asked zero questions about late-term abortion, the subject of her protest. She was instead quizzed on the bravery of her filibuster and the pink tennis shoes she wore. Hard-hitting stuff. Anything to avoid the ugliness at the core of her one-woman stand.

[5] A woman was thrown off an American Airlines flight for wearing a T-shirt with the same offensive (similarly censored) slogan in 2012. We find her opinion to be repugnant, but do not believe that putting it on a provocative T-shirt should merit booting a paying customer off a flight.

rights, they are just as pro-life, if not *more* pro-life, than older voters. A 2012 nationwide survey of millennials commissioned by Harvard University's Institute of Politics asked, "Which of these comes closest to your view on abortion?" The results:

It should be permitted in all cases: 32%

It should be permitted, but subject to greater
     restrictions than it is now: 14%

It should be permitted only in cases such as rape,
     incest, or to save the woman's life: 27%

It should only be permitted to save the woman's life: . . . 8%

It should not be permitted at all: 15%

Declined to say: 5%

So roughly two-thirds of young Americans support greater restrictions on abortion, with a majority adopting one of the three mainstream pro-life options. Incidentally, the same poll projected that this age group would vote for Barack Obama over Mitt Romney by 22 points. Obama won by 23, so Harvard wasn't relying on a fluky, right-leaning sample. Furthermore, in the Quinnipiac survey mentioned earlier, the results were broken down by age group. The cohort with the highest percentage of support for the late-term abortion ban? Young people.

Why the schism between gay rights and abortion? We suspect young people view both issues through a "rights" prism. They are unconvinced that there's any "victim" in gay marriage, and any theoretical harm to society is not a sufficient justification to prohibit their gay friends and siblings to marry. When it comes to abortion, however, there's a strong case to be made that the unborn child, whose life is terminated without her input or consent, is the severely wronged party in that moral equation. Republicans may want to pay attention to this dynamic as they plot their next moves on the "social issues."

We're not trying to be overly preachy on abortion here. Like many (most?) young people, we're pro-life—not only because of our faith, but also because of science, ethics, and a sense of fairness. It begins with a straightforward proposition: at some point prior to birth, unborn children become human beings worthy of legal protection. We don't claim to know precisely where that bright line exists ("viability," for example, is a shifting standard that has moved earlier and earlier as medical technology improves), so we'd prefer to err on the side of life. We understand that this is a tough issue for a lot of people and acknowledge that outright bans—in the first few months of pregnancy, in particular—could be logistically and politically unworkable. But *especially* after the first trimester, it's not really a close call in our minds. Most Americans, most young people, and most women agree with us. That's our point. The pro-choice side is entitled to its opinion and is welcome to make the case for legalized abortion. But declaring pro-lifers antiwomen extremists isn't just discussion-ending intimidation . . . it's empirically unsupportable.

And since some people can't resist tossing about charges of extremism on this issue, we might as well point out that the most recent Democratic Party platform abandoned President Clinton's "safe, legal, and rare" formulation on the question. The abortion lobby disagrees with the "rare" part—abortion is big business, after all. "Safe" sounds nice, but many Democrats have opposed legislation requiring that abortion clinics meet the same medical and sanitary standards as hospitals—while pushing to allow nondoctors to perform abortions, as we mentioned earlier. And lax oversight of abortion clinics, due to political considerations, led directly to the unspeakable horrors at convicted felon Kermit Gosnell's murder factory. If you think we're being hyperbolic with that description, google his trial. It's ghastly stuff.

One last thing: If you're through googling Kermit Gosnell and still aren't sufficiently sickened, punch in "Obama and Born Alive Infant Protection Act." As a state senator, Barack Obama was the only member of the Illinois legislature to speak against a bill to halt the practice—confirmed by whistle-blowers—of abortionists murdering babies who were accidentally born alive following unsuccessful abortions. He did so three times and has since whitewashed his record through a combination of flat-out misstatements and eye rolling. The latter approach is rather effective because his actual voting record is so genuinely radical that by simply recapitulating the facts, you yourself run the risk of sounding like you've opened up one too many of those Obama conspiracy/hoax chain e-mails.[6]

The rarely discussed de facto Democratic Party position on abortion is that it should be legal throughout pregnancy, for any reason whatsoever (including sex selection), and paid for by taxpayers. Who's extreme, again?

---

[6] Note: Please don't forward us yours.

7

(DIFFERENT) RULES
FOR "RADICALS"

Double Standards on Violence and Rhetoric

A TALE OF TWO SHOOTINGS

On the morning of Wednesday, August 15, 2012, a twenty-eight-year-old man named Floyd Lee Corkins left his parents' house in Herndon, Virginia. He drove to the East Falls Church Metro stop and boarded a train into Washington, D.C., with a backpack, three magazines of ammunition, fifteen Chick-fil-A sandwiches, a SigSauer pistol, a list of addresses, and a plan to murder as many people as he could.

Leonardo Johnson, Leo to friends, was just finishing his shift as a building manager at the reception desk at the Family Research Council when he watched the young man walk through the wood-paneled lobby toward him. Corkins told him he was there for an internship interview. Johnson, forty-seven, asked him for identification, and instead of reaching into his pocket, the young man unshouldered his bag and knelt to the floor to retrieve it. Acting on a gut feeling, Johnson walked from behind his desk and found Corkins pulling a loaded semiautomatic handgun from a backpack.

Corkins aimed the gun at Johnson's head. The unarmed former high school football player ducked and lunged at Corkins, who fired three shots. One shattered Johnson's forearm but he was able to subdue the shooter, wrest his gun from him, and hold him until police arrived, his injured arm swollen and bleeding as he watched over his attacker. "It's not about you," Corkins told Johnson after the twenty-second struggle. "I don't like the organization and what it stands for. I don't like these people and I don't like what they stand for." In some reports, Corkins is said to have uttered, "I don't like your politics" before he opened fire.

Family Research Council's politics are socially conservative. It's a national advocacy group that backs "traditional values" and opposes gay marriage.

Johnson was taken to the hospital, where he would undergo a long surgery and a week's stay to repair his arm, which still has bullet fragments lodged in it today. Corkins was taken for questioning by the FBI, where he openly described his motive. "He intended to enter the FRC that day to kill as many people as possible and smother Chick-fil-A" in his dying victims' faces, court documents state.

As Corkins told the FBI, the fried chicken was designed "to make a statement against the people working in that building . . . and with their stance against gay rights . . . They endorsed Chick-fil-A and also Chick-fil-A came out against gay marriage and I was going to use that as a statement." Corkins' parents told the FBI their son, who was a volunteer at the DC Center for the LGBT Community, had "strong opinions with respect to those he believes do not treat homosexuals in a fair manner." *Strong opinions.* That's one way of putting it.

His attack was not spontaneous. A week before the fateful Wednesday morning, Corkins bought a pistol at a Virginia gun shop. On Monday, he rehearsed his trip into the city, talking with someone at FRC headquarters—an edifice situated on a corner less than a mile from the White House. He bought his backpack at Kmart and the sandwiches the day before the attack. He had used an online map from the liberal Southern Poverty Law Center designating FRC and other socially conservative organizations "hate groups" to select and locate his target. He carried with him a handwritten list of four organizations, all "nationally recognized advocacy groups that openly identify themselves as having socially conservative agendas," according to court documents. The FBI has never released the groups on that list to our knowledge, but a Traditional Values Coalition employee later claimed investigators had told them they were on it.

The story was clear, the motive unmistakable. Corkins told his victim his reasons. He told cops on the scene. He told the FBI during questioning. Later, he told U.S. District Court judge Richard Roberts upon pleading guilty that he "hoped to intimidate gay rights opponents." The Department of Justice took him at his word. Corkins was charged with an act of domestic political terrorism, the first crime prosecuted in the District of Columbia under the Anti-Terrorism Act of 2002. Ever.

The charge came just two weeks before the presidential election of 2012. Had it been a spec script for a prime-time procedural, renowned for their ham-fisted political plots "ripped from the headlines," one would have critiqued it as a little too on the nose—the Chick-fil-A sandwiches scattered behind the crime tape, commingling with boxes of ammo a study in cartoonish stereotypes. There was a readily available video of the attacker being interviewed while buying his weapon—a chilling scene captured by a French news crew doing a story on the ease of getting a gun in the United States. "This is what I got," the calm, clean-cut man told the crew. "I guess it's a basic gun for starting out and what not," describing the pistol as he turned it over in his hands casually. There was video of him attacking "Leo the Hero," as he came to be called, from three surveillance cameras, and video of his interrogation by the FBI. The crime offered national media a chance to engage in three giant firestorms and pet issues: the policy debate about gun control in the wake of mass shootings; the cultural uproar over Chick-fil-A; and an occasion to hand-wring about the dangers of our overheated political rhetoric and the violence it might encourage.

The media largely passed on these opportunities. In the same way

Mayor Bob "Cop-a-Feel" Filner never became emblematic in press coverage of Democrats' treatment of women, the FRC shooting never became emblematic of some kind of dark threat posed by liberal activism.

But less than two years earlier, the media had seized upon a far less appropriate emblem in a huge way. In the parking lot of a Tucson Safeway in 2011, a horrific shooting rampage perpetrated by Jared Lee Loughner on a January Saturday morning ended the lives of six Americans, including a sitting federal judge and a nine-year-old girl. It left a sitting Democratic congresswoman, Representative Gabrielle Giffords, severely wounded.

But it was neither the good people lost that day nor the deranged man who murdered them that got the most attention in the wake of the crime. A child watching TV coverage might have been forgiven for concluding that the alleged shooter's name was Rhetoric, rather than Jared Lee Loughner. Rhetoric was the suspect most closely examined. The wounded were still being treated and transported when political blame started flying. A question about political motives was natural, especially given the nature of the targets, but the speculation was irresponsible, and from some, intentional. The same-day *New York Times* stories on the rampage were headlined, "In Attack's Wake, Political Repercussions," and "Bloodshed Puts New Focus on Vitriol in Politics."

Sheriff Clarence Dupnik used the spotlight afforded by the murders of his citizens to blame political pundits instead of the mentally ill twenty-two-year-old who opened fire on a crowd of innocents. "There's reason to believe that this individual may have a mental issue. And I think people who are unbalanced are especially susceptible to vitriol," Dupnik said during remarks the day of the shooting, before motive or full time line had been established. "People tend to pooh-pooh this business about all the vitriol we hear inflaming the American public by people who make a living off of doing that. That may be free speech, but it's not without consequences."

He also referred to his state as a "mecca for prejudice and bigotry," so he spoke about vitriol with some experience. These comments from a law enforcement officer allowed every media outlet to follow his lead, and follow they did, eagerly. The shooting "set off what is likely to be a wrenching debate over anger and violence in American politics," the *New York Times* conjectured, as it did just that. "While the exact motivations of the suspect in the shootings remained unclear, an Internet site tied to the man, Jared Lee Loughner, contained anti-government ramblings. And regardless of what led to the episode, it quickly focused attention on the degree to which inflammatory language, threats and implicit instigations to violence have become a steady undercurrent in the nation's political culture."

You'll notice there's very little actual information in that paragraph. It's not established that inflammatory language had recently increased or caused the incident at hand. All they had were ramblings on a website "tied to" Loughner, whatever that means. Heeding Dupnik's suggestion that the nation "soul-search" about this problem, the *New York Times* and the rest of the Left in the country started its search with the soul of a former Republican vice presidential candidate.

"Ms. Giffords was . . . among a group of Democratic House candidates featured on the Web site of Sarah Palin's political action committee with cross hairs over their districts, a fact that disturbed Ms. Giffords at the time," the *New York Times* mentioned, again with no evidence the map was at all connected to the murders. During President Obama's speech at the memorial service for those killed, he was careful to assure the country that a "simple lack of civility" didn't cause the murders. Good for him. But he also said that "at a time when our discourse has become so sharply polarized—at a time when we are far too eager to lay the blame for all that ails the world at the feet of those who happen to think differently than we do—it's important for us to pause for a moment and make sure that we're talking with each other in a way that heals, not in a way that wounds."

It turned out Jared Lee Loughner was a schizophrenic young man with no discernible political views beyond conspiratorial ravings. His obsession with Giffords had begun long before Palin's map[1] ever existed, a map that he reportedly never laid eyes on. Loughner was not connected with any Tea Party groups, the Republican Party, or conservative causes, nor was he even a passing fan of Glenn Beck's *The Christmas Sweater*. He did list both *The Communist Manifesto* and *Mein Kampf* as among his favorite books in an online profile, but a high school friend of Loughner's told *ABC News* that the killer was apolitical: "He did not watch TV. He disliked the news. He didn't listen to political radio. He didn't take sides. He wasn't on the left. He wasn't on the right," Zach Osler told interviewer Ashleigh Banfield. In other words, the national discourse played no role in his deadly spree.

That fact didn't stop several Democrats from promptly offering federal remedies for our discourse. Representative Bob Brady (D-PA) proposed a bill making it a federal crime to use "language or symbols that could be perceived as threatening or inciting violence against a federal official or member of Congress," broadening a law that already criminalizes threats against lawmakers. He was joined by Representative Rubén Hinojosa (D-TX). Representative Louise Slaughter's (D-NY) tool of choice was the FCC. In the national quest to cool our rhetoric, "Part of that has to be what we hear over the air waves," she told a New York TV station.

As Mary Katharine wrote at the time in a posting for the *Daily Caller*, the rhetoric police who count themselves as liberals were "happy to let political speech be the hostage with a gun to its head in their cynical negotiations over what Sarah Palin is allowed to say." She noted:

> *It is not wise for a nation that prizes free speech to conflate political speech and violence. Even if there were evidence that*

---

[1] Others have chronicled the many, many, many instances in which Democrats have used "targeting" imagery and verbiage, both before and after the Giffords shooting. That shorthand is commonplace in American politics on a bipartisan basis. It is not an incitement to violence.

a crime perpetrated by a clearly disturbed individual had been inspired by political speech, suggesting one's peaceful fellow citizens are therefore guilty of abetting murder is not terribly good for public discourse. In the absence of such evidence, it is the worst kind of rhetorical poison. People who deplore the rhetoric of "Second-Amendment remedies" cannot solve the problem by seeking remedies to the First.

Conservative writer David Harsanyi warned about the cynical nature of this "national conversation" on civility with a piece in the *Denver Post* in 2011, not knowing the White House and the press would prove him so very right a year and a half later. "[T]his impending conversation about civility and our climate of hate is not only a useless one but also meant to discourage dissent," he wrote. He maintained that it "leaves the person with two choices: Revise your viewpoint or shut up. Which, of course, is the point."

In August 2012, there was ample evidence that a crime committed by a clearly disturbed individual had been inspired by political speech, yet national media, Democratic lawmakers, and the rhetoric police were highly *un*interested in drawing any conclusions from Corkins's rampage or the map he admitted to using to target his victims. Two full briefings with White House spokesman Jay Carney, on the day of and the day after the Family Research Council shooting, featured a brief opening statement that the president had been made aware of the shooting and deplored the violence, and a total of two questions about the incident. By contrast, the press conference immediately following the Tucson shooting featured almost nothing but questions about the tragedy; most of them hinged on the nation's discourse.

We'll leave this section with a fitting bookend: conservative writer and researcher John Sexton noticed something unusual in March 2013, several months removed from the Corkins shooting at FRC headquarters. The *New York Times* had published a story about social conservatives. Sexton noted in his post at *Breitbart* that the *Times* piece quoted an official from the Southern Poverty Law Center, and "mentions the SPLC's designation of the Family Research Council as a 'hate group' . . . Not mentioned by the *Times* is the fact that the FRC's headquarters was targeted last August by Floyd Lee Corkins using an address he took from the SPLC's 'Hate Map.'"

Surreal. In response, Sexton tweeted the following question: "Can you imagine the *NY Times* talking to Sarah Palin about Gabby Giffords without mentioning [the Loughner] shooting?" We cannot. Again, Palin had *absolutely nothing to do with* the bloodshed in Tucson, whereas the would-be FRC butcher explicitly cited SPLC as a key resource for plotting his bloodshed. By the way, we take issue with the SPLC's criteria for designating "hate groups," but we don't blame them for Corkins's actions. We raise the issue to further highlight the breathtaking double standard in media coverage.

When national media implies the routine political speech of innocent Americans causes or encourages violence by mentally disturbed actors, the implied, and sometimes explicit, remedy becomes that innocent Americans should stop voicing their political opinions.

THE VIOLENCE OF THE LAMBS

I n August of 2009, a month filled with health-care town-hall meetings, a national chorus of reporters, anchors, politicians, and public intellectuals decided the Republic was going to burn at the hands of their ideological adversaries. This did not come to pass. Despite the presence of heated debate and vocal opposition to President Obama's health-care law, the month went by with barely a hint of political violence. But you would never have known it from watching media coverage.

"The American right has a deep-seated problem with political violence," wrote *Talking Points Memo*'s Josh Marshall in August 2009. "The ideological pattern is clear going back at least thirty years and arguably for longer."

Among the hyperventilators was Robert Kuttner, writing in the *Washington Post*, and promptly violating Godwin's law:

> *When economically stressed and frightened people are anxious and sullen, you never know who will capture their fears and hopes. In the 1930s, economic anxiety produced leaders as different as Franklin Roosevelt and Adolf Hitler. History shows that if the reformist left doesn't offer a plausible story and strategy of reform, the lunatic right will gain ground even with an implausible one.*

Nina Burleigh of *Huffington Post* raised alarms:

> *It remains to be seen how far the brownshirts will test their supposedly threatened Constitutional freedoms, but I put my money on seeing more menace and more outright violence as they come to terms with losing political power and the economy in the same year.*

Roland Martin, then of CNN, bemoaned "rhetorical thuggery" and a "lynch mob" mentality dominating the health-care debate. DeWayne Wickham, in *USA Today*, claimed white racism had resulted in an "uptick of hateful public speech and in the growing number of threats by activists who are armed and motivated to do harm."[2]

Jamie Stiehm, a scholar at the Woodrow Wilson International Center for Scholars, declared with no historical perspective at all that "when long-serving Sen. Arlen Specter and Rep. John Dingell are shouted down by hostile home crowds, then we've got trouble," suggesting that the health-care town halls of 2009 had brought a crowd similar to those of the Philadelphia race riots of 1837.

Scripps Howard columnist Ann McFeatters cowered in the face of a "lynch-mob" mentality. She bemoaned the "screaming and shouting

---

[2] Matt Welch of *Reason* magazine diligently tracked overhyped media forecasts of the "race war that wasn't," as he called it, at the beginning of the Obama administration.

Rhetorician, Heal Thyself!

New York Times columnist **Paul Krugman** wrote in 2011, "It's the saturation of our political discourse—and especially our airwaves—with eliminationist rhetoric that lies behind the rising tide of violence" in post-Tucson America's "Climate of Hate," as the column was entitled.

Krugman, in 2008, bragged of throwing an Election Night party at which partygoers were encouraged to craft and "throw in an effigy" into his backyard fire pit. In Paul Krugman's eyes, telling progressives to, "by all means, hang Senator Joe Lieberman in effigy" conveniently does not count as "eliminationist."

"Where's that toxic rhetoric coming from?" Krugman sputtered in his piece. "Let's not make a false pretense of balance: it's coming, overwhelmingly, from the right."

Sure, if you systematically ignore all the toxic rhetoric from one side, it will indeed look as if it's only coming from the other. It's a neat trick, and one former White House press secretary **Robert Gibbs** executed in jaw-dropping fashion at a White House press briefing on November 6, 2009:

> I will continue to say what I've said before. You hear in this debate, you hear analogies, you hear references to, you see pictures about and depictions of individuals that are truly stunning, and you hear it all the time. People—imagine five years ago somebody comparing health care reform to 9/11. **Imagine just a few years ago had somebody walked around with images of Hitler.**

Gibbs was referring to signs that had popped up at anti-Obamacare rallies featuring the president with a Hitler mustache, which belonged to hangers-on of left-wing crackpot Lyndon LaRouche, not Tea Partiers, but neither he nor the media was interested in such distinctions. The space of just several years had apparently relieved him of all memory of the Left's protest movements of the Bush administration, which relied so heavily on Hitler imagery that BusHitler is still a universally understood epithet for the former president. The "unprecedented opposition" fallacy strikes again. Evidence:

Vice President Joe Biden, so often good cop to his congressional buddies, likened Republicans to "terrorists," according to *Politico,* during debt ceiling negotiations in 2011.

Senator Tom Harkin called the Tea Party as dangerous to America as the Civil War.

White House communications director **Dan Pfeiffer** broke out comparisons to kidnappers, suicide bombers, and arsonists in describing GOP budget tactics (!) during a single interview with CNN's Jake Tapper in September 2013. These were our self-appointed language hawks in the not-so-distant past.

President Obama himself used the sexual slur "teabaggers" for Tea Party activists in 2009, according to Jonathan Alter's book *The Promise: President Obama, Year One.* He called them "hostage-takers" over a disagreement about tax margins in 2010 and the debt ceiling in 2013, while contemporaneously claiming he'd "purposely kept my rhetoric down."

In the end, our point is not to take to the fainting couch over these insults. They are words, and it is dumb and disingenuous and chilling to equate them with imminent violence. But it is worth noting two rules of thumb. Those who most strenuously call for civility in public discourse are often those most willing to abandon it for their goals. And, as we've said elsewhere, the first to say he wants to have a national conversation is least likely to want that actual conversation to take place.

Finally, **Obama** again in his 2015 State of the Union address:

So the question for those of us here tonight is how we, all of us, can better reflect America's hopes. I've served in Congress with many of you. I know many of you well. There are a lot of good people here, on both sides of the aisle. And many of you have told me that this isn't what you signed up for—arguing past each other on cable shows, the constant fundraising, always looking over your shoulder at how the base will react to every decision . . . A better politics is one where we debate without demonizing each other.

Imagine if we broke out of these tired old patterns. Imagine if we did something different.

Imagine indeed. Rhetorician, heal thyself.

down" of legislators and protesters throwing around "false rumors as if they were hand grenades." E. J. Dionne of the *Washington Post* called health-care town halls populated with Tea Party supporters "the politics of the jackboot."

And David Frum, who can often be relied upon to see the worst in his nominal ideological brethren, intoned in his *FrumForum* posting "The Reckless Right Courts Violence," "Nobody has been hurt so far. We can all hope that nobody will be. But firearms and politics never mix well . . . All this hysterical and provocative talk invites, incites, and prepares a prefabricated justification for violence." There were indeed people who raised their voices even—gasp!—in the presence of elected officials. Frum is also correct there were people with firearms at town-hall meetings across the United States, but there were no incidents involving them. Mary Katharine reported in the *Weekly Standard* in 2009:

> There were . . . two prominent reports of people carrying guns outside Obama town halls. Police told news outlets that William Kostric was within his rights to carry a holstered handgun in New Hampshire on August 11, even at a protest. In Arizona, where there's also an open-carry law, both Obama supporters and critics were spotted with [alleged "assault weapons"] at an August 17 rally against Obamacare in Phoenix. None of the armed protesters threatened anyone, but MSNBC's Contessa Brewer took the opportunity to crop out the face of a black man with a firearm, even while asking if all these "white people showing up with guns" evinced a dangerous "racial overtone."

None of the media elite's fears were realized, no matter how much they imagined them in their own fevered rhetoric. What the flurry of statements did was prepare a prefabricated justification for pinning any violent act one could find on conservatives and their political speech. Mary Katharine cataloged all this for the *Weekly Standard* in August 2009: "Obamacare critics flooding town halls . . . had been called 'extremist mobs' by the Democratic National Committee, pawns of the insurance industry by Senator Dick Durbin, 'un-American' by Nancy Pelosi and Steny Hoyer, 'brownshirts' by Representative Brian Baird of Washington, 'manufactured' and 'Astroturf' by White House press secretary Robert Gibbs, 'evilmongers' by Senator Harry Reid, accused of 'fear-mongering' by the president, and been deemed 'political terrorists' by Representative Baron Hill of Indiana." But if one went looking for real-life episodes of political violence to warrant the tone of media coverage, one came up very short, as Mary Katharine did in a thorough survey of all verifiable violent acts at health-care town-hall meetings in the month of August 2009.

> *That's the full list of documented violence from the August meetings. In more than 400 events: one slap, one shove, three punches, two signs grabbed, one self-inflicted vandalism incident by a liberal, one unsolved vandalism incident, and one serious assault. Despite the left's insistence on the essentially barbaric nature of Obamacare critics, the video, photographic, and police report evidence is fairly clear in showing that **7 of the 10 incidents were perpetrated by Obama supporters and union members on Obama critics**. If you add a phoned death threat to Democrat representative Brad Miller of N.C., from an Obamacare critic, the tally is 7 of 11.*

Most of these incidents were very minor. In the interest of fairness, Mary Katharine kept the definition of "violence" broad enough to encompass even the ripping of signs—once in Denver when a "woman in a 'HOPE' Obama shirt, ripp[ed] a homemade anti-Pelosi sign from Obama critic Kris McLay's hands as she yelled in protest," and once in St. Louis when a white male who seemed to be an Obamacare critic "tore away the sign" of an Obamacare supporter before they were both escorted out by police.

That's it. That's the tally of violence from more than 400 allegedly fevered, racist, roiling health-care town halls in August 2009. By almost any measure, that's a success in a widely diverse country of 300 million people engaged in contentious, sustained civic engagement over some pretty high-stakes legislation. Some might say, "Good job, America!" But not those who were reporting on the Tea Party movement who wanted to find a pattern of right-wing violence.

Instead, they "treat[ed] a handful of distinct crimes as a sign of a rising menace without so much as bothering to check if there's been more small-scale rightist terror this year than in previous years," wrote Jesse Walker, author of *The United States of Paranoia: A Conspiracy Theory*, in his June 17, 2009, article "The Paranoids Are Out to Get Me!" at *Reason*. Walker calls this tendency to impose patterns of right-wing violence the "paranoia of the center."

For those invested in seeing a pattern, there was a pattern. Every single incident that could possibly augment that pattern became an emblem of the frightening Right the media had fashioned in its reporting in 2009. At times, the national news media went beyond projecting a tone that implied pervasive violence where there was little. When violent events happened, they routinely concocted connections to right-leaning politics with no evidence, as they had done in the Loughner shooting.

Gabriel Malor, a lawyer and blogger in Washington, D.C., has spent several years cataloging the various violent incidents attributed to the political Right during President Obama's term in office that later turned out to be either apolitical or inspired in part by liberal politics:

"Media assumptions that violence is right-wing are routine—and routinely wrong," he wrote in a 2012 *New York Post* column precipitated by the occasion of ABC News investigative reporter Brian Ross's speculation in the aftermath of the Aurora, Colorado, mass shooting that killed twelve that accused shooter James Holmes was a member of the Tea Party. He was not, but Ross's casual association of the two with no verification is representative of the media's reactions to such incidents.

Malor offers this troubling list and explains the tautology that leads to these repeated mistakes: "Media figures sincerely believe the right wing is violent, so naturally they assume that violent people must be right-wing."

> ** September 2009: The discovery of hanged census-taker Bill Sparkman in rural Kentucky fueled media speculation that he'd been killed by anti-government Tea Partiers. In fact, he'd killed himself and staged his corpse to look like a homicide so his family could collect on life insurance.*

> ** February 2010: Joe Stack flew his small plane into an IRS building in Austin, Texas. The media immediately suggested that the anti-tax rhetoric of the Tea Party led to the attack. In fact, Stack's suicide note quoted the* Communist Manifesto.

> ** That same month, a professor at the University of Alabama, Amy Bishop, shot and killed three colleagues at a faculty meeting. The gun-loving Tea Party came under immediate suspicion. But Bishop was a lifelong Democrat and Obama donor.*

> ** March 2010: John Patrick Bedell shot two Pentagon security officers at close range. The media went wild with speculation that a right-wing extremist had reached the end of his rope. Bedell turned out to be a registered Democrat and 9/11 Truther.*

> ** May 2010: New York authorities disarmed a massive car bomb in Times Square. Mayor Bloomberg immediately speculated that the bomber was someone upset about the president's new health-care law. The media trumpeted the idea that crazed conservatives had (again, they implied) turned to violence. In fact, the perp was Faisal Shahzad, an Islamic extremist.*

> ** August 2010: Amidst the debate over the Ground Zero Mosque, Michael Enright stabbed a Muslim cabdriver in the neck. It was immediately dubbed an "anti-Muslim stabbing," with "rising Islamophobia" on the political right to blame. In fact, Enright, a*

left-leaning art student, had worked with a firm that produced a pro-mosque statement.

* September 2010: James Lee, 43, took three hostages at the Discovery Channel's headquarters in Maryland. The media speculation was unstoppable: Lee was surely a "climate-change denier" who'd resorted to violence. Oops: He was an environmentalist who viewed humans as parasites on the Earth.

* January 2011: Jared Lee Loughner went on a rampage in Tucson, Ariz. Again the media knew just who to blame: the Tea Party and its extremist rhetoric. In fact, Loughner was mostly apolitical—a conspiracy theorist who, to date, has been judged too mentally incompetent to stand trial.

In 2013, Malor added the initial reaction to the Boston Marathon bombing to the list. Because it happened on April 15, many in the media immediately speculated it was a crime of antigovernment or tax protesters commemorating either Tax Day or Patriot's Day. In fact, the date holds significance for Muslim Chechen separatists, whose cause the Tsarnaev brothers embraced.

We'll add another instance you probably haven't heard of: in the early morning hours of September 11, 2014, someone attempted to fire-bomb the district offices of Missouri congressman Emanuel Cleaver,[3] a Democrat.

An investigation determined that the perpetrator was a twenty-eight-year-old white male who held very intense political opinions, such as: "The Missouri congress has been a willing partner in the US governments [sic] capitalist war hungry agenda." Ah. The dude was a

---

[3] Cleaver, we should also mention, was one of the members who supposedly was spat upon and called the N-word by protesters gathered at the Capitol to protest an impending Obamacare vote in 2010. The late Andrew Breitbart offered to donate $10,000 to the United Negro College Fund if anyone would furnish evidence that either had taken place. Despite cameras and footage galore, no documentation of the offending actions and epithets was ever produced.

Far Left "Occupy" type. Rather than touching off a national civility emergency, the arrest of Eric King was met with ordinary, mostly local, news coverage. The Congressional Black Caucus released a statement offering a rote condemnation of "vandalism," and scolding King for his "ineffective means of voicing discontent or disagreement." If Eric King had been a conservative talk-radio junkie, he would have been treated exactly the same way, right?

Which brings us to another reminder that the Left isn't alone in pursuing demagoguery for the purpose of silencing ideological opponents. When two NYPD officers were gunned down in cold blood just before Christmas 2014, some on the Right quickly blamed the murders on those who'd encouraged or participated in recent antipolice protests over the killings of two unarmed black men earlier in the year. Perhaps some sensed a chance to dole out payback for the entirely undeserved bruising the Right sustained post-Tucson for a shooter wholly unconnected to its movement. Conservatives launched accusations in the immediate aftermath of the double murder and marshaled evidence of the shooter's motivations—which were far more obviously related to the Left's politics than Loughner's had ever been to conservative goals—to make liberals pay a price for this association.

Some accused Al Sharpton, New York City mayor Bill de Blasio, and even President Obama of having "blood on their hands," because the protests had fueled an anticop climate, pushing an unstable ex-con over the edge. Although some demonstrators came awfully close to incitement with disgusting chants about dead cops (certainly far worse than anything Sarah Palin or the Tea Party ever did), we still reject this mode of thinking. Attributing the heinous acts of a killer to a protest movement is, fundamentally, a form of speech suppression. Even if we concede that the murderer's actions were related to the protests' charged atmosphere and rhetoric (which it seems they were), then what? What's the endgame of this criticism beyond "Your political speech, which offends us, is dangerous and causing cop killings—so shut up"? A subsequent YouGov poll showed that a large majority of self-identified conservatives agreed that it is unacceptable for "elected officials to criticize certain police practices in public." *No, no, no.*

This impulse is uncharitable to fellow citizens, most of whom are not criminals, and antithetical to the conservative notion that a free people should have and exercise the power to check and critique the powers of the state. How, pray tell, do we limit government power without criticizing its practices in public?

Ask Not What the Facts Can Do for Your Ideological Assumptions

On the fiftieth anniversary of the assassination of President John F. Kennedy, the media dusted off an old chestnut. The cauldron of heated right-wing rhetoric that was Dallas in 1963 had inspired Lee Harvey Oswald to kill the president, the story goes. A *New York Times* op-ed called Dallas "the city with a death wish in its eye" and faulted it for not "grappling with its painful legacy." *Washingtonian* magazine declared, "The city of hate had, in fact, killed the president."

A *Washington Post* opinion piece by a Texas journalism professor was titled, subtly, "Tea Party has roots in Dallas of 1963," blaming a "strident minority [that] hijacked the civic dialogue and brewed the boiling, toxic environment waiting for Kennedy the day he died." The piece also name-checks retired General Edwin Walker as a potent part of this toxic mixture—an irony elucidated by a cursory understanding of Lee Harvey Oswald, the man who actually shot the president.

Oswald was a disgruntled former marine and Communist who defected to the Soviet Union. His first assassination attempt was against . . . the aforementioned famous anti-Communist, John Bircher, and segregationist, General Edwin Walker. That would make Oswald an odd right-wing extremist attacking his own.

WE'RE ALL EXTREMISTS NOW

The Department of Homeland Security issued a 2009 report, titled *Rightwing Extremism: Current Economic and Political Climate Fueling Resurgence in Radicalization and Recruitment*, warning of "rightwing extremism" early in President Obama's first term and giving credence to the exaggerated concerns of the commentariat with exaggerated warnings of its own. It defined *extremism* so broadly as to potentially ensnare most of the mainstream Right. "Rightwing extremism in the United States can be broadly divided into those groups, movements, and adherents that are primarily hate-oriented (based on hatred of particular religious, racial, or ethnic groups), and those that are mainly anti-government, rejecting federal authority in favor of state or local authority, or rejecting government authority entirely. It may include groups and individuals that are dedicated to a single issue, such as opposition to abortion or immigration," the report stated.

The threat warning from DHS, an armed, powerful law enforcement branch of the federal government, was based on the *thoughts* of citizens, not their deeds. "Threat reports that focus on ideology instead of criminal activity are threatening to civil liberties and a wholly ineffective use of federal security resources," wrote Michael German, senior policy counsel to the ACLU,[4] in April 2009 in a statement entitled, "Soon, We'll All Be Radicals." Jesse Walker of *Reason* magazine also reported that a publication distributed by the Missouri Information Analysis Center, a taxpayer-funded organization advising police, conflated anyone with a Gadsden flag, Constitution Party, Campaign for Liberty, Libertarian, Bob Barr, or Ron Paul sticker on their car as a probable member of extremist militias.

The combination of these cultural and governmental forces constitute what one researcher has called the third "brown scare" in American history. Philip Jenkins, a Baylor University historian of the

---

[4] Um, *thanks*, ACLU. No, really. They're not always wrong.

American Right, identifies these waves of fear of the Right as the lesser-known equivalents of Red scares. Red scares have a better publicist than their mirror image, in which the center-left engages in the same paranoid furor it decried in the Communist hunters of the past. In red and brown scare alike, not all wariness is unwarranted, but it's often taken too far in its tendency to demonize and discount fellow citizens, particularly when the government becomes the agent of enforcement.

THE RIGHT AND WRONG KIND OF PROTESTS

The absence of alarm in the national media is as instructive as its presence. When it comes to protest movements like Occupy Wall Street—a lefty amalgam of run-of-the-mill liberals, socialists, hippies, anarchists, and people who couldn't make it to the G8—the media hardly raised a concern about the threat they might pose to the Republic, despite a slew of quite clear pronouncements about destroying the current order.

At the birth of the Occupy movement, September 2011, one of the group's first major actions was a populist parade of protesters across the Brooklyn Bridge. They mustered the march, without a permit, and took over traffic lanes. Please cast your mind back to the volume and depth of the news coverage and investigations allotted to the temporary blocking of two lanes of traffic on the George Washington Bridge by some underlings of New Jersey governor Chris Christie.[5] Now, we want you to imagine the opposite of that, because that's what you heard when hundreds of Occupy protesters were warned they'd be arrested if they walked in traffic lanes. The protestors confronted police and pushed forward anyway, yelling, "Take the bridge," and then were arrested in numbers upwards of seven hundred. It was a disruptive act,

---

[5]Who, we might add, immediately fired those responsible and insisted that he had absolutely no knowledge of the scheme—a claim that three separate inquiries have effectively confirmed.

but not a violent one. The Republic was not on the verge of collapse, but the same people who decried the mere "shouting down" of legislators at health-care town-hall meetings suddenly had no problem with the much more aggressive tactics of Occupy protesters.

In many cities, the rules for Occupy protests using public parks, police, and other resources were totally different from the rules the Tea Party had observed. In Richmond, Virginia, the local Tea Party incurred about $10,000 in costs over three years to hold an annual rally in a public park, paying fees for security, police, insurance, and porta-potties. When Occupy squatted in the exact same park for two straight weeks in October 2011, costing the city thousands for security presence and cleanup, they were charged nothing.

"The City of Richmond's picking and choosing whose First Amendment rights trump someone else's First Amendment rights and we thought—well that's fine—then they can refund our money," Colleen Owens told the local CBS TV station after the Tea Party delivered an invoice to the City of Richmond for their costs. Curiously, shortly after pointing out their unequal treatment under the law, the Tea Party of Richmond got a notice they were being audited. "What did they send to Occupy (Richmond)? Obviously, there's nothing to send to them because they didn't have (a business license or rally permit)," Owens told the *Richmond Times-Dispatch*. "It's kind of adding insult to injury. We complained about the unequal treatment, and they turned around and piled on more."

In Boston, the story was the same. Occupy Boston never sought permits and was not required to obtain them, while the Tea Party painstakingly observed the rules. "It's always a dangerous precedent when the city treats one group differently than another," said civil rights attorney Harvey Silverglate to the *Boston Herald*. "I'm opposed generally to these requirements, but if they are required of one group, then they should be required of all. The precedent [the city is setting] is, if there are so many people joining a demonstration that the city doesn't want to tangle with them, then they will waive the requirements."

One political movement's speech was literally freer than the other's, and the difference was based on who they were and what they believed. Ironically, it was the allegedly dangerous, antigovernment Tea Party types who conformed to the government's onerous and expensive prerequisites to freedom of assembly and got called lawless mobs for their trouble.

Meanwhile, a mere month after the Tucson memorial service and President Obama's call to "be civil because we want to live up to the example of public servants like John Roll and Gabby Giffords, who knew first and foremost that we are all Americans, and that we can question each other's ideas without questioning each other's love of country," it was out with the new tone and in with the old in Madison, Wisconsin.

As we referenced earlier, the Badger State's newly elected Republican governor was trying to pass a bill designed, in part, to limit collective bargaining rights of public employee unions to tackle fiscal problems. The duly elected governor had a duly elected majority with which to do this, but the political machine of the entire Left in the United States of America was not having it. At its height, there may have been as many as 100,000 protesters in Madison, camping in and around the statehouse, leaving its atrium looking like an episode of *Hoarders*. Death threats and mob actions were played down, as news reports beamed images of protesters chanting "This is what Democracy looks like!" into homes across the country. Different ideology, different rules.

Semiautomatic Ignorance Edition

FIREARMS: FACTS VS. FABLES

When the politically opportunistic among us aren't using tragedies to go after the freedoms afforded us by the First Amendment, they're using them to attack the Second. In their defense, there is at least an established connection between a killing perpetrated with a gun and, well, guns. In this sense, national debates over gun control are a more reasonable reaction to mass shootings than post-tragedy speech stifling, but that does not make them more realistic or fact based.

Far from it. The drive toward gun control is so thoroughly guided by emotionalism and moral panic that the facts aren't as helpful as one might hope. The Second Amendment survives these national bouts of outrage only because an impassioned segment of the populace is committed to defending their firearms against encroaching regulations. Gun owners vote on guns; not nearly as many gun controllers do.

In the aftermath of the unspeakably horrific Newtown massacre, both sides of the debate mobilized. Adam Lanza, a mentally ill twenty-year-old, shot and killed his mother with four gunshots to the head before heading to a local elementary school. The black-clad young man shot through the front window of the school and turned down the first hallway toward the first-grade classrooms. His hands outfitted with black fingerless gloves, he wielded a Bushmaster AR-15, the civilian version of the military M16, and was immediately confronted by the school's principal and the school psychologist, both of whom he murdered on the spot.

He skipped the first classroom on the hallway, whose teacher had closed her door upon hearing shots. Fittingly, a black piece of construction paper over the window from an earlier safety drill in the school may have convinced Lanza there was no one inside. He instead entered the first-grade classroom of substitute teacher Lauren Rousseau. The children were huddled in a back corner near a bathroom. Lanza murdered fourteen of them. One six-year-old girl who played dead survived. The little girl, whose name has never been released, reportedly told her mother when they were reunited, "I'm okay but all my friends are dead."

In the next first-grade classroom, teacher Victoria Soto tried to throw Lanza off track by herding her students into a closet and a bathroom and under desks toward the back of the room. She was reportedly walking back to lock the classroom door when Lanza entered. She tried to misdirect him by telling him the students were in the auditorium, but when a handful of students tried to run to safety, Lanza mercilessly murdered Soto and them before he killed himself, less than five minutes and more than 150 rounds into his demented mission. None of his twenty child victims was over seven years old.

We recount these details again so that we can all acknowledge their truly epic horror. Epic, not in the glib Internet use of the word, but to connote the immense, nearly unfathomable scope of it. We should all also acknowledge that no one wants anything like this to happen ever again. The question is, how do we get closer to that goal?

In the wake of a shooting, our commentariat talked about how terrible the National Rifle Association is, though neither the shooter nor his mother, from whom he stole his guns, was a member. We talked about the ease of obtaining guns in the United States, even though the guns in question were legally owned and acquired in the tough-gun-laws state of Connecticut. We talked about "assault weapons," regardless of whether the guns used in the crime match that concocted designation (Connecticut actually had a state assault weapons ban on the books at the time of the crime, so it's a stretch to argue a similar federal ban would have stopped it). We referred to guns as "military style" and "automatic" when they were semiautomatic (automatic weapons fire multiple shots when the trigger is pulled; semiautomatic guns fire one shot per trigger pull). We talked about how important it is to *do something*, and how those (the NRA, for instance) who would stop us from doing something are moral monsters who want more children to die. We equated the act of passing federal legislation with solving a problem, yet there was little to no discussion of how new gun-control laws will prevent the bulk of gun violence in America, which is not due to mass murder. And we pretended there were virtually no gun laws on the books when there are 243 pages of federal gun laws and 480 pages of state gun laws, which the NRA spends much of its time and money informing its members about so they can be the kind of law-abiding gun owners who don't murder people.

Though a horrific incident can certainly spur citizens to action and change minds, divorcing the facts of a case from the solutions proposed is not a good way to make policy. The fact is mass killings are not on the historical rise, and violent crime in the United States is near all-time lows, while gun ownership has reached an all-time high. You're more likely to be killed by someone's hands and feet than a rifle, shotgun, or "assault weapon."[1] Each of these are statistical realities that are obscured in the wake of a tragedy.

"Why are mass shootings becoming more common?" asked *Wonkblog* blogger Brad Plumer at the *Washington Post* in the days after Sandy Hook, before adding an update that negated his entire thesis: "It's also possible that mass shootings simply aren't on the upswing at all. See this newer post for data suggesting these shootings have remained constant since 1980 and haven't increased at all." Criminologist James Alan Fox of Northeastern University, who has studied mass shootings since the 1980s told the Associated Press, "There is no pattern, there is no increase." The AP reported on Minnesota criminologist Grant Duwe, who found that "while mass shootings rose between the 1960s and the

---

[1] FBI's Uniform Crime Report statistics of 2011.

1990s, they actually dropped in the 2000s. And, mass killings actually reached their peak in 1929, according to his data."

Fox theorizes that the increased media attention and the more pervasive presence of such coverage make rare mass killings hit closer to home and feel more frequent. Further, because the incidents *are* relatively rare, a momentary uptick of one or two incidents, as we experienced in 2011 and 2012, can feel like a sea change. That's not necessarily a bad thing, as feeling the pain of one's fellow citizens is an important part of life as part of a community. But it's important to remember in assessing any crime story that humans are generally pretty terrible at risk assessment. We're often driven to make policy decisions based on feelings about risk, rather than facts, in the wake of such an incident.

That's fine if the mere passage of legislation is a goal unto itself, to feel better and safer, regardless of the law's efficacy. But especially in the case of such tragedies, the goal should be to actually do something that would help. That's the harder, but more worthy, goal.

If we'd like to tackle crime problems, we must deal with real crime data. Some mass shootings are perpetrated with long guns—rifles, shotguns, AR-15s, and the like that those who are unfamiliar with guns[2] classify broadly as "the scary-looking ones." But here's the thing: the vast majority of gun crime in America is not perpetrated with long guns, and banning them does little to curb overall gun violence.

"This politically defined category of guns—a selection of rifles, shotguns and handguns with 'military-style' features—only figured in about 2 percent of gun crimes nationwide before the ban," Lois Beckett wrote in the *New York Times* in 2012, a year in which "only 322 people were murdered with any kind of rifle, F.B.I. data shows." The FBI's Uniform Crime Report statistics for 2011 show you're more likely to be

---

[2] This group includes, by his own admission, humble coauthor Guy Benson, who has never fired a gun. There is a standing offer from Mary Katharine to take this poor Northeastern sap to the range.

killed by "personal weapons" such as hands, feet, and fists than by a rifle or a shotgun.

In fact, one of the most overlooked crime stories of the past decades is that violent crime has plunged so precipitously. Gun crimes in the United States dropped by almost 40 percent between 1993 and 2011, despite the expiration of the federal assault weapons ban, according to a 2013 Bureau of Justice Statistics report—with nonfatal crimes falling almost 70 percent. This is just part of an overall trend that saw violent crime in the United States at a forty-year low in 2010, leaving criminologists scratching their heads at the unexpected decrease, especially during an economic downturn. But this may be one of the best stories about America that no one knows, according to a 2013 Pew study:

> *Despite national attention to the issue of firearm violence, most Americans are unaware that gun crime is lower today than it was two decades ago. According to a new Pew Research Center survey, today 56% of Americans believe gun crime is higher than 20 years ago and only 12% think it is lower.*

There are plenty of theories about the empirical drop, which is present across crime categories, populations, and communities— including more sophisticated and targeted policing, higher incarceration rates (which both have downsides of their own, it must be said), the rise of electronic forms of theft that preclude the need for risky stickups, the decrease in lead children are exposed to via gasoline and paint, and the waning of the crack and cocaine use trends. But the point is, effective legislating to make us safer can't happen when more than half the country thinks the world is getting more dangerous when it's getting dramatically, demonstrably safer. In this regard.

Convincing America the world is scarier is more profitable for media and for some advocates and legislators.

Which leads us to the most popular of all the gun-control gambits in the wake of national tragedies—the gun buyback program. Post-Newtown, forty House members signed a letter asking for a $200 million federal buyback program. The number of buyback programs and the number of guns collected went up after Sandy Hook—some 2,000 in L.A. and 100 in Miami, according to a *Daily Beast* report. "They make for good photo images," Michael Scott of the Center for Problem Oriented-Policing in Wisconsin told the *Cincinnati Enquirer*. "But gun buyback programs recover such a small percentage of guns that it's not likely to make much impact." Study after study has shown, as with long-gun bans, buyback programs aren't getting guns off the street.

Both programs are symbolic measures. It's understandably hard to resist the urge of such a seemingly simple and seductive solution in the wake of a tragedy, especially when the friends and family of the innocents slaughtered are calling for increased regulations. Parents like the father of little Jesse McCord Lewis, Neil Heslin of Newtown, who called for the ban of long guns like Lanza's at a meeting of the Gun Violence Prevention and Children's Safety task force in Connecticut:

> *I don't know how many people have young children or children. But just try putting yourself in the place that I'm in or these other parents that are here. Having a child that you lost. It's not a good feeling; not a good feeling to look at your child laying in a casket or looking at your child with a bullet wound to the forehead. I ask if there's anybody in this room that can give me one reason or challenge this question: Why anybody in this room needs to have an, one of these assault-style weapons or military weapons or high-capacity clips . . . Not one person can answer that question.*

The gun-rights supporters in the room answered the question posed by calling out, "Second Amendment," and Piers Morgan of CNN, MSNBC, and numerous other media outlets turned it into a story of bloodthirsty, shameless gun nuts "heckling" a grieving parent. Erik Wemple, media critic for the *Washington Post*, reviewed the tape of Heslin's testimony and declared the exchange a "model of civil and patient discussion of a pressing public matter," if not for the distortions of those who used it to make their political adversaries into monsters. (From "Here's why Newtown victim's father was NOT heckled," *Washington Post*, January 30, 2013.) There was another voice in the wake of Newtown, one who was given very little attention and very little moral authority. Mark Mattioli, who lost his six-year-old James in the shooting, told the same Gun Violence Prevention task force, "The problem is not gun laws." "I don't care if you named it 'James' law,' I don't want [another law]," he told the commission. "I think there's much more promise for a solution in identifying, researching, and creating solutions along the lines of mental health issues—I think there's a lot of work that can be done there." He also called out the media for its gun ignorance, saying, "I think there's been talk about fear in the media, and I think a lot of it's been from the left, talking about what is a semiautomatic? You pull the trigger once, one bullet comes out." Mattioli also later backed the NRA's 225-page School Shield Task Force report, to very little fanfare.

Liberal columnist Tommy Christopher of *Mediaite* wondered about the blackout on Mattioli: "Whether I agree with him or not, though, Mark Mattioli deserves to be heard. I can't prove that his politics are the reasons he hasn't been, but it's tough for me to think of another complicating factor. To the pro–gun regulation crowd, he's an anomaly in a sea of victims they agree with, and maybe someone they're afraid to disagree with for fear of looking bad. That shouldn't be the case. Just as I've continually insisted that pro-gun legislators should have the courage to look parents like Neil Heslin in the eye, so should those in favor of gun regulations have the courage to engage Mr. Mattioli honestly and respectfully."

Indeed, hearing that two men, two fathers who lost children, can honestly disagree about this issue would be healthy for the debate. It would preclude the politically charged implication that everyone who disagrees with more gun regulations wants more children to die. But people with Absolute Moral Authority are sometimes hard to argue with, which is why the media often only grants it to one side. In the end, about one thousand pieces of gun legislation were considered nationwide in the wake of Sandy Hook—"about half to expand gun rights and about half to curtail them," according to PBS—*Frontline* and "by the end of 2013, only 43 gun-control laws had passed," often with grave political consequences for those who passed them.[3] By contrast, "27 states have passed 93 laws expanding gun rights." Second Amendment supporters mostly won the legislative battle.

Though they were portrayed mercilessly as nasty, violent, bought-off Neanderthals who want more people murdered, their efficacy demanded at least grudging respect from political commentators post-Newtown. When another grieving parent, Richard Martinez, called for congressional action and federal gun control in the wake of the Isla Vista shooting perpetrated by Elliot Rodger, the *Washington Post*'s Chris Cillizza conceded that mere "grief won't change the gun debate. It just won't."

Grief isn't an illegitimate catalyst for political action. But problem solving requires clear thinking and respect for evidence. Emotional efforts dressed up as compassion to silence dissenters won't get us there.

---

[3] Also, lots of unintended consequences. *National Review* writer Charles C. W. Cooke has done an exceptional job chronicling the wages of thoughtless overreach, particularly as it pertains to New York's uniquely shoddy law.

8

BAKE ME A CAKE, BIGOTS

Gay Rights and Authentic Coexistence

Let's talk about "Coexist" bumper stickers for a second. You've definitely seen them around. They're those blue strips with white lettering that assemble a collection of religious icons and mystical symbols (e.g., an Islamic crescent, a Star of David, a Christian cross, a peace sign, a yin-yang) to spell out a simple message of inclusion and tolerance. Perhaps you instinctively roll your eyes at these advertisements of moral correctness. Perhaps you find the sentiment worthwhile, but you're not a wear-your-politics-on-your-fender type of person. Or perhaps you actually have "Coexist" bumper stickers affixed to both your Prius *and* your Beamer. Whatever floats your boat, man; far be it from us to cast stones.

But we bring up these particular morality minibillboards to illustrate a bothersome dichotomy. If we were to draw a Venn diagram of (a) the people who flaunt their socially responsible "coexist" values for fellow motorists, and (b) the people who believe that, say, an evangelical Christian who owns a local flower shop ought to be sued and shamed for politely declining to provide floral arrangements for a same-sex wedding, the resulting circles would more or less overlap.

The coexist message: *You people* (i.e., conservatives) need to get on board and start coexisting with groups that might make you uncomfortable. It says so right here on my highly enlightened bumper sticker.

But don't you dare ask me to tolerate the "intolerance" of people with whom I disagree. Because that's different.

Is it, though? We believe that if Americans from across the political spectrum genuinely internalized and lived out the coexist message—rather than leaned on it as a form of social preening—the country would be much better off. Aggressive *anti*-coexistence permeates our national debate on gay rights, wherein activists on both sides seem to reflexively believe the worst about each other.

These wicked gays are trying to poison our morality, convert The Children, and bring down Western civilization through sexual anarchy!

Traditional conservatives are homophobic bigots who hate gay people and deserve to be drummed out of polite society!

Take a breath, everyone.

Cards-on-the-table time.[1] We're fairly liberal on a number of gay rights issues, including marriage equality—although we believe the right/left dichotomy on these questions is sliding into obsolescence. More on that in a moment. This book isn't really about policy prescriptions, nor does it fit into the "GOP comeback" genre, but here's our short pitch for gay marriage from a conservative perspective: conservatives should encourage, not oppose, stable, committed relationships, monogamy, and the family unit. Moreover, from a public policy perspective, a number of long-standing arguments against same-sex unions are less potent and persuasive than ever, including the "sanctity of marriage" slogan.

---

[1] Guy here. So, I'm gay. Friends and family have known for a number of years now, but I haven't mentioned it publicly for two reasons: First, I don't think it's most people's business, to be perfectly frank. Second, I didn't want my emerging career to be colored by identity politics. My aim was to allow my work and my character to speak for me, as opposed to some category into which I could be lazily pigeonholed. The thought of my sexuality hindering *or* helping my career trajectory is anathema to me, so I've chosen to remain strategically quiet. Why "come out" now? Because I'm coauthoring a chapter that addresses gay rights at length. I decided that I owed readers this relevant piece of personal context; it's the correct and respectful thing to do. And it's *literally* a footnote. So there you have it: I'm a Christian, an American, a conservative, a sports fan, a son, a brother, and a friend—who happens to be gay.

In terms of optics, it seems like many opponents of government-codified same-sex unions are fixated on blocking the expansion of the definition of what marriage entails vis-à-vis a tiny fraction of Americans. Heterosexuals have done far more to erode the sanctity and seriousness of marriage than gays could ever dream of, whether through rampant infidelity, or the explosion of no-fault divorce. When the vast majority of hand-wringing about "traditional marriage" focuses on roughly 3 percent of the population's inclusion or exclusion from the institution, rather than a full-blown marriage crisis taking root throughout the West, it smacks of hypocrisy, misplaced priorities, and narrowly tailored judgment.

On the flip side, we're not especially impressed with the "stop imposing your values!" argument in favor of gay marriage because virtually *all* laws involve the imposition of values. The people who employ this argument are more than happy to forcibly impose their values on the rest of us on any number of fronts, including this one. Still, we would respectfully challenge religious opponents of same-sex marriage on whether they would favor using the power of the state to outlaw other sexual behavior or unions that offend their moral code. Should there be a renewed push to legally prohibit adultery or premarital sex? If your position is that homosexual *activity* shouldn't be criminal, but marriages that codify such relationships shouldn't be permitted, would you also favor legislation proscribing heterosexual marriages for couples brought together by extramarital affairs? Wouldn't that marriage be rooted in immorality and sin? We're not moral relativists, and we obviously agree that some sexual behavior and manifestations *should* remain illegal (for instance, we're happy to "impose our values" on pedophilia as a criminal abomination). We're just encouraging you to engage in some introspection where you draw moral and legal lines, and *why*.

A final, important point on our own stance on this issue: we respect the fact that the vast majority of traditional marriage supporters are not mean-spirited bigots, and we don't pretend that society should blindly rush to reimagine a definitional, millennia-old institution without some significant measure of trepidation, reflection, and debate. Decent, kind people can harbor good-faith disagreements on these policy questions, and they should be afforded the space to articulate and advocate their views. This requires a generosity of spirit and *actual* tolerance.

Regardless of our personal opinions, the overall direction of America's marriage debate is indisputable. Public polling has measured a precipitous spike in support for same-sex marriage. According to Gallup's figures, just 27 percent of Americans expressed support for legally recognized gay marriage in 1996, with 68 percent opposed. Less than two decades later, the data lines have crossed; 55 percent of respondents said they favored gay marriage in a spring 2014 survey, with a 42 percent minority opposed. An astounding swing. Self-identified Republicans have adopted an increasingly open-minded posture on these issues, as well. A McClatchy/Marist poll released in late 2014 showed that nearly seven in ten Republicans "would be no less likely to support a well-qualified gay candidate, and 59 percent say they prefer that states decide same-sex marriage rather than the federal government—a stance that effectively is allowing such unions to take hold across the country," as summarized by the *Washington Post*. Both percentages were *higher* among Tea Party supporters. Quite a shift for a supposedly insular, radicalized, aging "anti-gay" party. The same survey revealed that 71 percent of American adults know a "friend, colleague or family member" who is gay. That number was just 39 percent in 1999. There's your flashing neon explanatory sign if you're looking for one. The more likely you are to know a real, living, breathing gay person, the less likely you are to oppose gay marriage.

A major underpinning of this sea change in public attitudes is a massive generational shift. Young people are overwhelmingly in favor of same-sex marriage. The numbers are striking and lopsided. A 2014 Pew Research survey of Republican-leaning Americans under the age of thirty pegged support for gay marriage at ($^{61}/_{35}$), a whopping margin.

Young millennials of faith are peeling away from traditional orthodoxy, too. A 2011 poll of Christians conducted by the Public Religion Research Institute found that nearly half of self-identified *evangelicals* under the age of thirty favor legalized gay marriage. The survey measured "at least a 20 point generation gap between Millennials (age 18–29) and seniors (65 and over) on every public policy measure in the survey concerning rights for gay and lesbian people."

Our purpose in recapitulating these statistics is not to demoralize gay marriage opponents, or to spike the football, or to, um, end the discussion on the matter. Polling isn't a reason for people to abandon religious or moral convictions, obviously. But, as we asserted earlier, productive discussions require eyes-wide-open assessments of relevant facts and information. These trends are empirically documented and hugely politically significant.

We're the first to admit that we don't have a neat, turnkey solution for the GOP to move forward in its vote-seeking mission when a sizable portion of its base would sit at home if the party "went wobbly" on marriage, while future generations of voters hold radically different views. For many young people, Republicans' continued opposition to gay marriage is a barrier to entry, period. They won't listen to our ideas on taxes, health care, and entitlement reform if they think we're denying basic fairness and rights to them or their gay friends. Marriage equality opponents' answers to that core complaint have failed to convince most young people, and the political implications of that reality cannot be ignored.

THE PURGE

While we've been pleased to see transformative, empathetic progress on one front of this issue, we've been seriously alarmed by what we'd call a malignant strain of gay rights "mission creep." A big reason why public opinion has moved so dramatically in recent years is that gay marriage supporters have delivered highly effective appeals to Americans' libertarian sensibilities and innate sense of fairness. Slogans like "our love and our marriage doesn't affect you" hit the mark. *Hey, it's a free country—whenever possible, live and let live.* But now that support for gay rights has claimed the political high ground, some activists' tactics are taking an ugly turn. The mind-set has moved from a "leave us alone" message of tolerance and equality to a vindictive campaign of score settling and enforced celebration. *You will validate our love, or else.* This mentality was crystallized by *Washington Post* columnist and MSNBC contributor Jonathan Capehart (who is openly gay) during the Michael Sam/NFL controversy. He explicitly argued that tolerance should *not* work both ways, and that dissenters on gay issues will be "made" to change their thinking:

> [T]olerance, no, is not—it should not be a two-way street. It's a one-way street. You cannot say to someone that who you are is wrong, an abomination, is horrible, get a room, and all of those other things that people said about Michael Sam, and not be forced—not forced, but not be made to understand that what you're saying and what you're doing is wrong.

"Made to understand." Does a more Orwellian formulation exist in the English language?

Look, we have no quarrel with the notion that personal slurs and identity-related put-downs aren't cool (actual homophobic harassment and abuse *does* exist, and should be roundly denounced), but the Capeharts of the world aren't merely promoting civility. They want to invalidate and eradicate an entire value set through a confection of lawsuits, shaming, bullying, and mandatory reeducation.[2] The laudable "win-

---

[2] Miami Dolphins defensive back Don Jones was fined and suspended for tweeting "horrible" as Michael Sam kissed his boyfriend on live television. The public display of affection came as Sam reacted to being drafted by the St. Louis Rams, becoming the first openly gay player in NFL history. The Dolphins said Jones would not be reinstated until he underwent "sensitivity training." We agree Jones could have been a *lot* more sensitive, but to put his sanctions in perspective, the League initially fined and

ning hearts and minds" stage has given way to an era of dissent-stomping recriminations and ideological vengeance—which, we might add, serve to validate some of the fears of traditional marriage supporters who predicted it. Illustrative examples of this phenomenon are demoralizingly plentiful.

Among the most alarming examples is the well-publicized case of former Mozilla CEO Brendan Eich, whose unceremonious ouster from the company he helped build was one of the catalysts that got us off our asses to write this book. Shortly after he assumed the chief executive position in March 2014, Eich's leadership encountered a sustained blitz from gay rights activists and Mozilla employees over a 2008 political contribution. Eich had donated $1,000 in support of Proposition 8, California's statewide constitutional referendum defining marriage as one man and one woman. That ballot measure ended up succeeding on the very same day that California's electorate also handed Barack Obama[3] a landslide victory. Prop 8 rode heavy support from Hispanics and blacks (just over half of the former group, and roughly seven in ten among the latter, according to exit polls)—among others—to secure passage. For the crime of engaging in political activism on behalf of a mainstream stance six years prior, the mob demanded that Eich publicly renounce his opinion and explicitly endorse gay marriage. "If he cannot," a petition signed by more than seventy-five thousand people read, "he should resign. And if he will not, the board should fire him immediately."

Eich pushed back initially, noting that he'd scrupulously left his political and religious views at the office door throughout his career at the tech company. In an interview with CNET, he rejected the comparison between gay marriage opposition and racism, and defended his right to free expression. "It's still permissible," he said. "Beliefs

---

suspended Baltimore Ravens star Ray Rice for just two games after he . . . severely beat his then fiancée, dragging her unconscious body out of an elevator in Atlantic City, on camera. The proportionality of NFL justice is a mysterious beast.

[3] Obama himself was "against" gay marriage at the time.

that are protected, that include political and religious speech, are generally not something that can be held against even a CEO." A gay Mozilla executive named Christie Koehler came to Eich's defense in a post on her personal *Subfictional Studios* blog, expressing her "disappointment" that he'd donated to the Prop 8 campaign, but praising his nondiscriminatory leadership style: "Certainly [the donation] would be problematic if Brendan's behavior within Mozilla was explicitly discriminatory," she wrote. "I haven't personally seen this . . . To the contrary, over the years I have watched Brendan be an ally in many areas and bring clarity and leadership when needed."

Here we have a gay employee vouching for Eich's character and skill set, while attesting to the fact that his personal beliefs on marriage impacted neither his treatment of colleagues nor his leadership of the company. But his actions and behavior were irrelevant to the purgers. He'd offended them by making a financial contribution that betrayed his privately held moral beliefs on a charged issue. His beliefs differed from theirs. Ergo, they moved swiftly to deprive him of his livelihood—again, not because of his work-related *conduct*, but because of his *thoughts*. Under intense pressure, Eich resigned, after which Mozilla quickly released an apparently unironic statement professing their commitment to free speech. GLAAD, a gay rights organization, one-upped them, cheering that the company's decision helped to ensure that corporate America is "inclusive, safe, and welcoming to all." The phrase "welcoming to all" did not contain an asterisk. Guy wrote about the episode at *Townhall* on April 3, 2014:

> *Are traditionalist religious people now* prima facie *unqualified to lead companies—or to hold any position of authority in the private sector, for that matter? This is madness. And it's corrosive to the soul of our country. Don't get me wrong: I'm not arguing that Mozilla didn't have the right to bow to a noisy and influential group of customers and investors (addendum: and employees). But the ability to boycott—or the success of a*

boycott—is not necessarily a reflection of its prudence, justice, or kindness. The impulse to purge and punish divergent political viewpoints does not enrich us as a nation. Nor does it make us more free—and we're a nation founded on liberty.

I appreciate that many gay people believe their claim on said liberty has been unfairly denied for too long. But most would also surely agree that much progress has been made on that front. The gay rights cause has been best advanced by winning hearts and minds, not by instilling fear or exacting perverse moral retribution. That's part of why these purges are so troubling. Anyone who values genuine *tolerance and freedom ought to reject them. But if one ultimately feels compelled to join the jackals in this spiteful, score-settling crusade, one should at least have the intellectual integrity to permanently surrender one's "tolerance" card.*

Andrew Sullivan is a prominent gay blogger who was an impassioned advocate for gay marriage long before it was cool. We have strenuous disagreements with Sullivan on many issues,[4] but he's written with admirable moral clarity about the Eich affair. Reacting to the CEO's departure, Sullivan fired off a cutting blog post at *The Dish* entitled "The Hounding of a Heretic," raising a number of how-far-does-this-go? questions. "Will [Mr. Eich] now be forced to walk through the streets in shame? Why not the stocks?" he asked, rebuking fellow gay rights champions. "The whole episode disgusts me—as it should disgust anyone interested in a tolerant and diverse society. If this is the gay rights movement today—hounding our opponents with a fanaticism more like the religious right than anyone else—then count me out. If we are about intimidating the free speech of others, we are no better than the anti-gay bullies who came before us." We could do

---

[4] His infamous and extended theorizing about the contents of Sarah Palin's womb was singularly bizarre, for example.

without the contemptuous shots at the "religious right," but that's how Sullivan rolls. Responding to incensed liberal readers, Sullivan expanded on the point Guy made about the distinction between rights and *what's* right:

> . . . *Of course Mozilla has the right to purge a CEO because of his incorrect political views. Of course Eich was not stripped of his First Amendment rights. I'd fight till my last breath for Mozilla to retain that right. What I'm concerned with is the substantive reason for purging him. When people's lives and careers are subject to litmus tests, and fired if they do not publicly renounce what may well be their sincere conviction, we have crossed a line. This is McCarthyism applied by civil actors. This is the definition of intolerance. If a socially conservative private entity fired someone because they discovered he had donated against Prop 8, how would you feel? It's staggering to me that a minority long persecuted for holding unpopular views can now turn around and persecute others for the exact same reason. If we cannot live and work alongside people with whom we deeply disagree, we are finished as a liberal society.*

Amen. We couldn't have said it better ourselves. Sullivan captures the essence of *End of Discussion* in a single paragraph of distilled truth. But while Sullivan forswears some gay rights activists' fanatical hounding impulses, others seem hungry for more. Richard Kim, the (obviously liberal) executive editor of the *Nation*'s website, appeared on the MSNBC show *All In with Chris Hayes* shortly after Brendan Eich was forced out at Mozilla. He recounted the following story, with some degree of concern, about a conversation he had with his "gay activist friends" after they'd whacked Eich:

> *Here's a disturbing thing. I did ask some of my gay activist friends, I was like, "Look, here's a list; 6,500 people gave the*

same amount that he did or more in California. Should we go down the list and sort of start targeting all these people?" And I asked this facetiously, and people were like, "Let's do it! Let's find out where those people live!"

We're not in Equalityville anymore, Toto.

The gay enforcement squad also set its sights on two reality shows in recent years, yielding mixed results. In December 2013, the Internet basically exploded when A&E announced its suspension of Phil Robertson, star of the cable network's runaway reality hit *Duck Dynasty*. Robertson is the family patriarch on the show, known for his camo-patterned bandannas, flowing gray beard, and devout Christian faith. He credits God with plucking him from a dark path earlier in life and leading him to salvation and redemption. Phil Robertson's blunt, take-no-prisoners approach to life isn't much of a secret. It's part of the reason he has a show, in fact. He doesn't think much of political correctness, an attitude he made abundantly clear in an interview with *GQ* magazine. When asked about the nature of sin, Robertson included homosexuality in a long list of sexual behaviors forbidden in biblical passages, including adultery and bestiality.

Later, he expressed personal puzzlement over how any man could prefer—shall we say—men's nether regions to women's, but added that it's not his place to judge: "We never, ever judge someone on who's going to heaven, hell," he averred. "That's the Almighty's job. We just love 'em, give 'em the good news about Jesus—whether they're homosexuals, drunks, terrorists. We let God sort 'em out later, you see what I'm saying?"

We do, actually: Love thy neighbor as thyself, and judge not, lest ye be judged. Perhaps lumping gays in with alcoholics *and terrorists* isn't the most artful phrasing of all time, but we suspect Phil Robertson isn't overly concerned with artful phrasing. This is an old-school man of the bayou, saved through grace, articulating traditional Christian doctrine with his own inimitable verve. We may disagree with some of his beliefs and wince at some of his answers, but we understand that this is an authentic person being authentic. You know, actual *reality*. Others weren't as understanding. Following an orchestrated outrage campaign—petitions, blog posts, press releases, tweets, and so on— A&E condemned Robertson's comments and placed him on indefinite hiatus from the show.

The network's official statement assured the grievance mongers that A&E has "always been strong supporters and champions of the LGBT community," adding that Robertson's opinions "in no way reflect those of A & E networks." Well, yeah. Is there a solitary person in the world who would assume that an unscripted, un-PC statement from a Louisiana swamp person/reality TV personality might somehow represent the views of Manhattan-based executives of the channel that airs his show? C'mon. The outrage SWAT team at GLAAD, ever at the ready to take offense "on behalf of" an entire community, weighed in with a rote denunciation from spokesperson Wilson Cruz:

> *Phil and his family claim to be Christian, but Phil's lies about an entire community fly in the face of what true Christians believe. He clearly knows nothing about gay people or the majority of Louisianans—and Americans—who support legal recognition for loving and committed gay and lesbian couples. Phil's decision to push vile and extreme stereotypes is a stain on A&E and his sponsors who now need to re-examine their ties to someone with such public disdain for LGBT people and families.*

As Mary Katharine quipped at the time, that statement "doesn't really seem to match Robertson's actual comments, but I'm guessing they're just in cut-and-paste mode at this point." The suspension and apology triggered a furious backlash from *Duck Dynasty* fans, who melted down social media in support of Robertson. Amid threats of boycotts and counterboycotts, and public complaints from public officials like Louisiana governor Bobby Jindal, A&E reversed its decision after nine short days. It took an organic tidal wave of fury to beat the outrage machine, and sanity eventually prevailed—but not before an outpouring of *outrageous outrage* from all sides. Is this what "victory" looks like?

In 2014, David and Jason Benham—twin brothers tapped by HGTV to cohost a new home renovation show—were dropped by the network when a left-wing website, called *Right Wing Watch*, attacked David for holding "anti-choice, anti-gay extremist" views. Benham reportedly took part in a prayer vigil outside the 2012 Democratic National Convention in Charlotte in which he decried "homosexuality and its agenda that is attacking the nation." Benham was also active in the campaign for North Carolina's sweeping ban on same-sex unions.[5] The usual suspects came out of the woodwork, scandalized that someone with an opposing viewpoint (expressed in caustic terms) would have an opportunity to host an entirely apolitical television program. HGTV, seemingly caught flat-footed by the controversy, severed ties with the duo in a tweet: "HGTV has decided not to move forward with the Benham Brothers' series."

But Jason Benham told CNN's Erin Burnett that HGTV was absolutely aware of his brother's comments, having raised them during the vetting process many months earlier. "When [the network]—a year and a half ago—saw some of the footage where my brother was saying the things he was saying, they spoke with us," Benham said. "They got to know us a little better and then they made a judgment call, recognizing that David and I have no hate in our heart for anyone. We've been running a successful real estate company for the last 11 years and we help all people. There is no discrimination." But as we've seen, a dearth of tangible acts of bigotry and discrimination isn't sufficient anymore. The punishment crowd kicked up the decibels, and the

---

[5]Amendment One passed overwhelmingly (61 to 39 percent) on May 8, 2012. The state constitutional amendment prohibited gay marriages *and* civil unions. We would have voted "no."

Incivility as a Virtue

S ome gay rights proponents are pleased as punch with the impo- sition of this emerging, toxic environment of viewpoint punish- ment. Acerbic *New York Times* blogger Josh Barro, son of famed economist Robert Barro, made this explicitly clear in a series of online exchanges with Heritage Foundation scholar Ryan Anderson. Barro is gay[6] and an atheist; Anderson, a Catholic, is one of the country's lead- ing academically oriented opponents of same-sex marriage. Both are bright, erudite, young men who disagree profoundly on public policy questions in this vein. The latter engages (persuasively, and other- wise) in respectful discourse on these issues; the former, not so much. "Anti-LGBT attitudes," Barro declared on Twitter, are "terrible," so "we need to stamp them out, ruthlessly." He later magnanimously clarified that he wasn't advocating *killing* people, just casting their opinions as

---

[6] Barro has written and tweeted separately about gay people's "duty" to come out, and he was critical of NBA player Jason Collins's "belated" decision to do so. We anxiously await Mr. Barro's all-important verdict on the timing and nature of Guy's "duty fulfillment," or whatever—which transpired several pages ago, in case he missed it.

Benham brothers lost their show. Here's how HGTV once promoted the erstwhile program in a press release:

> *After a decade of flipping houses for profit, brothers David Ben- ham and Jason Benham now help families buy the homes they never thought they could afford. In each episode, the guys help a deserving family find a fixer-upper and transform it into their forever home—with a healthy dose of sibling rivalry between the brothers along the way.*

Thank goodness *that* hate fest got the axe. Kudos, outrage foment- ers, for sparing all those needy families from being exposed to such bigots. So what if they're also being deprived of a transformational home construction experience? It's for the greater good.

"shameful, like segregation." These people should be made pariahs, not made dead. How generous.

In a string of back-and-forths, Barro taunted Anderson, asking him why Anderson would expect him "to be civil toward you . . . [since] you devote your life to promoting anti-gay public policies." Anderson countered, "I think even in the midst of disagreement we should treat all people with respect." Barro disagreed. "Some people are deserving of incivility," he shot back, citing the hypothetical of shunning someone promoting the reinstitution of slavery. "You just don't like where I'm drawing the line," he concluded. True enough, and neither do we. There are millions of kind, caring, compassionate people in this country who may oppose altering the institution of marriage, and who are worthy of respect and civility. These people do not deserve public shaming, nor have they earned the dishonor associated with having one's values "stamped out." We may be quite a bit closer to Barro than Anderson on several of these policy questions, but we're on Team Ryan regarding the manner in which these debates ought to be conducted. Anderson wants to have the conversation, treating participants on all sides with basic courtesy and respect. Barro and others like him are hell-bent on ending the discussion. "Ruthlessly."

The ideological retaliation against the Benhams wasn't quite through. Having their dream show yanked away by a craven television network, the brothers returned to their successful renovation business, only to discover that their longtime banking partner was dropping them as clients. The *Daily Caller* reported, "The brothers confirmed that SunTrust Banks has pulled all of its listed properties with the Benham brothers' bank-owned property business, which includes several franchisees across four states." In an interview with the publication, David Benham admitted to feeling shell-shocked by the turn of events. "We were caught off-guard with this one," he said. "Keeping us off television wasn't enough, now this agenda to silence us wants us out of the marketplace." Brother Jason added, "If our faith costs us our HGTV show and our business, then so be it."

It didn't come to that. An irate response from conservative and Christian customers led the bank to reverse its decision within hours, pointing the finger at a third-party vendor. Again, via the *Daily Caller*: "We clarified our policies with our vendor and they have reinstated the listings with Benham Real Estate," SunTrust spokeswoman Beth McKenna said. "While we do not publicly comment on specific vendor relationships, we don't make choices on suppliers nor base business decisions on political factors, nor do we direct our third party vendors to do so . . . SunTrust supports the rights of all Americans to fully exercise their freedoms granted under the Constitution, including those with respect to free speech and freedom of religion." In another big "win," conservative Christians who'd been dumped from their forthcoming television show weren't *also* stripped of the small business they'd spent years developing. The bar for victory is getting awfully low. And the price for holding mainstream beliefs is getting awfully high.

MANDATORY CELEBRATION

As we've demonstrated time and again, the outrage brigade doesn't train its fire exclusively on public figures. Whether it's the guy who tweeted a quasi-defense of Donald Sterling's right not to be secretly taped in private, or the college town DJ booted from a gig for playing a major billboard hit, ordinary people aren't immune from the circus's wrath. Coercing an average Joe is, in many respects, much easier than targeting someone with a major platform from which to fight back. This has been true on the gay rights front, as local business owners have been forced to enlist the assistance of pro bono advocacy groups like Alliance Defending Freedom to fend off and combat lawsuits filed by celebration-imposers. Here's how ADF describes one of the most well-known cases in this legal struggle, which has dragged on for years (the U.S. Supreme Court declined to take up the case in its current iteration in the spring of 2014):

Alliance Defending Freedom attorneys represent Elane Photography and its owners, Jonathan and Elaine Huguenin. In 2006, Elaine received an e-mail from a woman about photographing a "commitment ceremony" between her and her same-sex partner and asking if Elaine would be "open to helping us celebrate our day . . ." Elaine politely declined to use her artistic expression to communicate a message at odds with her beliefs. The woman who approached Elaine, Vanessa Willock, easily found another photographer for her ceremony—and for less money. Nevertheless, Willock filed a complaint with the New Mexico Human Rights Commission. After a one-day administrative trial in 2008, the commission ruled against the Huguenins and ordered them to pay $6,637.94 in attorneys' fees to Willock. The case then made its way through the New Mexico state court system, and the New Mexico Supreme Court upheld the ruling. In a concurrence accompanying the court's opinion, one of the justices wrote that the Huguenins "now are compelled by law to compromise the very religious beliefs that inspire their lives," adding "it is the price of citizenship."

Violating one's core beliefs, rooted in religious teachings, is now "the price of citizenship" for any person of faith who decides to enter the marketplace, according to New Mexico's high court. We'd imagine that would be news to the Founders. The Huguenins have learned firsthand how quickly the coexist crowd's message ("Our love doesn't affect you!") can morph into, "You must betray your beliefs and actively validate our love, or we'll sue your ass."

A judge and a "Civil Rights Commission" in Colorado issued similar rulings against Masterpiece Cakeshop, whose religious owner declined to bake a cake for a gay couple's commitment ceremony in 2012. Jack Phillips was "ordered to change his store's policy, and revamp training for his staff" forthwith, according to *National Review*. A sad conga line of similar cases is snaking its way through the courts, featuring family businesses from a florist in Washington State to a print shop in Kentucky.

Then there's the husband and wife from New York who were fined $13,000 by an administrative law judge and the state's Human Rights Commission in 2014 for declining to host a lesbian wedding *at their home* two years prior. The couple lives at the farm, which they sometimes rent out for events. "Cynthia Gifford, who along with her husband offer a corn maze, market and events at the 100-acre farm, told Melisa McCarthy her same-sex marriage would cause 'a little bit of a problem' because the Giffords have a 'specific religious belief regarding marriage,' according to court papers," reported *Capital New York*. The judgment required the Giffords to pay the couple $1,500 each for "mental anguish," and an additional $10,000 "for the goal of deterrence." That's a direct quote. *"Let this be a warning to the intolerant fanatics who continue to labor under the ludicrous misconception that they're free to live out their religious beliefs within the confines of their own personal homes."* Thus is the state of "freedom" in America today.

We're aware that we're entering a thorny legal thicket as we explore these questions. Equal protection and public accommodation laws prevent discrimination based on specific factors (sexual orientation isn't covered in many states), which most people agree should almost always be illegal. There is a libertarian argument to be made that private businesses *should* be permitted to discriminate as they see fit, and that the market has every right to react accordingly with boycotts and protests. But an endless cycle of boycotts and protests by aggrieved parties doesn't sound like an appealing outcome to us, especially since our general message is "Relax with the constant outrage, America!" Clearly, circumstances exist wherein the State *does* have a moral imperative to intervene aggressively (Alabama in the mid-1960s). Such governmental action should be limited to extraordinary and extreme circumstances, in our view. But once again, we find ourselves in a murky, subjective area. What constitutes "extreme," and who gets to make those decisions? Jonah Goldberg tried to address these philosophical questions in an eloquent August 2013 "The Gold-berg File" column:

> *The market's not perfect, to be sure. Sometimes the state does need to break down illegitimate barriers or, you know, crush slavery. But such intrusions should be for the really important cases, not the trivial ones. Instead, what we do today is make the trivial cases into important ones. Indeed, we've turned vast swaths of the government into an industry that searches out boutique and often ridiculous arguments for new "civil rights" and then mints them accordingly. Each newly minted coin di-minishes the value of more legitimate rights and trivializes the responsibility of liberty.*

Speaking of trivialization, can we please dispense with the melo-dramatic fiction that if a same-sex couple "only" has access to 98 out of 100 area flower shops in planning their wedding, that's somehow indistinguishable from Jim Crow? The hyperbolic heavy breathing is ridiculous.

Nevertheless, forging balancing tests that grapple with "where does it end?" questions is real, and difficult. Should a devout Muslim caterer be legally required to provide her services at a gay couple's wedding? Should she be coerced into violating her conscience and/or religious edicts, in order to preclude the possibility of a punitive lawsuit? Must a Jewish pastry chef bake a cake for a wedding between two Palestin-ian Hamas supporters? And what if the couple wanted "Free Gaza" and "death to Zionism" inscribed in the frosting? Yes, these are far-fetched hypotheticals,[7] by design. But what are the outer limits of what

---

[7] Far-fetched, but not ludicrous. In 2008, a supermarket in New Jersey refused to dec-orate a child's birthday cake with his given name: Adolf Hitler. But that's what the poor kid's parents—trolls and bigots extraordinaire—demanded. Were they entitled to that cake? If the point of public accommodation laws is to protect unpopular or minority groups, wouldn't . . . white supremacist anti-Semites fit the bill for a protected class? And no, we're not comparing gay couples with skinheads. Stop it.

a free society will accept, in the name of "tolerance"? Where does the reasonable protection of one group's rights cross a threshold into the trampling of another's?

It occurs to us that there's a meaningful distinction to be drawn between issuing a blanket denial of service (no, black/gay/white couple, you cannot stay at this hotel, or eat at this restaurant) and seeking an effective waiver from being forced to *actively participate* in a wedding or commitment ceremony, specifically, the purpose of which is to celebrate the consecration of a union. The editors of the *Los Angeles Times*, editorializing in favor of Elane Photography in 2013, frame the argument less through a religious lens, and more as a free expression issue. "Compelled speech is a bad idea," they wrote, referring to photographers, graphic designers, and others, whose work cannot be separated from artistic expression. After reiterating their commitment to legalized gay marriage and opposition to discrimination, the *Times* editors concluded by exhorting the Supreme Court to "find a way to protect" people like the Huguenins.

In spite of the dramatic uptick in public support for gay marriage, most Americans agree. A 2013 Rasmussen poll found that "if a Christian wedding photographer who has deeply held religious beliefs opposing same-sex marriage is asked to work a same-sex wedding ceremony, 85 percent of American adults believe he has the right to say no." Eighty-five percent of Americans might not be able to agree that the sky is blue, yet an overwhelming supermajority coalesced on this question to come down on the opposite side of New Mexico's Supreme Court and Colorado's Civil Rights Commission—each of which issued unanimous rulings. (We should note that a September 2014 Pew survey found a much closer split on the religious liberty issue, while a 2015 Associated Press poll fell somewhere in between Rasmussen and Pew; question wording and emphasis were definitely a major factor in these disparities.)

The jaw-dropping legal reasoning from the New Mexico decision included this brief lecture from Justice Richard Bosson: The case "teaches that at some point in our lives all of us must compromise, if only a little, to accommodate the contrasting values of others." He's obviously directing his lesson at the Huguenins, but doesn't that sentence apply perfectly to the gay litigants? If that couple had "compromised, if only a little, to accommodate the contrasting views" of Elane Photography, they would have found another photographer who was delighted to commemorate their special day (which they did), and left the Huguenins in peace to conduct their business in accordance with their sincere convictions (which they did not). *Contra* Jonathan Capehart and Justice Bosson, genuinely progressive tolerance *is* a two-way street.

We're not constitutional lawyers and we don't pretend to have clean solutions for these challenging gray areas. But we don't view the First Amendment, the first clause of which enshrines religious freedom, as a mere legal nicety, subservient to stacked commissions' whims. Defining down and severely limiting the scope of our religious freedoms betrays our founding and isn't healthy for the country. And we're pretty confident that we'd be a lot better off as a society if people of all backgrounds resisted the temptation to act like litigious, trolling assholes upon experiencing even an inkling of offense. Tolerance. Let's try it. How might such a nonoutraged, shrug-it-off mentality manifest itself? Here's one example, selected for reasons that will become immediately clear. Over to you, *Washington Times* (in a January 23, 2014, article by Valerie Richardson):

> *Alan Sears doesn't know what it's like to be refused service for being gay, but he does know what it's like to be refused service for being a conservative . . . [A] Southern California photographer turned him down flat when he asked her to take a Christmas card photo of his family, explaining in an email, "I oppose the goals and objectives of your organization and have no interest in working on its behalf." That was fine with Mr. Sears, CEO and general counsel of the conservative Alliance Defending Freedom, who is leading the legal battle on behalf of*

photographers, florists, cake decorators and others sued for re-fusing to create products for same-sex weddings. What applies to wedding cake designers asked to violate their core beliefs, Mr. Sears argues, applies equally to liberals who decline to fill certain orders to conservative customers.

A lawsuit would have escalated the outrage arms race. Instead, Sears adopted a "suit yourself" posture, found someone else to snap the Christmas pics, and left the liberal photographer to stew in her principles. More of that, please.

TRANS-GRESSIONS

We're going to go ahead and guess that many Americans aren't en-tirely sure what "transgender"—the *T* in LGBT—actually is. The transgender community, for its part, demands to be understood and respected. But confused parties may not ask certain questions of the "T" group, no matter how innocent their intentions, nor may they use incorrect terminology (mastering the rules for which requires an ad-vanced degree in queer studies from Wellesley), lest they be denounced as "transphobic." Infractions can include such horrors as adding a su-perfluous "-ed" to the end of words.[8] For a basic primer, please con-sult the "transgender terminology" online guide, published by the National Center for Transgender Equality. It defines nearly two dozen phrases and words, such as "genderqueer, gender non-conforming , bi-gendered, and two-spirit." The list we're working off is actually labeled

---

[8] No, really. Mary Katharine has a friend, a gay liberal man, who has worked on behalf of the LGBTQ community in myriad ways, who was nonetheless castigated for saying "transgendered" instead of "transgender." He was mildly distraught at the upbraiding, blaming himself for insensitivity. Mary Katharine asked him, "If your friend can't give enough grace to quickly forgive a misplaced '-ed' from a friend and political ally, doesn't the problem lie with your friend, not you? Tolerance should cover suffixes, at the very least, or we're in very serious trouble."

"updated January 2014," suggesting that these permissible working definitions may be, let's call it, permanency nonconforming.

Every human being is imbued with inherent dignity, and people should make an effort to be caring and compassionate to those who are different from themselves. This applies to the transgender community as much as anyone else; their struggles, frustrations, and feelings of exclusion are difficult for most people to grasp. What makes empathy more difficult to achieve, though, is the ultrasensitive manner in which questions and discussions of that community's collective and individual experiences are regulated. Even as we write these words, we aren't entirely sure which of our insights will be deemed "acceptable" versus transphobic by the people who adjudicate this stuff hyperzealously.

Kevin Williamson, a conservative author and *National Review* editor, published a provocative and blunt piece in May 2014 entitled "Laverne Cox Is Not a Woman." Cox is an actress who stars in the Netflix original series *Orange Is the New Black* and who was featured on the cover of *Time* magazine, accompanying a feature story called, "The Transgender Tipping Point." Cox was born as a male, but identifies as a woman. Based on "do unto others" ideals, we refer to "her" and "she" in describing Cox, out of respect for her self-conception, but we also cannot contend that Cox is, as a matter of biological fact, a woman. It's complicated. Williamson's column, though nuanced and forgiving in many respects, refused to refer to Cox as anything other than "him" and "he." These excerpts may not be diplomatic, and they may make you squirm in your chair, but they make serious points:

> *Regardless of the question of whether he has had his genitals amputated, Cox is not a woman, but an effigy of a woman. Sex is a biological reality, and it is not subordinate to subjective impressions, no matter how intense those impressions are, how sincerely they are held, or how painful they make facing the biological facts of life. No hormone injection or surgical mutilation is sufficient to change that.*

. . . As a matter of government, I have little or no desire to police how Cox or any other man or woman conducts his or her personal life. But having a culture organized around the elevation of unreality over reality in the service of Eros, who is a sometimes savage god, is not only irrational but antirational. Cox's situation gave him an intensely unhappy childhood and led to an eventual suicide attempt, and his story demands our sympathy; times being what they are, we might even offer our indulgence. But neither of those should be allowed to overwhelm the facts, which are not subject to our feelings, however sincere or well intended.

For writing this candid defense of empirical reality—perhaps at the expense of subjective sensitivity, which isn't unimportant—Williamson was immediately reviled as a transphobic hater. The *Chicago Sun-Times,* a newspaper that printed the syndicated column, was excoriated by groups like GLAAD, which wrote that Williamson's piece was "dangerous" and amounted to "ugly and insulting propaganda." *BuzzFeed* reported that after more than six hundred people signed a petition circulated by a group called WAM! (Women, Action and the Media), the *Sun-Times* pulled the column from its website and apologized for publishing it in the first place. "VICTORY!" exclaimed WAM!'s website. GLAAD posted a comment from a *Sun-Times* editor explaining the paper's decision to spike the piece, which happened to parrot several points from GLAAD's original statement protesting the existence of Williamson's column. The editor wrote that Williamson had "failed to acknowledge" various facts related to transgender issues, few of which were germane to the point of the column. "Offensive" content → complaints to the exclusion of tangential qualifiers dressed up as "factual errors" → 600 signatures → BANNED. End of discussion. Also known as "VICTORY!"

But Williamson is a knuckle-dragging right-winger. Such antediluvian h8norance is expected of him. Surely liberal personalities who've warmly welcomed transgender guests onto their television shows to discuss their identities and personal journeys would fare better, right? Wrong, even if you're Katie Couric or Piers Morgan. "Transgender advocate" Janet Mock (who was born a male but now identifies as female) appeared on Morgan's since-canceled CNN show in February 2014, only to complain afterward that the host and producers had "sensationalized" her story. Among Morgan's grievous errors were (a) listing Mock as "a boy until age 18" in an on-screen graphic, and (b) referring to an anecdote in Mock's book in which she relays the story of informing a man she was dating that "You used to be yourself a man," as Morgan put it to her. But Mock has "never identified as a man," explained *BuzzFeed's* Chris Geidner, so in her mind, she never was one. Even though she was, physically. Which was presumably the whole point of sharing this anecdote. Which, again, appeared in the book she was on the show to promote. How is it offensive to ask about an incident she herself has raised?

Couric fell into a similar trap when interviewing two transgender guests, the aforementioned Laverne Cox and Carmen Carrera. Couric was slammed online for using the word *transgenders* as a noun, and was literally shushed by Carrera as she stammered through an awkward question about Carrera's surgeries and "private parts." We get that these matters are both awkward and private, but . . . when you're on a television show to talk about your transgenderism, is it unreasonable to anticipate curious and confused questions about such matters? Does hissing "shhh" at the host who's stiltedly trying to figure things out really help "educate" the people whose ignorance you lament? Or does it feed the ignorance? For her efforts on a segment branded "Transgender Trailblazers," Couric was treated to the following *Slate* headline: "Laverne Cox and Carmen Carrera Endure Transphobic Katie Couric Interview."

Okay, but even if a conservative like Williamson and well-meaning but underinformed mainstream lefties can't get it right, surely someone like gay activist and sex columnist Dan Savage[9] "gets it." He resides in the LGBT space for a living, so he's safe. Yeah, *nope*. We're going to just go ahead and let the University of Chicago's student newspaper, the *Chicago Maroon*, do the heavy lifting in describing the following May 2014 incident, followed by our analysis (emphasis ours—also, "T-slur" means "tranny," which the carefully parsed report goes to great lengths to avoid spelling out for readers):

> *After a terse exchange about the use of a transphobic slur between a guest speaker and student at an Institute of Politics (IOP) event last week, students in the LGBTQ community have started circulating a petition calling for a formal apology from the IOP. At press time, the petition had more than 1,100 signatures. The event was an* **off-the-record Fellows seminar** *held by Ana Marie Cox, a political columnist on U.S. politics for* The Guardian. *It featured Dan Savage, a relationship and sex advice columnist and founder of the It Gets Better project, as a guest speaker.*
>
> *The incident occurred when, according to several sources, Savage and Cox began discussing his personal history as a gay man. According to a first-year student and member of the LGBTQ community who asked to be identified as Hex, Savage used the slur t– as an example in an anecdote about reclaiming words. Cox then added, "I used to make jokes about t-ies," audience members recounted. "That was one of the most hurtful parts," Hex said, explaining [that] the perceived insult was that Cox used the slur to refer to the group of people she joked about. "In that context, it was like being applied to all transgender people," it said. (***"It" is Hex's chosen pronoun.***)*
>
> *. . . Hex asked Savage and Cox to use the term "T-slur"*

---

[9] President Obama's antibullying "czar" who, well, *bullied* Christian high school students during a profanity-laced, Bible-attacking presentation. He then reportedly ridiculed them as "pansies" as they walked out of the seminar. *You had one job,* Dan.

instead of the actual word. According to second-year Sara Rubinstein, an executive director of QUIP (Queers United in Power), and Hex, Savage then named other slurs, asking if they were suitable to use instead. "Obviously [he attempted] to threaten me and make me feel uncomfortable in that space, which was pretty successful," Hex said.

So Dan Savage behaved, in some people's eyes, like a provocative jerk—as is his wont *and his reputation*. He offended a handful of students at the off-the-record fireside chat–style seminar by using the term *tranny* in a historical context (see Savage's explanation to follow). When he was scolded by "Hex"[10] for doing so, he rattled off some other "offensive" terms to drive home the point that he wasn't about to be censored, and to prove a separate point about "reclaiming" slurs (again, stay tuned). Being an in-your-face discusser of sexual issues is what he does. Sarcasm, needling, and general assholery are sort of his thing, so none of this should have shocked anyone. In fact, Savage was "glitter-bombed" (in which a bucket of glitter is poured over the head of a gay rights opponent) by LGBT activists (!) in 2011 for alleged transphobia, and emerged from the experience unbowed—although he stopped using *tranny* around the same time.

We repeat: Nothing about his behavior in this little kerfuffle should have been surprising to anyone. But gripped by a fresh bout of outrageous outrage, several students crafted a Change.org petition insisting that the Institute of Politics program issue a formal apology and make "a commitment to preventing the use of slurs and hate speech in the future." They also asserted that the tacit confidentiality agreement of the off-the-record session was made null and void by Savage's

---

[10] How is *it* not a dehumanizing, offensive pronoun? And, if the "rules" are entirely subjective from person to person, how are people supposed to navigate this stuff without a personalized style guide? Is this not insanely unreasonable? Good luck in the real world, Hex!

commission of a "hate crime." To the school's credit, administrators greeted the petition with a swift back of the hand:

> *By definition, views will be expressed on occasion with which some will strongly disagree or even find deeply offensive. But we cannot remain true to our mission and be in the business of filtering guests or policing their statements to ensure they will always meet with broad agreement and approval and will not offend.*

Thank you, University of Chicago.[11] Savage reacted to the contretemps in a withering blog post at the *Slog*, the meat of which we've reproduced below. To paraphrase Dos Equis's Most Interesting Man in the World, we don't often agree with Dan Savage, but when we do, we prefer that our concurrence take the form of *exquisite awesomeness* like this (per usual, emphasis ours):

> *I never suggested that the trans community ought to reclaim "tranny." I wasn't giving orders to the trans community. Just sharing a little queer history with IOP students in a confidential, off-the-record conversation.*
>
> *During this part of the talk a student interrupted and asked me to stop using "the t-slur." (I guess it's not the t-word anymore. I missed the memo.) My use of it—even while talking about why I don't use the word anymore, even while speaking of the queer community's history of reclaiming hate words, even as I used other hate words—was potentially traumatizing. I stated that I didn't see a difference between saying "tranny" in this context and saying "t-slur." Were I to say "t-slur" instead of "tranny," everyone in the room would auto-translate*

---

[11] As a graduate of Northwestern—Chicago's *much* more well-rounded and fun "elite" university—Guy doesn't frequently dish out compliments to U of C. Savor the moment, Maroons.

Michael Sam and the Right to Say "Meh"

Michael Sam's journey to becoming the first openly gay player in NFL history was a legitimate news story. Some conservatives who insisted that the development wasn't worthy of any significant attention seemed cranky and out of touch. Others' critique that the resulting media coverage dwarfed the importance of the actual news itself might be closer to the truth. We're happy for gay people and their allies who were excited and empowered by Sam's blazing of this trail. We couldn't help but smile when Sam sacked Johnny Football in the 2014 preseason, leaping to his feet after the whistle to taunt the quarterback with his own, obnoxious "dollar bills" hand gesture. We're also fine with others who thought the whole thing was overblown. It seemed for a while as if everybody on planet Earth was required to state their opinion on the entire episode—the more dramatic, the better. We just wanted to say that it is an entirely reasonable course of action to have witnessed the spectacle, shrugged, and gone on with your life. Exercising the right to say "meh" is what separates us from those who live the soul-sucking politicized life, as described in chapter 2.

"t-slur" to "tranny" in their own heads. Was there really much difference between me saying it and me forcing everyone in the room to say it quietly to themselves? That would be patronizing, infantilizing, and condescending. Cox gamely jumped in and offered that she had used "tranny" in the past but that she now recognizes its harm and has stopped using it. **The student who objected interrupted: as neither Cox nor I were trans, "tranny" was not our word to use—not even in the context of a college seminar, not even when talking about why we don't use the word anymore.** I asked the student who objected if it was okay for me to use the words "dyke" and "sissy." After a moment's thought the student said I could use those words—permission granted—and that struck me [as] *funny because I am not a lesbian nor am I particularly effemi-nate. (And, really, this is college now? Professors, fellows, and guest lecturers need to clear their vocabulary with first-year students?) By the not-your-word-to-use standard, I shouldn't be able to use dyke or sissy either—or breeder, for that matter, as that's a hate term for straight people. (Or maybe it's an ac-knowledgment of their utility? Anyway . . .)*

*This student became so incensed by our refusal to say "How high?" when this student said "Jump!" that **this student stormed out of the seminar. In tears. As one does when one doesn't get one's way. In college.***

We can't help but wonder if Savage might actually enjoy chapter 5 of this very book! But in light of his "transphobic" history, requisite glitter-bombing (heretofore reserved for the Michele Bachmanns of the world), and subsequent "hate crimes," he's quite clearly not the man to offer tips on avoiding the silencing mob's wrath, since they've nailed him, too. There must be a better choice to help us navigate these confusing cultural waters.

We've got it! How about cross-dressing pioneer RuPaul, arguably the most famous drag queen in the history of the planet. Though Ru-Paul doesn't identify as transgender, she's[12] been at the forefront of introducing mainstream American culture to alternative gender constructs and lifestyles for decades. Her current show, *RuPaul's Drag Race*, premiered in 2009 on Logo, a cable network geared toward LGBT programming. It's featured dozens of contestants over a half-dozen seasons—a mix of gay men and transgender women. When the show aired a "minichallenge" in season six called "female or she-male?" LGBT activists protested, calling the latter term "transphobic." The uproar resulted in a spate of bannings by Logo, which pulled the

---

[12] He wrote in his autobiography that he doesn't care whether people refer to him as "he" or "she."

offending episode altogether and scuttled a long-running gag called "you've got she-mail." RuPaul's catchphrase "Grrrl, you got she-mail," was also forcibly retired, according to *Vox*.[13] Evidently mystified by accusations of transphobia from ever-enraged "activists" (do these people ever sleep?), RuPaul took to Twitter to vent. "I've been a 'tranny' for 32 years. The word 'tranny' has never just meant transsexual. #TransvestiteHerstoryLesson," she tweeted, adding, "The absurdity! It's as if Jay Z got offended by Kanye using the word 'Nigga.'"[14]

That's right, RuPaul—*Ru-f***ing-Paul*—was forced to fend off transphobia allegations and was compelled by her network to abandon a silly branded segment on her own show. We're *all* the way through the looking glass, guys. If RuPaul can't approach these issues without being dragged under by the Outrage Circus, what chance do the rest of us stand?

Obama's "Evolution"

On May 9, 2012, President Obama made history by affirming his support for same-sex marriage. *This is stunning, groundbreaking news,* said nobody who'd paid any attention to his "evolution" on the issue. Running in the 1996 Democratic primary for a state Senate seat in Chicago's ultraliberal Hyde Park district, Barack Obama unequivocally asserted his strong support for gay marriage. Responding to a candidate questionnaire from *Outlines* newspaper, Obama wrote, "I favor legalizing same-sex marriages, and would fight efforts to prohibit such marriages." By the time he needed to win statewide in his epochal 2004 U.S. Senate run, Obama had "evolved" into *opposing* same-sex marriage. "What I believe is that a marriage is between a man and a woman," he stated in a televised debate.

---

[13] We know, we know.

[14] RuPaul is black, so this is okay.

Obama's "Evolution" *(continued)*

Four years hence, Obama's progression was frozen in place, as he ran for president. "I believe marriage is the union between a man and a woman. As a Christian, it's also a sacred union," he said to loud applause at a candidate forum hosted at Rick Warren's Saddleback Church in California. As we mentioned earlier, Obama carried that deep blue state easily several months later, among the same electorate that approved Proposition 8 on the same day. By 2010, with pressure mounting from gay megadonors, Obama pronounced himself "evolving" on the issue. Two years later, with public support for gay marriage maintaining its steady upward climb—and after Vice President Joe Biden prematurely let the cat out of the bag—the White House orchestrated an interview with ABC News to seal the deal. Obama sat down with host Robin Roberts and offered this verbose and self-referential endorsement of gay marriage:

> *At a certain point I've just concluded that for me personally it is important for me to go ahead and affirm that I think same-sex couples should be able to get married.*

Obama later intoned that his experience meeting the mother of Matthew Shepard, a young gay man murdered in Wyoming in 1998, helped inform his change of heart on gay rights. May we remind you that he was on the record as favoring same-sex marriage (the first time) two years *before* Shepard's death, but pulling that heartstring was a classy touch. And that, friends, is how Barack Obama's sixteen-year metamorphosis on gay marriage reached its completely inevitable (if premature) conclusion. The various twists and turns of this special journey, oddly enough, directly coincided with the immediate political interests of Barack Obama. Positively heroic. His closest adviser, David Axelrod, confirmed this cynical "bullshit," as Obama reputedly labeled his official position in private, in his 2015 memoirs.

And by the way, we should also note that Barack Obama is by no means the first politician to exploit gay issues for political gain. For instance, the 2004 Bush/Cheney reelection campaign was given a strategically choreographed boost in the form of antigay marriage ballot initiatives in eleven states, including the key battleground of Ohio. The idea was to generate a surge in turnout among social conservatives who weren't necessarily reliable voters. If your gut reaction to this maneuver is, *Hey, it worked*, keep that feeling in mind the next time you're on the brink of castigating Democrats over ends-justify-the-means politics. For the record, no, we're not the least bit regretful that President John Kerry was never a thing.

9

THE UPTIGHT CITIZENS BRIGADE

The War on Comedy

In our hypersensitive, self-righteous, constantly offended society, it took an octogenarian woman with cojones to lead us.

Joan Rivers was never one for observing conventions. Fittingly, the legendary comedienne's death at age eighty-one relieved our society of two conventions we generally observe upon the death of a prominent figure: (1) the custom of promptly and politely forgetting anything that could be construed as negative about the recently deceased; and (2) the obligation to refrain from joking about that figure's demise for a culturally appropriate cooling-off period.

For a brief moment, our sensitivity culture loosened up, and it stands to reason Rivers would have approved. Because Rivers's meanness was her signature, nothing could be "too soon" for her. Minutes after her death, a headline on Fark.com declared, "Joan Rivers' face dies at age 25." Journalist Toby Harnden spotted evidence of international derision with this placard in a London railway station: "As a tribute to the late Joan Rivers, parts of this station will be gradually replaced over the next 40 years." Sure, it was all tasteless and rude, but it was funny. And Joan gave us the license to laugh. It was a great parting gift.

Rivers went out doing what she loved—undergoing surgery. (You see what we did there?) She went out making jokes, offending people, and telling the perpetually offended to shut up. Rivers's loud mouth and ribald performances on *The Tonight Show* with Johnny Carson, starting in the late 1960s, put her on her way to the pantheon of iconic comedians. She made her mark by treading, as a woman, on network TV, in the midcentury, on topics many feared to tread on. And she didn't apologize for it.

Many comedians and entertainers are fond of declaring themselves unapologetic, but very few can own the description so literally. Months before her 2014 death, Rivers made a joke on *The Today Show* that got our cultural hall monitors calling for the principal. She was promoting a reality show about living with her daughter, Melissa: "Those women in the basement in Cleveland had more space," she said, referring to the three missing teenagers found captive in Ariel Castro's basement, enslaved and abused by the madman for years after their abductions.

Yes, the tragedy those three women endured is gravely serious. But here's the thing: Comedy isn't. When the world demanded an apology, Rivers refused. Her statement is one to live by: "I'm a comedienne," she told the *Cleveland Plain Dealer*. "I know what those girls went through. It was a little, stupid joke. There is nothing to apologize for. I made a joke. That's what I do. Calm down. Calm f—— down. I'm a comedienne. They're free, so let's move on."

"Calm f***ing down" is right. The fact that "Comedian refuses to apologize for telling joke" amounts to news is a cultural indictment on its own. If nothing else in this book motivates Americans to rebuke the outrage machine, let it be our desire to laugh. We have always been a country that prizes its entertainment.

Too many comedians have begun to feel that they must police their every word, which is not exactly conducive to comedy.

Comedian Neal Brennan, host of Sundance network's *The Approval Matrix*, put it this way, begging for a little leeway for levity: "I say it's like irregular shirts at the outlet mall. These are irregular jokes," Brennan said. "If thoughts are my business, every once in a while, weird jagged thoughts are going to come out, and maybe just put them at the outlet mall."

Chris Rock, speaking in an interview on November 30, 2014, with Frank Rich for *New York* magazine, also explained how a directive not to offend does not lend itself to great comedy.

> *It is scary, because the thing about comedians is that you're the only ones who practice in front of a crowd. Prince doesn't run a demo on the radio. But in stand-up, the demo gets out. There are a few guys good enough to write a perfect act and get onstage, but everybody else workshops it and workshops it, and it can get real messy. It can get downright offensive. Before everyone had a recording device . . . you'd say something that went too far, and you'd go, "Oh, I went too far," and you would just brush it off. But if you think you don't have room to make mistakes, it's going to lead to safer, gooier stand-up. You can't think the thoughts you want to think if you think you're being watched.*

Rock doesn't even bother to play his sometimes racy show at colleges anymore because they're "too conservative (in their) . . . willingness not to offend anybody." He lamented that you can't even "be offensive on your way to being inoffensive" anymore.

Stephen Colbert, the satirical anchor of Comedy Central's *The Colbert Report* until late 2014 who modeled his character on Bill O'Reilly for years, found this out when a joke satirizing racism sparked a Twitter campaign to cancel his show. On a Thursday in March, the *Colbert Report* Twitter account tweeted: "I am willing to show #Asian community I care by introducing the Ching-Chong Ding-Dong Foundation for Sensitivity to Orientals or Whatever."

The joke, which also aired on the show, was a send-up of Washington Redskins owner Dan Snyder's new organization, the Washington Redskins Original Americans Foundation. Snyder started the nonprofit in the wake of national, well, outrage about the Redskins' name. When Colbert used various outdated terms for Asians in his tweet mocking Dan Snyder's outdated term for Native Americans, outrage begot outrage.

A twenty-three-year-old hashtag activist[1] named Suey Park saw the tweet and urged her followers to tweet #CancelColbert until it became popular on Twitter. Thus, a national news story was born, and Colbert explained himself. He didn't exactly apologize, but said, "When I saw the tweet with no context, I understand how people were offended."

Colbert's show was not canceled, but it's unclear if a figure with less slobbering acclaim among liberal tastemakers would have survived the brouhaha. He did abolish the Twitter account that tweeted the joke, so Park did succeed in shutting down some form of speech.

Keegan-Michael Key and Jordan Peele, the titular talents of Comedy Central's *Key & Peele* wrote in *Time*, "Make fun of everything," suggesting that declining to make fun of a certain group is a form of insensitivity of its own:

> *It's amazing to think how popular television shows like* All in the Family *and* Good Times *might fare today in a Hollywood pitch meeting. Films like* Blazing Saddles *and* Silver Streak *wouldn't make it past the development stage at a studio. Too edgy. Somewhere along the line, we've forgotten the true purpose of humor: to help people cope with the fears and horrors of the world. Sure, sometimes at* Key & Peele *we swim in the shallow waters of pratfalls, airplane observations and simple old-school punnery. But what we strive for—and what we think more people should strive for—is deeper: to make fun of everything.*
>
> *It can be scary. We don't want to lose our audience. Can*

---

[1] Yes, that is a thing. Park is also credited with the prominent hashtag campaign #NotYourAsianSidekick.

we make them laugh at a sketch about slavery? Terrorism?
The Holocaust? At the same time, though, it's our duty. To not
make fun of something is, we believe, itself a form of bullying.
When a humorist makes the conscious decision to exclude a
group from derision, isn't he or she implying that the members
of that group are not capable of self-reflection? Or don't possess
the mental faculties to recognize the nuances of satire? A group
that's excluded never gets the opportunity to join in the greater
human conversation.

One antifun activist decided to prove Key and Peele's point over a game of cards in the summer of 2014, dramatically demanding to be excluded from the "greater human conversation" comedy can offer by ritually burning a card that offended him.

First, an explanation of this particular card game. Since the night in 2010 a couple friends developed Cards Against Humanity as a party game for a New Year's celebration, the game has been winning devotees with its funny, crass simplicity. Essentially a dirty version of Apples to Apples in style of play, the game's title consciously references the phrase "Crimes Against Humanity" for a reason. Its cards are meant to be as offensive as possible, taking potshots at public figures, children, the disabled, all races.

The game, funded by a *Kickstarter* campaign, became the most popular game on Amazon and was on backorder for months at a time, as is each "expansion pack" of newly offensive cards. In its sheer unabashed embrace of the offensive, it somehow made it past our cultural sensitivity gatekeepers, and many a liberal in good standing has had a couple shots of Fireball at a party and played the "Not giving a shit about the Third World" card or "Kids with ass cancer." Charles C. W. Cooke encapsulates the game's nature in *National Review*:

Among the other topics at which Cards Against Human-
ity routinely pokes fun are incest, abortion, genocide, race,

homosexuality, death, the disabled, those with crippling dis-
eases, and the religious. A typical combination: "What will al-
ways get you laid? Date rape." Another: "In 1,000 years, when
paper money is but a distant memory, black people *will be our*
currency." Within the pack there are ready made Holocaust
jokes, jokes about the massacre of American Indians, jokes about
the molestation of altar boys, jokes that make light of black peo-
ple and of slavery, jokes about fatal drug addiction, and an end-
less supply of gross, semi-pornographic nonsense. Oh, and more
Holocaust jokes. (Oh, and even more *Holocaust jokes.)*

But it was bound to come to pass that the game's clear, satirical
nature would be no defense against an outrage, just as with Colbert's
joke. So, in the summer of 2014, an activist and Tumblr user appropriately named "horriblewarning" objected with loud, self-righteous, In-
stagrammed offense to a particular card. This teen, Jonah from Boston,
who identifies as transgender, took photos of the burning of one card—
"Passable transvestites." The caption: "DEATH TO TRANSPHOBIA."

"A lot of my friends are LGBT, emphasis on the T," Jonah told the
Fusion TV network. "Somebody played that card, and somebody else
was like, 'That's not OK.' I decided I didn't want it in my deck." One of
the cocreators responded by apologizing for the card: "I regret writing
this card, it was a mean, cheap joke," Max Temkin wrote. "We took it
out of the game a while ago." Temkin revealed that the creators of a
game *designed solely to be offensive* have lately been writing cards to be
less offensive:

Temkin says he and the other creators know there's a big dif-
ference between cards that make fun of public figures and ones
that victimize people in marginalized groups . . . To that end,
some of the newer cards have a decidedly social-justice-friendly
edge: You can now play "heteronormativity," "the patriarchy"
and "white privilege."

Sounds like a riot. Here's the problem, once one has confessed that one card in Cards Against Humanity is too offensive for a game, again, DESIGNED TO BE OFFENSIVE, where does it stop? Are transgender teens more worthy of protection from this party game than, say, Holocaust survivors, about whom there are several cards? Jonah learned this quickly, as in a turn of events poetic in its self-righteous stupidity, the rest of the perpetually offended began to ask Jonah why he wasn't offended by all the cards? *Hmm?* Jonah genuflected, acknowledging his privilege[2] and correcting himself to be offended by all the things:

> *When I first posted this, I did not realize that it was problematic. I was fine to say "I can't find this specific card funny, it is too close to being about me, I wanted it out of my game and since I like fire I decided to burn it." I did not comprehend that I was essentially saying "Well I personally have never experienced racism, so it doesn't really matter to me and I can still laugh at it, and it's okay because I'm not racist." And I see now that that is what I was doing. I was only looking at the issues which affected me personally, and I was allowing myself to find everything else funny because I wasn't the person to whom it's directed. I truly regret making this post, not because I've gotten a bit of shit for it but because I am appalled at myself that I didn't see what I was doing.*

Sigh. In the end, Jonah did on behalf of the trans community exactly what Key and Peele bemoan. Jonah made a "conscious decision to exclude a group from derision." In a card game called Cards Against Humanity, there can be no cards against trans people. Ironically, in the quest to be treated with humanity, Jonah declared himself apart from it.

---

[2] Drink!

There's an old, hackneyed, probably offensive joke about the self-serious among us.

Q: *How many feminists does it take to change a lightbulb?*
A: *That's not funny.*

Sure, it was originally about feminists, but it could apply to most of the Left these days, as illustrated by the ludicrous "comedy" panel at the annual liberal gathering Netroots Nation. Conservative writer Jon Gabriel sat through a discussion almost entirely devoid of laughs, the premise of which turned out to be something like "creating one-ness" through "comedic social justice media." Sounds funny, at least unintentionally.

Members of the comedy panel began by listing which jokes no one should tell, according to Gabriel's reporting, which he posted at *Ricochet*, January 16, 2015: nothing including a disenfranchised population, nothing about "ugly historical crimes, sexism, or racism."

"Sure, it might get a laugh—if that's what you want," said Julianna Forlano, host of a parody news show called *Absurdity Today*, with seemingly no appreciation for the absurdity of that sentiment in a discussion of comedy.

> To ensure a joke isn't unintentionally offensive, Forlano even recommended running it by a professional comedian first. Everyone on the panel agreed . . .
>
> The audience had several questions about what they were allowed to joke about, and even how comedy works. A white septuagenarian proudly stated that she no longer tells jokes to black people because that might expose them to unwitting racism. Two panelists sadly noted that her preface of "I'm not a racist, but . . ." confirms that she is, in fact, a racist.
>
> Another audience member asked how progressives can shut down funny, effective lines coming from the right on talk radio,

blogs and Twitter. "*The right has short, pithy things to say because they lie,*" *another participant replied.*

Are you not entertained? Joan would roll over in her grave. We'll let you fill in the blanks with your very own offensive pun about rolling over, sex, and Joan that we can't think of right now because we're still laughing too hard at the Netroots Nation humor panelists.

FIGHTING BACK WITH FUNNY

Recently, comedians Mindy Kaling and Michael Che did not heed this panel's advice, declining to run their sitcom plots and silly tweets by a panel of liberal activists. The outrage machine exacted a cost, but the actions of Kaling and Che show a comedian's reaction can mitigate the machine's damage.

Kaling, most famous for her portrayal of ditzy Kelly Kapoor on *The Office*, started as a writer on that show and now writes her own sitcom, *The Mindy Project*. In an episode entitled "I Slipped," Mindy and her on-screen love interest, Danny Castellano, face relationship hijinx when a sexual encounter becomes, ahem, more anal than she anticipated. The show treats the sexual incident as a miscommunication, not an attack by Castellano. The couple works through it humorously, finally talking openly about it.

> **Danny:** You want the truth about the other night? Here's the real truth: It didn't mean anything, and I don't want you to be anything. I just tried something, all right? That's it. Because America was built on trying things.
>
> **Mindy:** If you want to try something freaky, just run it by me first.

Though the sitcom explicitly dealt with sexual consent, which feminists and outrage mongers had been screaming for, and though it was a groundbreaking female comedian of color who addressed it, the show didn't do it exactly right, critics whined. *Ms. Magazine* declared "'The Mindy Project' slips up on consent," the writer declaring she was "squirming in her seat."

Kaling, a Dartmouth-educated adult, quelled the outrage, not by apologizing but by explaining things to these emotional children like a smart, confident adult. There was no "sexual peril" for her beloved character, she told a New York audience at the New Yorker Festival after a fan asked about criticism of the episode.

> *I would say this: I think I disagree with you. And I think that Danny is a wonderful character, a wish-fulfillment character, and he loves Mindy, and they have a relationship that is very understanding with each other, and he tried something because he was trying to see what he could get away with. But I don't think that in that relationship that Mindy's reaction to it was "I feel violated"; it was "Hey man, run that by me!"*

Kaling explained her position with her signature good humor and smarts instead of immediately admitting fault and apologizing, as critics often demand. In so doing, she gave her audience the credit it deserves, and a real conversation.

Che, the new cohost of *Saturday Night Live*'s "Weekend Update," found himself on the wrong side of the outrage crowd just weeks after his debut. A viral video of a woman walking the streets of New York being catcalled by men more than one hundred times in a day had generated reams of online commentary. Some of the catcalling amounted to sexual harassment and creepy behavior, but many of the exclamations were benign if taken on their own.

Che tweeted about the video:

> *I wanna apologize to all the women I've harassed with statements like "hi" or "have a nice day" or "you're beautiful." I can't imagine what that must feel like.*

When the backlash came, he didn't apologize, but tweeted a concise explanation of the theme of this book and why it should make us all worried.

> *I wanna apologize for my last apology. Sometimes I forget that I belong to all of you now and that any thought I have should be filtered through you, and receive ur approval. It's tough because I'm used to taking risks and finding humor in places of discomfort. But that's all over cause I have a job on TV. And, if I say the wrong thing, you'll see to it that it's taken away. So, next time I have a silly thought, I'll giggle to myself, keep my mouth shut, & post a picture with my arm around a more famous person I met somewhere.*

We feel you, Michael. We really do.

Comedian Patton Oswalt has also skewered outrage merchants who come at him from right and left (but mostly left) with admirable regularity on Twitter, particularly the writers at *Salon*, who must have a fainting couch in every office judging by the frequency with which they lose their minds over tiny perceived cultural offenses.

Oswalt sat down in 2015 with the speech-policing gadflies at *Salon* and has this to say about the turn of classically liberal society toward politically correct Puritanism:

> *What I'm saying is, that comes down to someone like a Charlie Hebdo, or a Larry Flynt—they are necessary. We need people that will go all the way out on the edge and ask the most disturbing fucking questions that are out there. We need them. Otherwise, if you start having a society where people are policing their own thoughts, now we're back in Salem, Massachusetts, where literally, they didn't do anything for fun, and then that pressure built up and they all went nuts. . . . Everyone now has this litmus test, where if you do not agree on every single*

point, then we can't talk to you or that guy's got to lose his job. You're not going to ever agree perfectly with everybody.

But sometimes an even more direct approach is called for.

For that, how about another comedian adept in the fine art of offending and giving zero f—s—Adam Carolla. Name an outrage group, and he's been on the wrong side of it. We've commented on the way the Internet can exacerbate the culture of outrage, but we're no Luddites. The Internet, with its ability to host an ever-increasing number of channels, shows, podcasts, and distribution networks, can also allow an entertainer to untether from the skittish corporate overlords who require one to kowtow to the outraged community *du jour.*

After a successful career ruffling feathers in traditional outlets like MTV, terrestrial radio, and Comedy Central, Carolla found himself fired from a morning radio show and looking for somewhere to go.

He started Carolla Digital, a self-published podcast network with plenty of listeners, plenty of advertisers, and a whole lot less censorship. Carolla calls this oasis of free expression "the pirate ship." From there, he can happily tell anyone to stuff it if they're offended, and he is more than happy to do so.

We talked to Carolla about his advice for those facing the buzz saw of the outrage machine:

The only way we're ever gonna claim the streets back from these nutjobs is to literally tell them to "fuck off." That's what I do. They've created this culture where everyone's scared shitless and we're oversaturated and we're at a tipping point and we need to claim it back.

Just because someone is on the offense doesn't mean you have to get back on your heels on defense. Just because someone is pointing the finger at you and accusing you of being xenophobic, homophobic, whatever they're accusing you of, which they'll never stop doing. Just because they're doing that doesn't mean you have to retreat and go "whoa whoa whoa, you misunderstood" . . . The answer should be "Fuck you! You think I'm a racist? I think you're an asshole."

I've been broadcasting from my own studio in my own warehouse for going on six years. Nobody demands an apology anymore because they know they're not gonna get one. These guys are like the mob and we're just like store owners, and we're all living on the same street. And, if you start doing business with them, then I have to start doing business with them, and the place on the corner has to do business with them. The point is we need to have a block party where all the business owners get together on the street and say we're not doing business with the mob.

Hear, hear.

Watching comedians grapple with the outrage machine is disheartening because one might assume that even if the outrage economy is unwilling to let the rest of us have any fun, it'd be willing to let comedians tell jokes. On the other hand, the comic community is heartening in that many of them do push back on these orthodoxies. Perhaps more than any other group, they recognize an immediate danger to their art and livelihoods.

Rivers will be sorely missed because attitudes like hers are sorely needed. One can imagine a tombstone[3] with a tastefully carved, marble middle finger atop it. *Rolling Stone* once asked Rivers if she ever shies away from certain topics:

No. Part of my act is meant to shake you up. It looks like I'm being funny, but I'm reminding you of other things. Life is tough, darling. Life is hard. And we better laugh at everything, otherwise we're going down the tube.

Thank you, Joan.

---

[3] In another videotaped interaction with a paparazzo posted by *TMZ* weeks before her death, Rivers was asked what she would want on her tombstone. She reflected for a beat, then responded definitively: "She had a great time." So she did. RIP.

10

RESIST WE MUCH?[1]

Advice, Sort Of

"The time for talk is over." —*Barack Obama, many, many times*

Welp, looks like we've made it. We've reached the point in the book where we, as your sagacious authors, are charged with drawing important conclusions and imparting brilliant advice that addresses some of the problems we've enumerated over the course of this book. Here's the thing, though: many of the challenges we discussed are too entrenched, too irresistible for demagogues, too insidious to uproot in three easy steps. Which is not to say that we believe conservatives and defenders of true dialogue ought to throw their hands up in despair. What follows isn't a satisfying, tidy conclusion along the lines of the "if only everyone else were smart enough to agree with us, everything would come up roses" variety. But there are things we can do. Let's start with the fun stuff.

Many of our peers will be familiar with the 1990s children's cartoon series *Captain Planet and the Planeteers*. Looking back on the show today, it's blindingly obvious that it was left-wing propaganda to the point of parody. The cartoon's opening sequence explains, "Our world is in peril! Gaia, spirit of the earth, can no longer stand the terrible destruction plaguing our planet. She sends five special rings to five

---

[1] If this chapter title puzzles you, that means one thing: you ignored our previous exhortation to search Al Sharpton vs. the teleprompter on YouTube. For shame.

special young people . . . when the five powers [earth, wind, water, fire, and heart] combine, they summon Earth's greatest champion, Captain Planet!"

This squad of "special young people" is, needless to say, composed of an approved mix of ethnicities and genders, hailing from all over the world. They summon the show's superhero by slipping on their magic rings and pointing them skyward. Their "powers combined" would awaken Captain Planet, who would rocket up from the depths of the earth, joining them to beat back the show's villains: unscrupulous factory owners, greedy businessmen, "deforestation," "smog," and "hate," natch.

Although we could go on, we're not here to bitch and moan about a long-canceled afternoon cartoon.[2] But we're captivated by the entertaining, if wildly implausible, image of conservatives employing a similar model to hunt down and harass the Left's Outrage Circus across the country. Whenever a pop-up outrage emerged, a team of carefully selected conservative provocateurs would be dispatched to ground zero of the controversy to address the Left's arguments head-on and force the media to cover the other side. Team members would be selected based on criteria typically valued by the Left: take-no-prisoners attitudes, Absolute Moral Authority status, and "diversity."

We don't have the whole cast and script quite worked out just yet, but we're thinking about folks like radio host Dana Loesch (female, media personality, gun rights champion), radio host Tammy Bruce (female, gay—double points), syndicated columnist Deroy Murdock (black, gay—double points), and Ayaan Hirsi Ali (female, black, atheist, victim of misogyny, fighter of male privilege—quadruple points). Perhaps additional specialists could be called in, depending on the nature of the hoopla. Thomas Sowell might be the on-call economist, the Federalist Society founders could head up the legal department, while attorney John Yoo and former CIA clandestine service chief Jose

---

[2] We have blogs for that.

Rodriguez would run the national security shop. We're open to additional candidates and suggestions for this undertaking.

Now, on a slightly more practical level, may we suggest the creation of a . . .

COALITION TO CHILL THE HELL OUT

The sound, fury, and economic impact of a boycott—or even jitters associated with the *threat* of a boycott—can serve as salient societal change agents. In our view, as we hope we've made clear by now, such tactics should be employed very sparingly. Some on the Left go to this well with alarming regularity, whipping up "outrage" and demanding punishment for even the slightest departures from their current acceptable standards. Their efficacy depends on the degree to which their targets fear the consequences—which, in turn, is often linked to the volume and intensity of organizers' outrage output. The resulting state of play allows a relatively small handful of agitators, sometimes posing as "grassroots" activists with untold hordes of supporters at their back, to create the impression of a popular groundswell that targets ought to take seriously.

As Juan Williams can attest (see chapter 4), even a trickle of e-mails can do the job. We're not suggesting that boycotts and social media campaigns can't be righteous and important from time to time. We are suggesting that they're overused and allow small circles of zealots to wield disproportionate influence by purporting to speak "for America." In many cases, what America would probably prefer is for people to chill the hell out. Feel free to voice your displeasure with business decision X, or individual Y. But let's dial back the scalp-claiming business. To that end, perhaps it would be edifying and worthwhile to develop a vast e-mail list or a turnkey petition function that would allow millions of ordinary people to affix their signature to a document declaring their profound neutrality/apathy/indifference on the latest dustup. Such a system could give voice to the silent *vast* majority in most circumstances and imbue pressured parties with the confidence associated with a timely reminder that their tormenters aren't necessarily speaking for a significant chunk of consumers.

To wit, "We the undersigned hold differing views on same-sex marriage, which we understand to be a controversial political issue. We also enjoy the delicious chicken prepared six days per week by the fine employees of Chick-fil-A and would prefer that they concentrate their efforts on cooking their delectable offerings, which we will continue to purchase and consume—even as we agree and disagree with the ownership's political or religious beliefs. Signed, the Coalition to Chill the Hell Out and Eat Mor Chikn.™"

George Will cited Chick-fil-A as one reason to, well, chill the hell out about the Outrage Circus in general. The merchants of outrage "shout at the margins of public discourse," Will said in an interview with us. "We should view this with a bemused disdain because they're making a ruckus, perhaps noted by people of similar persuasions, but I don't think they're having many consequences. Remember, not long ago, when the CEO of Chick-fil-A expressed support for the traditional understanding of marriage, taking the position that Barack Obama held when he ran for election in 2008. There was an immediate outcry from a small but clamorous minority that people should boycott Chick-fil-A. So while the spirit of these people is disreputable, their effect is often negligible."

Yep. In the year following the Chick-fil-A boycott, the family-owned restaurant surpassed KFC's market share for the first time ever and was identified in internal McDonald's documents as a "serious and growing competitive threat."

We're still a bit less sanguine than Will is on the topic, but some of his points are well taken and should be instructive for those who may find themselves in the center of a future whirlwind. Our alliance of shruggers could offer a shot-in-the-arm reminder to the besieged that while self-reflection is healthy and sometimes needed, this too shall pass. The disreputable few's bark is louder than their "often negligible" bite. Chill the hell out.

WHEN "OUTRAGE CIRCUS" TENTS COLLAPSE

W e've spent much of this book warning about the growing influence of the conversation-ending demagogues, so we think we owe it to our conservative readers to cite a few encouraging examples of the Outrage Circus throwing everything they've got at political opponents—and going down in flames. On that score, we were keen on tracking the respective fates of two candidates for office in the 2014 elections: Wisconsin governor Scott Walker and Colorado Senate candidate Cory Gardner. Each was subjected to relentless and often dishonest fear tactics from the Left—and we're delighted to see that each man stuck to the issues and prevailed.

We've already reviewed liberals' extraordinary opposition to Governor Walker, chronicling Wisconsin Democrats' obstructionist efforts that culminated in a mass exodus from the state in an ill-fated attempt to block votes. When that failed, they gathered signatures and spent millions to try to recall the governor from office—not over an alleged crime or ethical breach, but over an ideological dispute in which they'd lost fair and square. The climate surrounding the collective bargaining fracas[3] and subsequent sore-loser-do-over election was chaotic. Mass protests. Squatting in the Capitol. Death threats. Hitler comparisons. Madison had it all.

After Walker thwarted them a second time with his recall triumph

---

[3] Which was really rooted in unions' terror over a provision in Walker's reforms that made it—gasp!—voluntary for many government sector union members to pay dues. Since those objectively successful reforms were implemented, dues-paying public union membership in the state has cratered. The *Milwaukee Journal Sentinel* reported that membership "has declined by 50 percent or more" in some public sector unions since the passage of Act 10. It seems that many working folks think they can spend their earnings better than Democrats and their union boss benefactors.

(the first time in U.S. history that a sitting governor won a recall election), Democrats geared up to defeat him in his 2014 re-re-election campaign. Their nominee, Mary Burke,[4] began her campaign with an ad flagrantly lying about Walker's jobs record, earning a "Pants on Fire" rating from left-leaning *PolitiFact*. DNC chairwoman Debbie Wasserman Schultz—the Cal Ripken Jr. of political lying—visited the state to denounce Walker's record on "women's issues" (sigh—see chapter 6), which she graphically compared to domestic abuse. She mused that the governor's policies had dragged women around by their hair, and that Walker had given female Wisconsinites "the back of his hand." Because Democrats take violence against women very seriously, you see.

Perhaps the most enraging component of the Left's "kitchen sink" anti-Walker outrage fest was the media's treatment of a so-called John Doe investigation by partisan Democratic prosecutors into Walker-allied groups in the state. The secret probe imposed gag orders on its targets, including organizations like the Wisconsin Club for Growth, and kneecapped a large component of the Right's activist network in the state leading up to the 2014 election. It even featured dramatic pre-dawn raids at private homes, designed for maximum humiliation and retribution. Two separate judges—one federal, one state—looked at the prosecutors' evidence and effectively ordered the investigation halted in its tracks for lack of evidence. (This led to much legal wrangling, including a series of appeals, which are ongoing as of this writing.)

The federal judge even allowed a lawsuit by targeted conservatives against the prosecutors to move forward. Months later, as that pushback lawsuit pressed ahead, reams of documents from the original thrown-out-of-court case were made public. This cache of papers spelled out old allegations that had been advanced long ago, and that

---

[4] Burke ran on her business experience at Trek, her family's bicycle business. It emerged just before the election that she'd been . . . "downsized" at said family bicycle business, with several former executives confirming that her leadership had been shambolic. Ouch.

had been tossed out of court by two judges because the persecution team couldn't establish sufficient probable cause. But you'd never know any of that from the resulting media coverage.

Local and national media outlets breathlessly plastered this "bombshell" story across front pages from Madison to Manhattan. Much of the coverage misleadingly adopted the present tense: "Prosecutors allege x, y and z . . ." No, prosecutors *alleged* those things, then two judges reviewed their case and basically said "Get lost." Oh, and Walker himself had never even been the target of a single John Doe subpoena, let alone a candidate for indictment or conviction. Yet all that humongously relevant context was either buried deep within stories or elided altogether. When some of us raised these issues, Walker's critics responded by sniffing, "When you're explaining, you're losing," a familiar and often-accurate political adage. *Seriousness of the allegation*, and all that. Naturally, the Burke campaign cut an ad on the alleged shocking development within hours. The investigation—spearheaded by a man whom respected journalist and Brookings scholar Stuart Taylor later revealed to be a hard-core partisan whose wife's hatred of Walker bordered on the pathological—had served its true purpose.[5]

The Outrage Circus emptied their tactical clip on this guy. They tapped the full arsenal. And he beat them, for the third time in four years. How'd he manage that?

"All too often, people get freaked out by the people who are right there in front of them, and they forget about everybody else," Walker tells us in an interview, recounting a story that illustrates his point. "At

---

[5] If conservatives really wanted to fight dirty, they'd recruit unscrupulous lawyers who are willing to deploy the frivolous indictment/ethical cloud playbook against elected Democrats. The negative headlines created by Representative Tom DeLay's (later-reversed) downfall, or Senator Ted Stevens's (later-reversed) conviction days before an election, or Governor Rick Perry's (truly groundless) indictment, or the sundry outlandish claims that grew out of Governor Chris Christie's "Bridgegate" brouhaha (after which three separate inquiries found no evidence he'd been untruthful) take political tolls. Find some yahoo prosecutor to indict a public figure, then drone on about "abuse of power" and "corruption" until the intended target's polls take a hit. The media would surely go along with that GOP smear project, right? *Right??*

the height of the [anti-budget reform] union protests, when we were approaching 100,000 protesters at and around the Capitol, I finally got wise. I started holding press conferences at 5:00 because I knew that if I kept it concise, local television and some national outlets would cover it live. So I had an unfiltered way to talk to the state for about ten minutes. The protesters figured it out, too. They started to get really loud right around 5 p.m. I'd be speaking to the press, and they'd make lots of noise. On one particular day, they were louder than they'd ever been, and a reporter asked me if those people had a right to be heard. And I said that they had every right to be heard, but that I wasn't going to let tens of thousands of people—and some were bused and flown in from other states—drown out the voices of millions of people around Wisconsin who elected me to do exactly what I was doing."

So he had the courage of his convictions and chilled the hell out and kept in mind his duty to the millions when faced with the screeching few.

Walker said that the darkest days of the battle over his Act 10 reforms steeled him for future challenges, making recall and reelection campaigns seem tame by comparison. "I was getting lots of threats [at the time]," he recalls. "One day, the leader of my security team came to me with a letter they'd intercepted that had been sent to my real home, our private home, that was addressed to my wife. It said that while there had never been a Wisconsin governor who'd been assassinated before, there was a first time for everything. It told my wife that she needed to stop me, and that the sender knew where my boys attended high school and where her father lived. It was scary, but it made me furious. I decided I'd be damned if I was going to let these people terrorize me. Rather than retreating, I was resolved to move forward, and I realized that if I could get through this, there wasn't anything I couldn't sustain."

The governor calls the Madison meltdown of 2011 a "case study" in the Left's tactics of outrage and intimidation. "They were trying to rattle us. They literally tried to shut down the legislative process and the debate by disrupting votes and trying to block entrances to the chambers. There were times when lawmakers, including myself and my staff, legitimately felt threatened. I'm not talking about political risks, I'm saying we were literally afraid that people were going to physically attack us." Walker says protesters trailed him everywhere, sometimes learning where he was planning to hold official events in advance. At one ceremony, agitators had filled the entire room and began shouting when the event's official program began. "You couldn't hear anything," he remembers. An elected Democrat in attendance got up to address the crowd, telling the mob that although he disagreed with Walker on big issues, it was wrong to shout him down and ruin an event. "He was booed and called a traitor just for asking that we be able to speak," Walker says.

Asked what he'd say in a short pep talk to fellow conservatives who find themselves in the Outrage Circus's political crosshairs, Walker doesn't flinch. "Be bold, be firm and be united." He said that some of the more moderate Republican members of the legislature who may have been more reluctant in the past were able to withstand the fire and hold the line because of the unity of purpose the party maintained in the crucible. "[The Left] is never going to treat you better if you retreat," Walker says, at least not in the long run. "They went after people regardless of what their past track record had been." He adds that conviction and guts in defense of a strong policy doesn't have to be a political liability. "Being bold and sticking with it doesn't just help you with your 'base,'" he says. "It also helps you with general voters. A lot of times, voters don't want moderation. They want leadership."

As Walker was fighting and winning his 2014 contest, Democrats halfway across the country in Colorado were applying a full-court press to defeat Republican Senate challenger Cory Gardner, a conservative congressman who was seeking to unseat incumbent Senator Mark Udall. Gardner has been widely credited with running a virtually flawless campaign, beating back the Left's deranged and dishonest attacks with almost otherworldly positivity. He proved uniquely adept at fighting back against Team Udall's comically relentless focus on birth control, and Gardner's nonexistent scheme to "ban" it. Gardner ran several ads setting the record straight from the get-go, highlighting his actual position, which entailed *expanding* access to affordable contraception by making the pill available for adult women over the counter, without a prescription. When Udall refused to let it go, Gardner began challenging the hapless Democrat on the issue of OTC birth control, knowing full well that Udall couldn't embrace the plan because his Planned Parenthood benefactors opposed it, largely out of financial self-interest. Consequently, Udall looked like a mumbling buffoon in debates, as Gardner grinned ear to ear. It's no small wonder that the Udall campaign had taken the extraordinary step of declining to participate in a single televised statewide debate.

Udall's fixation on birth control became so one-note and stale (*The Hill* reported roughly a month before Election Day that approximately *half* of all Udall ads focused on the issue) that the left-leaning *Denver Post* editorial board lambasted the candidate in its eyebrow-raising endorsement of Gardner. The money line: "Udall is trying to frighten voters rather than inspire them with a hopeful vision. His obnoxious one-issue campaign is an insult to those he seeks to convince." We practically did backflips when we first read that sentence.

In the home stretch of the campaign, a report published on the *Gawker*-owned sports blog *Deadspin*—which is often quite funny—accused Gardner of having fabricated his high school football career. Democratic operatives virtually high-fived online, with some crowing that the story was a crushing game changer. Except it was nothing of the sort. Within minutes, Gardner personally tweeted two contemporaneous photos of himself in his . . . high school football uniform, accompanied by good-natured quips about his unimpressive athletic career. Real journalists followed up with sources and quickly dismantled the core of *Deadspin*'s "scoop," which was ultimately retracted. What appeared to be a potential threat was reversed and pounded into dust within hours. The Republican once again turned an attack line to his benefit. Team Gardner approached both the serious "war on women" challenge and the silly-season football nonsense with a smiling, but determined, game face.

"On the issue of birth control, we recognized early on that too many Republicans had lost because they'd played defense," Senator Gardner explained in a postelection chat. "We've tried to win on a message of 'oh, no, no, no—I really do support birth control!' What we recognized was the need to have an offensive message. So what we did was talk about the good policy of over-the-counter contraception, and by doing this focused on policy, not politics. The drive of the Democrats was always about politics. There's an old saying that good policy is good politics. So we were able to push back, on offense, with a very popular thing, and the people of Colorado looked at that and said, 'That is a good idea. And if he's for that, we obviously cannot believe the charge that [Democrats] are making, which is outrageous, that he wants to ban birth control.' So we had something to be *for*. To stand *on*. Instead of just denying a negative charge."

When his high school football career was called into question by *Deadspin*'s article, Gardner knew the real attack was on his integrity and honesty. He recalls how his campaign deployed its masterful and nimble rapid-response strategy that afternoon: "I knew that I did play football, obviously, but the only proof that I could think of was at home. I called my mom and said, 'Mom, this is a very, very important thing, and I hope you're not busy. But I need you to immediately go over to my house and find my high school [yearbooks] down in the basement, and find the pictures of me from football and take photos with your iPhone and text them to me. Please.' And within ten minutes, she had done that. We determined that we couldn't handle it from a sense of outrage because that's what they wanted. The best way to fight back to the absolute snark and cynicism we were seeing on Twitter was to be humorous and make fun of myself. It ended up resulting in days of good press for us."

Gardner eschewed the angry/indignant temptation and used a

pair of self-deprecating tweets to demolish a potential problem. He estimates that the whole tumult went from red-hot controversy to the discredited butt of jokes in the span of forty minutes. Spending even a short time with Gardner reveals that his earnest, upbeat sunniness is his secret sauce. Though it comes naturally to him, Gardner believes a positive outlook can help conservatives connect better with people and neutralize the outrage peddlers. "We need to remember that the people of this country have plenty to worry about. Plenty to worry about at work, at home, abroad. One thing they do not need is for conservatives to give them more things to worry about by being too negative or fear-driven. Or being too shrill. We believe in what we stand for as conservatives. We should be excited and energetic and enthusiastic. If people perceive you as energetic and enthusiastic about what you believe in, there's a contagion there that can spread. And it results, ultimately, in an optimistic worldview. You can't just do it as a campaign persona. You have to carry it out in real life, too."

So there you have it. Two candidates. Two sets of challenges. Two wins. After several hundred pages of outlining the frustrating, pernicious obstacles the Left erects for conservatives, we felt like we owed you some good news in our conclusion. So take heart, friends. All is not lost. At least in the electoral politics realm, if Republicans can train themselves to confront the Outrage Circus in a smart and disciplined manner, employing the right mix of targeted cold-bloodedness and good cheer, sanity can still win the day. Just ask thrice-elected Governor Scott Walker, or freshly minted United States senator Cory Gardner.

ADVICE, SORT OF

Perhaps the biggest challenge in writing this tome was the task of crafting actionable advice to impart in our farewell chapter. The core tension we've grappled with from the earliest writing stages is whether or not conservatives should attempt to fight the Left blow for blow, "outrage" for "outrage." On one hand, recusing ourselves from getting our hands a bit dirty amounts to unilateral disarmament. Losing with honor is still losing.[6] On the other hand, diving into the outrage arms race is depressing. It's exhausting. It's soul-crushing. And, thanks to the mainstream media's heavily documented double standards, it's often counterproductive. The deck is stacked. The correct approach entails striking an appropriate balance, wherein the Right declines to cede the playing field altogether without needlessly escalating the outrage wars, which would threaten to officially push our national conversation over the "beyond repair" Rubicon. So, without further ado, here are our closing thoughts.

To Everyone

(1) Stop narcing on each other. It's not our job as friends, family, coworkers, or even political adversaries to spend all our time picking out what is wrong with someone else. Yes, you have a recording device at your disposal at all times in the smartphone era. No, that does not mean you should record every incidence of boorishness you come across and send it to *TMZ*. If we take it upon ourselves to tattle to authorities about our fellow citizens' every moment of weakness, questionable behavior, and "incorrect" thought, we're just opposition researchers in this campaignlike existence we're creating. We should not view ourselves as agents of the righteous state, or a righteous activist group, or a righteous media, rooting out minor infractions to make the world a better place. Sometimes shining a light on misbehavior

---

[6] Nope, we're not saying that one side of the political spectrum has a monopoly on dishonorable people or tactics. If you think that's what we're saying, you might be a lazy opposition researcher who hasn't read the book you're holding, or who has suppressed entire elements of it. Don't be that guy. (We acknowledge that "that guy" is a heteronormative and sexist microaggression that likely merited a trigger warning.)

is important, but it is the right of every American to occasionally be a jerk, to occasionally say the wrong thing, especially in the privacy of their homes, without being reported. If you enjoy such a courtesy, extend it to others. Let's not elevate the tattletale to a place of cultural exaltation he does not deserve.

(2) Don't allow yourself to be cowed into silence. Sometimes keeping your thoughts to yourself is the polite and proper thing to do. Sometimes it's best to do further research, or to self-edit a bit, before spouting off. But it's unhealthy for our society if you self-censor out of fear of crossing the self-stylized thought police. Finish that sentence. Post that status. And if your friend, relative, or coworker sputters, "But that's ___ist!" try to avoid default defensiveness. Consider that they may not have any earthly idea how to refute the point you're actually making. Ask them simple questions like, "Why do you say that? Without calling me a ____ist or getting upset, why do you think I'm wrong on the merits? I want to have this conversation, don't you?"

(3) By the same token, don't be afraid NOT to have an opinion on something. (This goes doubly for us, as people who are literally in the business of having opinions.) The outrage mongers thrive on making every single American act like a political candidate, declaring his or her position on every subject no matter how big or small. It's ludicrous to try to keep up. Attempting to do so causes more context-free opinions, more groupthink as citizens simply pick the side to which their political affiliation seems to be migrating, more fatigue, and less fun. We're a free people who have every right to say, "meh." Hold that dear. It is more honest and more healthy than handing your life over to the outrage brigades.

To Our Fellow Conservatives

(1) Pick your battles with wisdom and great care. This means letting some things go. Figure out what's important, and why, and don't sweat every single thing that comes down the pike. Your blood pressure will thank you.

(2) Stop taking yourselves *so* superseriously. Enjoying interests beyond right-wing politics, and, you know, *laughing*, aren't signs of weakness or betrayals of "the cause" or whatever. To convince normal people who are not political junkies, it helps if we at least seem relatable. Anger, like desperation, is not a political aphrodisiac.

(3) Quit spending much of your time and energy attacking one another. This may be slightly beyond the scope of this book, but good heavens. If the center-right spent *half* the time focusing on winning as we do on RINO-huntin' and TrueCon-bashin', who knows what we might manage to accomplish?

(4) Ask yourself, "Might I fit the lefty stereotype of a close-minded conservative?" Do you tailor your media consumption habits such that you almost exclusively consume viewpoints with which you're heavily disposed to agree? What is the last issue on which you've genuinely listened to a left-of-center friend, and perhaps changed your opinion? If you can't answer that, do you really, truly believe that your ideological canon is that infallible? That our "side" is right about literally *everything*? Occasional self-examination is healthy. It's a rare person indeed who isn't some kind of political hybrid. We all have our ideological oddities. We should be honest about them and unsurprised and understanding when others have them, too.

To Moderates and Independents

We imagine that you've found yourself nodding along through portions of this book, while gritting your teeth at other passages. We're not asking you to agree with us on every single issue (although we certainly wouldn't object!); that's not the point. The point is that the core American value of free exchange is under sustained, deliberate attack. If you agree with the overall warning we've issued, please consider actively joining the Coalition to Chill the Hell Out, and perhaps try to be more skeptical and aware consumers of future political and cultural controversies. Beyond contemplating "Which side do I agree with?," then moving along, also ask questions like "Regardless of my own personal feelings, is either side trying to shut down this debate altogether?" And "Is the other side's stance so fundamentally unacceptable that it doesn't deserve a reasonably fair hearing?" We can't imagine the answer to the latter question will often be yes.

To Our Open-Minded Friends on the Center-Left

Thanks again for reading. The mere fact that you did so suggests that you're probably not part of the problem we're addressing in the book. Though an ideological conversion would be splendid, you can absolutely stand firm on your liberal principles while reminding your brethren what tolerance and open-mindedness (some of the most admirable, if decreasingly applicable, tenets of liberalism) truly look like in practice. Also, see item four in our message above to our conservative colleagues, and challenge yourselves with the same questions.

To Those Currently in the Crosshairs

Stop giving in so easily. The storm is probably not as bad as it seems. The boycott is not as effective as its perpetrators hope. Sometimes apologies are truly necessary, and when you offer one, it should be complete and sincere. But our society demands them far too often for far too little, precipitating nonapologies and insincere apologies. Many are under the impression that an apology will stop the outrage, but it often feeds, rather than quells, the storm. Take a page from the late great Joan Rivers and employ your middle finger liberally, in spirit if not literally. Guess what happened when Rivers refused to apologize for a joke? The outrage purveyors looked at her, confused, screamed briefly about her stubbornness, and moved on to the next outrage. Our short attention spans aren't good for much, but perhaps we can harness them to save us from ourselves. Like so many cranky magpies, the perpetually aggrieved will move to the next shiny offense. And there will always be one.

To the End-of-Discussion Outrage Circus

Please stop, or at least replace your "Coexist" bumper sticker with an aesthetically similar one that reads "Coerce." Be honest about who you are and what you're really trying to accomplish.

And with that, we're done here. Thanks for listening. This is the end of our discussion, but let's all keep talking. *For America.*

ACKNOWLEDGMENTS

T ackling a project of this magnitude was challenging and intimidating, even with the workload divided two ways. There's a reason why neither of us had summoned the fortitude to write a book before, and our maiden voyage couldn't have happened without a great deal of help.

We are grateful to the excellent team at Crown Forum whose enthusiasm for this project was infectious and evident from the earliest stages. Special thanks is owed to promotions gurus Campbell Wharton, Megan Perritt, and Ayelet Gruenspecht; creative genius Michael Nagin; and publisher Tina Constable, who presided over everything with confidence-inspiring class and warmth. And then there's our editor, Mary Choteborsky, whose steady, insightful guidance over many months of work, on every front imaginable, was indispensable.

To our agents at Javelin, Keith Urban and Matt Lattimer, thanks for handling the business side of this project with such aplomb and apparent ease from wire to wire.

We'd also like to give a special shout-out to J. T. Hebden, our liberal secret weapon, who graciously helped us identify ideological blind spots and refine our arguments. Our end product is stronger and more persuasive because of his efforts. We owe him a nice bottle of Sancerre.

One of the hardest tasks throughout the intensive book-writing process was making sure that we didn't neglect our primary day jobs at Townhall Media. Perhaps the biggest reason we managed to pull this balancing act off is the fact that our boss, Jonathan Garthwaite, is basically a saint. He offered us critical minisabbaticals during our heaviest writing periods, and afforded us flexibility and patience when we needed it most. It is a true pleasure to work for him.

Our colleagues at Townhall and Hot Air were also incredibly supportive and prolific, offering encouragement along the way, and picking up our online slack when we were slammed with deadlines. Thanks to Ed Morrissey, Allahpundit, Noah Rothman, and Jazz Shaw at Hot Air—and Dan Doherty, Kevin Glass, Conn Carroll, Cortney O'Brien, Leah Barkoukis, Sarah Jean Seman, Christine Rousselle, Matt Vespa, and Amanda Munoz at Townhall. We owe unique gratitude to Katie Pavlich, who (despite being several years younger than us) has already written *two* successful books. Her pep talks and tips—especially during crunch time—were reassuring and invaluable. And we'd be terribly remiss if we failed to mention our mentor Hugh Hewitt, a prolific writer in his own right, who has been as generous to us as any person possibly could be. He's a joyful cheerleader, an indefatigable advocate, and a dear friend.

We are also extremely thankful to be members of the Fox News team. It is a blessing to work with such a talented and successful group of people on a regular basis, and it's an honor to be afforded such a formidable platform from which to share our views. We're never told what to say, or how to say it—and that's priceless. Many thanks to the hosts and producers who entrust us with their airtime, and to the extraordinary management team—Roger Ailes, Bill Shine, John Moody, and Suzanne Scott, in particular—who brought us into the fold. We *never* take it for granted.

Finally, we'd like to say how much we appreciate everyone else who's helped us in the writing and promotion of this book, from those who agreed to interviews (in many cases finding time amid extremely busy schedules), to those who endorsed the finished product, to those who toiled behind the scenes. This entire project has been a remarkable collaboration, which could not exist without many willing and generous collaborators.

And now, a few customized thank-yous.

MKH

Huge thank-yous to my parents, Jon and Kay, the best damn newspaper man and elementary school librarian in the world. My dad taught me history, storytelling, a broad appreciation of the music of the American midcentury, geography, and how to make mirepoix, sometimes all in the space of one day. My mom taught me that a fulfilling career and a bustling family life are without question compatible. She punctuated a noble intellectual pursuit—teaching kids to read and love books—with a flair for performance and the perfect silly costume in a way I hope to emulate with half her creativity, kindness, and hard work for the rest of my life.

Thanks to my amazing husband, Jake, who has always had a firm belief that we can do the seemingly impossible, like have a baby and write a book in the same year. Thanks to all of my in-laws. I count myself lucky to have acquired them by marriage, and couldn't have made this work without their constant support, and frequent availability for child care help. Thanks to our daughter, who is wise beyond her two years and sixteen vocabulary words, as graciously chill and flexible as her insane parents need her to be, and basically the coolest chick I know. In close competition for the title, my friends Emily, Susannah, Jenica, Angela, Joy, Emily, and Kelly, who are always there.

Thanks to my brothers, Jon and Owen, for making me rough-and-tumble, both literally and figuratively, for making me laugh, and for a relationship that can be constant with basically no emotional maintenance while I'm busy with a baby and a book. Brothers, God bless 'em.

Thank you to the late Conrad Fink, the most impressively gruff, worldly, and tough professor one could hope for. Even at the University of Georgia, I was a bit of an ideological oddity, and Fink's true fairness was a model for journalists, professors, and students alike.

Thank you to the Bull City—Durham, North Carolina, my cool, quirky, incredibly liberal hometown. Its insularity made me seek out different ways of thinking, and its charming idiosyncrasies made me appreciate all that those who disagree with me have to offer. I would never trade the upbringing that brought me here, made me stand my ground even when hopelessly outnumbered, and left me with a giant group of lifelong friends who look and think differently than I do, and may disagree with everything in my book.

Thanks to Community Newspapers, Inc., the Heritage Foundation, and Townhall for giving me a shot when I was very young. Thanks to Bill O'Reilly and his dedicated crew for the privilege and pleasure of appearing, and occasionally disagreeing, with the most-watched man in cable news every week.

Thank you so very much to Guy for being the one who keeps the trains running around here. The value of his perfect understanding of my sometimes exasperating, loopy, scatterbrained work process cannot be overstated. It has been a privilege to undertake this with a person who so clearly complements my own weaknesses with his considerable strengths. I wouldn't be here without you, nor would I want to be!

Thanks, every day, to God for protection, for health, for love, and for listening.

GUY

Thanks to Him, from whom all blessings flow.

My friends have been incredibly loyal and kind during this journey—from encouraging me to take the plunge at the outset, to putting up with my occasional whining, to understanding when I disappeared into hermit mode. They are too numerous to name-check, but a few went above and beyond the call of friendship duty: Thank you to "the Family," Lauren, Mitch and Carolyn, Rob and Suzanne, Steve and Susan, Colin and Alyse, Gabe, Dave, Kelly, Dan, and especially James.

I also feel indebted to the many strong teachers and professors under whom I studied during my academic career, from HKIS to RHS to Northwestern. One man whose decency, good humor, and character have always stuck with me is Brian Vanicky, my high school history teacher from my sophomore year through graduation. He left us far too soon, but I hope that if he were still here, he'd be proud of the work we've done in these pages. It's a cliché, sure, but teachers really do matter. And we really do remember.

To my family, I don't say it enough, but I love you all very much. I'm blessed with an incredible extended family, all of whom regularly remind me that they're rooting for me, regardless of our political agreements or differences. Particular thanks are due to Uncle Peter, Aunt Pip, and Cousin Chris and Simon. And to my immediate family—Mom, Dad (Lisa and Nick), Jab and Olivia—thank you for your unconditional love, unswerving support, and useful advice, solicited and otherwise (I'm looking at you, Dad). You guys were there to answer every call, return every text, and offer every hug that I needed. From the bottom of my heart, *thank you.*

Finally, unorthodox as it may be, although I see she's already beaten me to it, I'd like to thank my coauthor, Mary Katharine. You're a lovely, conscientious, thoughtful, creative, funny, and charming person. You've been a wonderful friend for many years, through peaks and valleys. It's been a privilege to work (and share countless head explosions) with you. We make a great team.

INDEX